Literary

This classic and longstanding series has established itself making a major contribution to literary biography. The books in the series are thoroughly researched and comprehensive, covering the writer's complete oeuvre. The latest volumes trace the literary, professional, publishing, and social contexts that shaped influential authors—exploring the "why" behind writers' greatest works. In its thirtieth year, the series aims to publish on a diverse set of writers—both canonical and rediscovered—in an accessible and engaging way.

More information about this series at
http://www.palgrave.com/gp/series/14010

Matthew C. Augustine

Andrew Marvell

A Literary Life

palgrave
macmillan

Matthew C. Augustine
School of English
University of St Andrews
St Andrews, UK

Literary Lives
ISBN 978-3-030-59289-9   ISBN 978-3-030-59287-5   (eBook)
https://doi.org/10.1007/978-3-030-59287-5

This Palgrave Macmillan imprint is published by the registered company Springer Nature Switzerland AG.
The registered company address is: Gewerbestrasse 11, 6330 Cham, Switzerland

For Julian

Acknowledgments

One of the themes of this book is the 'manyness' of Marvell's authorship, his patronage relations, his collaborations with the living and the dead, his habits of borrowing and ventriloquism, of transprosing and transversing. So nothing could be more appropriate than to acknowledge, with humility and pleasure, the various debts and borrowings that underwrite my own endeavours in these pages.

The historical spine of the book relies extensively on the work of seventeenth-century historians which can in no way be adequately acknowledged by means of the minimal apparatus of books in this series. Where specific citations are given, a more general debt may usually be assumed. Some of the historians to whom I have most often turned in writing the book include Glenn Burgess, Patrick Collinson, Barry Coward, Tim Harris, Ann Hughes, Mark Knights, Ronald Hutton, John Miller, Steven Pincus, Jacqueline Rose, Conrad Russell, Jonathan Scott, Paul Seaward, Quentin Skinner, John Spurr, Nicholas Tyacke, Austin Woolrych, and Blair Worden. Reading them more deeply than I had done previously has been its own reward, and I can only hope they think their work was put to good use.

My debts to the most recent generation of Marvell's editors and biographers—Annabel Patterson, Martin Dzelzainis, Nicholas von Maltzahn, Neil Keeble, and Nigel Smith—are more substantial still. With respect to Martin, Nick, and Nigel, they are also personal. Not only have they encouraged my work for many years, they have also responded to my numerous queries with the same diligence and patience for which they are known in their scholarship. I can't thank them enough.

Friends and colleagues in the Andrew Marvell Society have provided a lively community for the sharing of work in progress, and their own writings have of course variously shaped and challenged my view of Marvell's life and work. For their wisdom and fellowship, in addition to those named above, I am especially grateful to Steph Coster, Geoffrey Emerson, Joan Faust, Alex Garganigo, Blaine Greteman, Nick McDowell, Ryan Netzley, Brendan Prawdzik, Tim Raylor, Jonathan Sawday, and David Simon. Here Joanna Picciotto deserves special mention: her boundless enthusiasm for the project urged it forward in low moments, and amidst much other more pressing business, she generously read the whole manuscript before it went to press; to her I am very grateful indeed. Within my home department, Christina Alt, Harriet Archer, Giulio Pertile, and Nick Rowe read and commented on versions of several chapters; I thank them for their care and for their untiring collegiality. I am also grateful to Emma Buckley and Edward Paleit for advance sight of their edition of Thomas May's *Lucan's Pharsalia*. The timely completion of this book was made possible by a semester of teaching leave in Spring 2019, and I am grateful to the School of English and the College of Arts and Divinity at St Andrews for that sabbatical.

At the Hull Charterhouse, the resident historian Ann Godden provided much valuable information concerning the historical buildings and grounds. The Master, Rev. Canon Paul Greenwell, welcomed me with extraordinary grace, and indeed, we sat with the ghost of his predecessor, Andrew Marvell Sr, and with the poetry of the Charterhouse's most famous son, a communion unlikely to be repeated in this life. For that experience, Paul is most warmly remembered.

Years ago, on submitting my first article for publication, a reviewer tartly commented that the essay seemed too much an argument with the author's teachers. But who better to argue with about Marvell's poetry than Derek Hirst and Steven Zwicker? This slightly childish response is I hope at least partially vindicated by the publication of this book, the product of a now decades-long conversation with those incomparable scholars, teachers, and friends. Amidst the isolation of intense work on the manuscript compounded by the arrival of a global pandemic, the company of their writing, their emails, and Steve's regular phone calls from across the Atlantic has been sustaining in ways far beyond the recompense of these acknowledgments, but I thank them all the same.

I would also like to thank the Press's two anonymous readers for their many fruitful suggestions.

The privilege of writing this book has been paid for most dearly by those most dear to me. To Katie, as ever, thank you for all that you are and do. To Julian, of indefatigable cheer, this book is dedicated, as promised.

MCA
August 2020

A Note on the Text

The presentation of the text in this book reflects a set of imperfect compromises. At the advice of the press and in keeping with the series' aim 'to publish in an accessible and engaging way', quotations from texts in old spelling have been silently modernised throughout. This decision bears most vexingly on the presentation of Marvell's prose, the original appearance of which is preserved with great care (though not unvaryingly) in the standard Yale edition. But to make an exception of Marvell's prose and retain its original spelling, capitalisation, and so on would be to make it stand out as awkward and old-fashioned when what one wants to emphasise about Marvell's prose is exactly its modernity. At the same time, one *does* want to retain aspects of orthography and typography which are deliberate and rhetorical, for instance, when medial capitalisation serves to personify a noun or italic type is used to identify quoted language or for purposes of visual debate. When quoting from texts in old spelling, I have thus sought as far as possible to convey the effect achieved in the original while upholding the standard of modernisation. I have preserved initial capitalisation of honorific nouns in quotations, for example, 'King', 'Church', and 'State', but not that of ancillary forms, for example, 'kingdom'. Where it seemed best to reproduce original spelling or punctuation, it is so noted parenthetically.

Contents

Abbreviations

ELH   English Literary History
ELR   English Literary Renaissance
HJ   Historical Journal
HLQ   Huntington Library Quarterly
MP   Modern Philology
N&Q   Notes & Queries
RES   Review of English Studies
SC   The Seventeenth Century
SEL   Studies in English Literature 1500–1900
SP   Studies in Philology
TLS   Times Literary Supplement

Frequently Cited Works

1681   *Miscellaneous Poems, by Andrew Marvell, Esq.* (London, 1681)
Chameleon   Nigel Smith, *Andrew Marvell: The Chameleon* (New Haven: Yale
            University Press, 2010)
Chronology Nicholas von Maltzahn, *An Andrew Marvell Chronology* (New York:
            Palgrave Macmillan, 2005)
CJ   *Journal of the House of Commons (1547–1699)*, 12 vols. (London:
            His Majesty's Stationary Office, 1802)
ConstDoc   *The Constitutional Documents of the Puritan Revolution*, ed.
            S. R. Gardiner, 3rd ed. (Oxford: Clarendon Press, 1906)
CPW   *Complete Prose Works of John Milton*, gen. ed. Don M. Wolfe, 8 vols.
            (New Haven: Yale University Press, 1953–82)
HPHC   *The History and Proceedings of the House of Commons (1660–1739)*,
            14 vols. (London: Richard Chandler, 1742)
ODNB   *Oxford Dictionary of National Biography*

OED   *Oxford English Dictionary*

Pepys   *The Diary of Samuel Pepys*, ed. Robert Latham and William Matthews, 11
        vols. (London: George Bell, 1970–83)

P&L   *The Poems and Letters of Andrew Marvell*, ed. H. M. Margoliouth, rev.
        Pierre Legouis with E. E. Duncan-Jones, 3rd ed. (Oxford: Clarendon
        Press, 1971)

Poems   *The Poems of Andrew Marvell*, ed. Nigel Smith, rev. ed. (London:
        Longman, 2007)

PW   *The Prose Works of Andrew Marvell*, ed. Annabel Patterson, Martin
        Dzelzainis, Nicholas von Maltzahn, and N. H. Keeble, 2 vols. (New
        Haven: Yale University Press, 2003)

1

Introduction: A Literary Life?

What is a 'literary life', and why should Andrew Marvell be in need of one? Certainly not for want of recent attention. A century ago, in a famous essay published in the *TLS*, T. S. Eliot proposed to 'bring the poet back to life' by squeezing the drops of two or three poems (Eliot 1975, 161). Seventy years later, in 1990, Frank Kermode and Keith Walker's Oxford Authors edition of Marvell could proclaim him 'the most important seventeenth-century poet after John Milton'. And indeed, the mass of literary, biographical, and editorial commentary devoted to Marvell's relatively slim body of work over the last several decades is little short of astonishing. The emphasis on 'poet' in the OUP brief might give us pause, however, insofar as the study of Marvell in the latter part of the twentieth century can be characterised by a paradigm shift, from Eliot's poet of 'tough reasonableness beneath the slight lyric grace' to what Annabel Patterson has called 'the writer in public life'. In the course of this shift, scholarly attention has been broadly transferred from the domains of lyric invention and lyric possibility to the more civic preoccupations of panegyric, satire, and animadversion.

Modern biography of Marvell follows much the same pattern. Pierre Legouis's *André Marvell: Poète, Puritain, Patriote (1621–1678)* was begun in the same year as Eliot's essay and completed in 1928; an English abridgement was published in 1965. Legouis's would remain the standard biography until 2010, with the publication of Nigel Smith's deeply researched and essential study *Andrew Marvell: The Chameleon*. Highlighting his differences with Legouis, Smith observes that by page 20 of *Poet, Puritan, Patriot*, 'Marvell has arrived at Nun Appleton, but his life was more than half over' (*Chameleon*, 6). Nun Appleton, the Yorkshire estate where Marvell served as tutor to the daughter of Thomas Lord Fairfax, is where we think Marvell wrote much of

© The Author(s), under exclusive license to Springer Nature Switzerland AG 2021
M. C. Augustine, *Andrew Marvell*, Literary Lives,
https://doi.org/10.1007/978-3-030-59287-5_1

his greatest poetry, including his masterpiece, 'Upon Appleton House'. Legouis hastens towards this idyll in Marvell's career; his section on 'The Lyrical Poet', at 64 pages (of 252), is the longest in the book. By contrast, Smith has Marvell arrive at Nun Appleton on page 88 and depart on page 110 of a Life that runs to some 350 pages. Attuned as it is to actions and events, *The Chameleon* turns resolutely from the world of private *otium* to that of public *negotium*, where it is led by the rich archive of material associated with Marvell's state employments, first as a secretary in Cromwell's Protectorate, then as MP for Hull, a position Marvell held for the last twenty years of his life. The biography's literary vantage point is thus shifted away from the languishing numbers of Nun Appleton and towards the Cromwell poems and Marvell's satires and pamphlets of the Restoration.

The advantage, the rationale of a 'literary life' is a degree of liberty from the standard biographer's duty to life records and the material trace. My account of Marvell's life places his body of lyric verse at the centre, ordering and illuminating everything else. With the 'Horatian Ode', Marvell wrote perhaps the greatest political poem of the seventeenth century, indeed some would say in the English language. But he also wrote superbly when he turned his hand to the poetry of carpe diem ('To His Coy Mistress'), to the lover's complaint ('The Definition of Love'), to philosophical meditation ('Eyes and Tears', 'On a Drop of Dew', 'The Garden'), to sacred verse ('The Coronet'), to the fictions of pastoral (the Mower poems), to epicedium ('The Nymph Complaining'), and to chorography or country-house poem ('Upon Appleton House'). Indeed, it is hard to think of another poet in Marvell's time, or any time for that matter, who mastered so many of the prevailing genres of his age. It is the more remarkable that Marvell seems to have withheld much of his lyric verse from public view, writing for only select coteries and indeed often just for himself—his *Poems* were not published until 1681, 'being found since his death among his other papers' ('To the Reader').

Reemphasising the poems that have appealed to generations of readers need not mean slighting Marvell's turn in the mid-1650s to a more public mode of writing and to the work of politics. That career is compelling in its own right, and Marvell's advocacy for religious toleration and freedom from arbitrary government still speak urgently to the present. Moreover, this book shares the view that Marvell was often just as witty and as 'literary' in his political satires and prose pamphlets as he is in his lyrics. A varied genius is still the same genius—it makes little sense to treat Marvell as if he were split in two by the forces of history. But neither does this book purport to unravel 'the figure in the carpet' of Marvell's writing. It is tempting to suppose the existence of such a key to Marvell's work, some ethical ideal, some metaphysical quiddity 'to make a whole man out of this poet with too many personae' (Patterson 1978, 5). And indeed, as is implicit in the very project of fashioning a 'literary life', this book seeks at least a measure of such coherence in writing itself. Like previous biographers and critics, I seek to contextualise and to explain apparent gaps, elisions, and contradictions in both Marvell's real and his imagined life. Where others have sought to see through Marvell's masks and ironies or see past his chameleon shifts, however, this book holds that contextualisation often brings us to the brink of mystery but no further, making room for the delight many readers take in the sense that Marvell's poetry holds an unfathomable secret.

Needless to say, Marvell gave little thought to the figure he would cut in future biographies, or to having or leading something that we might call a 'literary life'. He withheld most of his poetry from view, and, with a few exceptions, maintained his anonymity even in those works he did choose to publish or circulate. And unlike, say, his friend John Milton, who could hardly resist writing about himself, and who cast himself variously as a second Homer or Orpheus, or as touched by holy fire like the prophet Elijah, Marvell typically holds himself aloof in the shadows of his work. Marvell's literary lives have thus been significantly shaped by the interests of those who saw fit to provide such a life for him. Soon after his death, for instance, he was celebrated as a Whig patriot and hailed in some circles as 'the poet laureate of the dissenters'. This (still active) image of Marvell belies, however, the changeability of his political allegiances, the complexity of his patronage ties, his scrupling over being 'mistaken' for a dissenter. Such labels are also prone to backfilling—to the discovery of clues or traces which point to the future. Eliot's aestheticizing of Marvell is of course no less motivated, no less 'political' than the Whig history it disrupts: Eliot holds up 'the really valuable part' of Marvell's verse as an emblem of European culture before the onset of a spiritually deadening modernity. In the absence of a knowable author, Marvell's writings mark out a discursive space unusually open to the projections and idealisations of critics.

It would be at once deceiving and self-deceiving to suggest that *this* life of Marvell was not also conditioned by the values of the people and institutions which have produced it. Nonetheless, I have tried to honour Marvell's reticence to be made an icon, even for those causes he courageously supported (to say nothing of causes which he scarcely imagined). We must be responsive as well to some of the particular challenges posed by the nature of Marvell's literariness. Under the tutelage of modern criticism, we have learned to see him as a ventriloquist, a magpie, a great 'borrower of other men's words' (Patterson 2000, 4). His most famous poem, 'To His Coy Mistress', combines overt parody of Cavalier tropes and the figurative excesses of metaphysical verse with subtle but pervasive echoes of neo-Latin poetry—a remix, as it were, of other poets and other poems. This habit of recall, and what we might term pastiche, extends also to Marvell's polemical work and is part of what makes it so difficult to pin down Marvell's own convictions. When he chose to enter the arena of Restoration prose controversy, for instance, he did so by reworking ('transprosing') a popular dramatic burlesque called *The Rehearsal*, hence *The Rehearsal Transpros'd*. It is a basic principle of post-Romantic literary theory that all art comes from other art; this is acutely so in the case of Marvell, whose whole poetic may be summed up in that Latin prefix *trans*—crossing 'from one place, person, thing, or state to another'. For this reason, Marvell's texts are often best viewed in terms of their encounters with other texts, viewed, in other words, as scenes of reading.

This idea allows us to chart precisely some of the junctures between Marvell's life and art: for reading, as scholars increasingly recognise, is an inherently embodied and historically conditioned activity. As Thomas McLaughlin (2015) remarks, 'Reading is a physical practice that requires a vast social pedagogy. Hands and eyes and brains need to learn the procedures and respect the logic of the practice. Reading socialises the body, subjects it to a powerful discipline. Yet, all reading bodies are unique, differently capable, differently socialised. Reading practices are enacted by specific, idiosyncratic bodies in concrete, complex physical and social environments' (2). This book is an attempt to trace out the history of a specific, idiosyncratic body reading (and writing) within a series of concrete, complex physical and social environments: under the roof of Marvell's father, the Rev. Andrew Marvell, in the East Riding of Yorkshire; at Trinity College, Cambridge; on the Continent and in London during and just after the English civil wars; at Nun Appleton, in the employ of Lord Fairfax; in service to Cromwell, both at home and abroad; and back in London, at Westminster, and in the coffee houses, print shops, and libraries Marvell frequented during the Restoration.

Such an approach finds sanction in the fact that reading, writing, and their attendant pedagogies figure importantly across the body of Marvell's work. As a professional tutor, as a literary client to various patrons and constituencies, as a government functionary with specific responsibility for diplomatic correspondence, as a highly valued gatherer of intelligence, and as a writer who, after the Restoration, largely operated outside the law, Marvell was uniquely attuned to the application of linguistic acts and arts. Reading and its pedagogies are engaged in even the tenderest of circumstances. In a letter from Marvell to his friend John Trott, for instance, Marvell consoles Trott on the loss of his son. 'Only, as in difficult things,' Marvell advises the grieving father, 'you will do well to make use of all that may strengthen and assist you. The word of God: the society of good men: and the books of the Ancients' (*1681*, 69). Reading's pedagogy is a balm against the 'dissoluteness of grief' and 'prodigality of sorrow' (67). But it is not hard to see that the letter itself is a fruit of the reading practices it prescribes, in its bounty of instructive parallels and scriptural allusions. In this way, it is also a token of 'the society of good men'. The letter cements the social and affective bond between Marvell and Trott and speaks to a shared culture of 'exemplary reading' and epistolary (not to mention poetic) exchange (see Zwicker 2002).

But the experience of reading could also be the locus of all-too-real abrasions. In *The Rehearsal Transpros'd*, Marvell chides the intemperance and cruelty of the Oxford cleric Samuel Parker, commenting archly: 'I must confess at this rate the nonconformists deserve some compassion: that after they have done or suffered legally and to the utmost, they must still be subjected to the wand of a verger, or to the wanton lash of every pedant; that they must run the ganteloop [gauntlet], or down with their breaches as oft as he wants the prospect of a more pleasing nudity' (*PW*, 1:82). Marvell speaks here to the common experience of early modern schoolboys, who were routinely beaten for fumbling their grammar exercises. But he also points to the repressed drives that structured such a manner of teaching by schoolmasters and churchmen. In his poetry, Marvell is repeatedly drawn to representing scenes of endangered innocence, often in tones which do not altogether belong to the conventions of pastoral. As a Member of Parliament and Restoration polemicist, he inveterately opposed what he saw as the rapacity of the clergy; the so-called Bishop's Bill of 1677, which would have deputed the education of royal children to the bishops, was the occasion of Marvell's longest speech in the House and moved him to a vehemence for which he felt obliged to apologise (see Grey 1769, 4:322). Such evidence is admittedly fragmentary and open to interpretation, but it has been taken by some to suggest, as indeed I take this evidence to suggest, that Marvell understood perhaps too well the collocation of reading, authority, and abuse, and moreover that such knowledge was integral—if painfully so—to Marvell's writing life (see Hirst and Zwicker 2007, 2012).

*   *   *

Here we might acknowledge the more immediate occasion of this book, which is the approaching quatercentenary of Marvell's birth in March 2021. The marking of a four hundredth birthday is surely as good a reason as any to reassess a major author, and in the century since Eliot's 'resurrection' of Marvell, a major author is undoubtedly what he has become. Perhaps more decisive for the writing of this book, however, is the sentiment expressed by Rosalie Colie at the outset of her brilliant study *'My Echoing Song'* (1970), the only justification any work of literary criticism could ever have or need: 'Marvell's work was and remains too hard for me' (vii). When we have said all there is to say about a writer, when our understanding seems more or less sufficient to its object, we turn elsewhere. The endurance of Marvell in the critical consciousness of the last century, and in particular the flowering of Marvell scholarship over the last forty years, speak clearly to the fact that Marvell is a writer who continues to fascinate (and perplex) not just those new to his work but also—perhaps especially—the community of readers most devoted to him, that is, his critics, historians, and biographers.

It may be that this book will be read mainly by students and scholars, but I have tried to write it for the benefit of anyone who wants a way of putting this writer, if not exactly together, at least into perspective: the life within the world, the work within the life. Care has been taken to cover Marvell's career from beginning to end, and though my account concentrates most deeply on matters of poetry, it honours the potency and historical force of the prose as well. From the beginning, it was important to me that the book should also give an adequate account of the political developments that shaded Marvell's historical experience, and which found reflection—both directly and indirectly—in his writing. Achieving a suitable depth of political narrative sometimes came at the cost of this narrative appearing to run parallel to that of Marvell's life. My hope is that readers will find connections between the national and the personal biography in the contingent flux of interest and allegiance thematic of both. With respect to commenting on the poetry, my strategy has been to privilege depth over breadth, eschewing potted readings of dozens of poems in favour of detailed and original explorations of a smaller number of texts in different genres.

In organising the contents of the book, I have deliberately tried to avoid the impression that Marvell's writing life falls into a series of discrete chapters, that he is first a lyric poet, then a writer of panegyric, then a satirist and politician, and so on. Marvell's writing habitually blurs the boundaries of genre, and his preoccupations are not linear but recursive, appearing and reappearing without respect for tidy biographical narrative. Above all, I have tried to foreground here the acts of reading that comprise Marvell's art no less than they comprise the historical reception of that art—the ways in which Marvell found his voice in and through the voices of others and the ways in which we continue to make him speak anew. Like most all stories of reading and writing, this one begins at home, and it is to Marvell's early life, at home in east Yorkshire, that we now turn.

References

Colie, Rosalie. 1970. *'My Echoing Song': Andrew Marvell's Poetry of Criticism.* Princeton: Princeton University Press.

Eliot, T.S. 1975. *Selected Prose of T. S. Eliot.* Ed. Frank Kermode. London: Faber.

Grey, Anchitell. 1769. *Debates of the House of Commons, from the Year 1667 to the Year 1694.* 10 vols. London.

Hirst, Derek, and Steven N. Zwicker. 2007. Eros and Abuse: Imagining Andrew Marvell. *ELH* 74 (2): 371–395.

———. 2012. *Andrew Marvell, Orphan of the Hurricane.* Oxford: Oxford University Press.

Kermode, Frank, and Keith Walker, eds. 1990. *Andrew Marvell.* Oxford Authors. Oxford: Oxford University Press.

Legouis, Pierre. 1928. *André Marvell: Poète, Puritain, Patriote (1621–1678).* Paris; London: Henri Didier; Oxford University Press.

———. 1965. *Andrew Marvell: Poet, Puritan, Patriot.* Oxford: Clarendon Press.

Marvell, Andrew. 1681. *Miscellaneous Poems by Andrew Marvell, Esq.* London.

———. 2003. *Prose Works of Andrew Marvell.* Ed. Annabel Patterson, Martin Dzelzainis, Nicholas von Maltzahn, and N. H. Keeble. 2 vols. New Haven: Yale University Press.

———. 2007. *Poems of Andrew Marvell.* Ed. Nigel Smith. Rev. ed. London: Longman.

McLaughlin, Thomas. 2015. *Reading and the Body: The Physical Practice of Reading.* Basingstoke: Palgrave Macmillan.

Patterson, Annabel. 1978. *Marvell and the Civic Crown.* Princeton: Princeton University Press.

———. 2000. *Andrew Marvell: The Writer in Public Life.* New York: Routledge.

Smith, Nigel. 2010. *Andrew Marvell: The Chameleon.* New Haven: Yale University Press.

Zwicker, Steven N. 2002. Habits of Reading and Early Modern Literary Culture. In *The Cambridge History of Early Modern English Literature*, ed. David Loewenstein and Janel Mueller, 170–200. Cambridge: Cambridge University Press.

2

Andreae Filiae: East Riding, Yorkshire, 1621–1633

Details of Marvell's early life are sparse; however, the essential facts are no longer in doubt. Marvell was born on 31 March 1621, a Saturday, in the rectory at Winestead, a tiny parish to the east of Hull in the East Riding of Yorkshire. As late as the middle of the nineteenth century, records show that Winestead had only 139 inhabitants. Marvell's father was the Rev. Andrew Marvell (b. 1584), the parish's incumbent minister. Andrew Sr had married the poet's mother, Anne Pease (d. 1638), at Cherry Burton near Beverley, a village some twenty-five miles northwest of Winestead, on 22 October 1612. Their union produced three children prior to Marvell's birth: Anne (b. 1615), Mary (b. 1617), and Elizabeth (b. 1618). They would have one more child after Andrew, another son, John (b. 1623), who would not survive infancy. Marvell's sisters, however, all lived into adulthood, eventually marrying prominent Hull townspeople, respectively James Blaydes, Edmund Popple, and Robert More. Marvell's connection with the Popples was especially close and remained so throughout his life. His brother-in-law, Edmund, helped ensure Marvell's election as MP for Hull when Marvell's fledgling career in government was threatened by the collapse of the Commonwealth. But it was with his nephew, William Popple, that Marvell enjoyed the warmest personal relationship in his adult life. Perhaps the closest we get to an unguarded Marvell is in his letters to Will, his 'beloved nephew'.

While Marvell's mother had Yorkshire roots, his father was a recent arrival. Marvell's grandfather had been a yeoman farmer in Cambridgeshire, and the Marvell family seems to have been well established there. Andrew Sr was born in the village of Meldreth, ten miles southwest of Cambridge. But his was not to be a farmer's life—a 'rising man', the poet's father matriculated to Emmanuel

College, Cambridge in 1601, graduating BA in 1605 and taking his MA in 1608. Founded by the Puritan Sir Roger Mildmay in 1584, Emmanuel had rapidly expanded to become the largest college in Cambridge by the 1620s and was known as a centre of reformist zeal. After being ordained as deacon in 1607, the elder Marvell gained an appointment as curate and schoolmaster at Melbourne, a village in his home shire, in November 1608. We find the Rev. Marvell's signature in the burial register for Flamborough, in the East Riding, in January of the following year, and in May 1609, he would be ordained as priest at York Minster. It was in the course of his tenure at Flamborough that Marvell Sr met and married Anne Pease.

In April 1614, the young minister was presented with the living of Winestead-in-Holderness, about forty miles south of Flamborough and four-teen miles east of the bustling port of Kingston-upon-Hull. The Winestead Parish Register records that 'Andrew Marvell parson of Winestead was inducted into the corporal and peaceable possession of the said parsonage by Mr Marmaduke Brooke, dean, parson of Ross, upon Easter even, being [St] George's day' (*Chronology*, 16). Anne and Andrew Marvell's children would be born there. Shortly after the death of his infant son John in September 1624, however, Marvell Sr was elected Master of the Hull Charterhouse, which stood just outside the walls of the town, in Sculcoates, and at the same time began to preach at the Holy Trinity Church in Hull. Originally an alms-house adjoining a Carthusian monastery, the Charterhouse survived the dis-solution of the priory, being re-endowed for 'the living of the master and relieving of poor and impotent people'. Marvell would revisit such structures and dissolutions when he came to write 'Appleton House', with its recollec-tion of the manor's former life as a nunnery. It was the Master's responsibility to render the hospital's accounts, see to the upkeep of the building and grounds, and of course to minister to the spiritual needs of its residents. According to ordinances passed in 1571, 'Daily, or at least thrice a week, the master was to say divine service, viz., morning and evening prayer from the Book of Common Prayer, and further instruct the brethren and sisters in the catechism, and procure that the brethren and sisters should each communi-cate at least four times a year' (see Page 1974, 310–313).

It was once thought that Marvell's father had been Master of the Hull Grammar School rather than Master of the Hospital. The correction of this error—which persisted for more than 150 years—effectively relocated the young poet's everyday life from the busy centre of Hull to the rural suburbs beyond the city walls. The Charterhouse stood merely fifty yards from the River Hull. Having been rebuilt in 1644, after it was destroyed during the

Siege of Hull, torn down and rebuilt again in 1780, and restored by architects after the Blitz (1940–1941), the Charterhouse is still in operation today as supported living for pensioners. Visitors there will be shown the mulberry tree in the garden, under which Marvell is supposed to have read as a child. Like the anecdote of Newton and the apple, this story is probably too accommodating of Marvell—that poet of gardens—to be true, though there is often a regressive patina to Marvell's fantasies of ease and satiety. In 'The Garden', 'Ripe apples drop about my head; / The luscious clusters of the vine / Upon my mouth do crush their wine'—lines which perhaps recode the child's unrestrained sensual pleasure (feasting on mulberries, for instance) in more adult terms. The stanza ends, 'Stumbling on melons as I pass, / Ensnar'd with flow'rs, I fall on grass', thus enacting the fall in reverse, a stumble into innocence (ll. 33–40). Much of the pathos of Marvell's pastoral poetry derives from a sense of longing for such a backward fall, mingled with an awareness that you can't go home again.

To be sure, the Yorkshire landscape made a deep and lasting impression on Marvell. In 'Upon Appleton House', Marvell will become the great chronicler of that country's meadows, woods, and riverbanks. More elementally, Marvell's abiding fascination with perspective owes something to the undulating topography of the Yorkshire Wolds, which run in a crescent from the Humber estuary west of Hull to the chalk cliffs of Flamborough Head, and to the squashed horizons of the lowland plains of Holderness which lie east and south of the Wolds. In 'Appleton House', one critic observes, the reader 'will have to experience a series of inversions, metamorphoses, and tricks in perspective before he will find himself once more standing erectly … Men will change to grasshoppers, mowers to Israelites, and the meadow which seemed a sea will in fact become a sea' (Roth 1972, 272). The poem ends, it may be recalled, with that striking image of topsy-turvydom, 'But now the salmon-fishers moist / Their leathern boats begin to hoist; / And, like Antipodes in shoes, / Have shod their heads in their canoes' (ll. 769–773). Walkers of the Wolds will know that the ground can appear much flatter at a distance than is the case, as the glacial valleys cutting the plain tend to deceive the eye. Also, whereas typically low-lying land is farmed, and livestock graze the hills, the fact that the arable land in this area is on top of the Wolds means farming appears 'upside down', with hills used for crops, and the valleys for grazing. Smith describes Holderness as 'one of England's ends, a place of dunes seldom rising more than three yards, with seawater all around' (*Chameleon*, 12). Indeed, the land here is slowly tilting into the sea: according to a Eurosian Case Study, the East Riding coastal zone is the fastest eroding in Europe, and there are signs that over thirty villages have been lost to the sea here since Roman times (see Sistermans and Nieuwenhuis 2013). The eroded material gives the water off the Holderness coast its characteristically muddy appearance. Marvell's youthful perception was formed within a matrix of liminality, inversion, and the visually counterfeit.

England in the 1620s

'Let's in', says the poet to the reader in the closing lines of 'Appleton House', and it remains to explore the experiences of young Marvell in the Charterhouse and the Hull Grammar School and to discern what we can of his family life and upbringing. First, though, let us turn our attention outward, from shire to nation, so as to situate Marvell's early years within the unfolding political history of England, a story in which he will eventually have a part. By 1621, King James the VI and I was entering the last years of his reign. He had come to the throne in 1603 following the death of the childless Queen Elizabeth. In 1625, James would be succeeded by his son Charles, crowned Charles I. James was the first British monarch to rule, in both name and fact, over the multiple kingdoms of England, Scotland, and Ireland. Although Henry VIII had been proclaimed king in Ireland in 1541, the island was not brought under effective political control until the last years of Elizabeth's reign. James had long been king in Scotland before inheriting the English throne, and even after the union of the crowns in 1603, Scotland remained semi-independent, retaining its own Parliament as well as its ancient grudges towards England. For their part, James's English subjects were no less prejudiced against Scots for having a Scottish king. Then as now, English people grumbled that the joint monarchy served merely to siphon off English wealth and taxes. James's proposals for uniting Scotland and England under one constitution were decisively quashed in Parliament.

The political and ethnic tensions among James's kingdoms were exacerbated by religious difference, a consequence of the uneven progress of the Reformation across the British Isles. Though Ireland was ruled by a Protestant Ascendancy of English landowners, the majority of the country remained Catholic, as the independent Republic of Ireland is today. In Scotland, the winds of Reformation had by the end of the sixteenth century thoroughly transformed the Scottish Church, which was staunchly Calvinist in doctrine and Presbyterian in structure, though still nominally episcopal (that is, governed by bishops). As we shall see, it was Charles I's ham-handed intervention in Scottish church government which set in motion the crisis that would lead to civil war.

Religious matters in early Stuart England were internally pressurised and would only become more so under James and especially Charles. Since the Elizabethan Settlement of 1559, an element of English Protestants had more or less continuously agitated for further reform in the doctrine and discipline of the Church. These 'precisians' or 'Puritans', as first called by Archbishop Matthew Parker, stressed Bible reading and systematic preaching at the expense of sacramentality and clericalism, and on the whole fostered an intensity of religious experience greater than that of their Protestant neighbours. Though episcopacy was generally accepted in England before 1640, a wide swathe of Anglicans and Puritans could nevertheless agree that bishops were too worldly and corrupt, local clergymen often inept, and that a galling proportion of Church tithes ended up in lay hands. There was also broad consensus within the English Church on Calvinist predestinarian teaching, though this too was threatened by an insurgent group of powerful bishops, led by William Laud, with whom Charles would fatefully cast his lot. This 'Laudian' or 'Arminian' wing of the Church rejected the Calvinist theology of grace, arguing instead for the free will of man to obtain salvation (after the Dutch theologian Jacobus Arminius). With this apparently liberal theology, however, came a renewed (and self-interested) emphasis on liturgical ceremony with the priest at its centre. This struck more precise Protestants as a return to Roman Catholic ritual and reignited fears of popery and absolutism in church and state. The outbreak of the Thirty Years' War in 1618—which pitted various Catholic and Protestant powers against each other for control of central Europe—lent further urgency to the question of the future of English Protestantism.

'A Most Excellent Preacher': Rev. Marvell and Life in the Charterhouse

Anticipating the religious context of the English civil war prompts questions about the character of Marvell's father, a clergyman, and about the temperature of religious feeling in the Marvell household. Conveniently, Marvell the controversialist has left us a pithy description of his father, the force of which has perhaps been lost in the rush to confirm Marvell's dissenting credentials. 'But as to my father', Marvell wrote in 1673, addressing Samuel Parker in the second part of *Rehearsal Transpros'd*, 'he died before ever the war broke out, having lived with some measure of reputation, both for piety and learning: and he was moreover a conformist to the established rites of the Church of

England, though I confess none of the most over-running or eager in them'
(*PW*, 1:288–289). In his debate with Parker, Marvell would defend Charles
II's Declaration of Indulgence to dissenters against those, like Parker, who
wished to see nonconformity excluded and persecuted. Marvell is responding
here to a riddle of Parker's in his *Reproof to the Rehearsal Transprosed* (1673),
which Marvell interpreted as an attempt to smear his late father (d. 1641) by
associating him obscurely with the revolutionary governments which had dissolved episcopacy and abolished monarchy in England. Parker was hardly
scrupulous about his evidence; no doubt he would have seized on any sliver of
reputation Marvell Sr may have had as a radical preacher or Puritan revolutionary. As it was, the self-consciously weak gambit of impugning Marvell's
paternity backfired: Marvell scorched Parker's own pedigree in the early
going of *RT2*.

Further evidence of the Rev. Marvell's moderate conformity to the Church
of England may be found in Church administrative records and in his surviving papers. On more than one occasion in the years 1638–1639, at the height
of the Laudian Church's emphasis on ceremonial and liturgical conformity,
Marvell Sr was called before higher-ups in the diocese of York. There he was
ordered, when holding services at Holy Trinity Church, to read from the
Book of Common Prayer as prescribed and admonished to wear his hood and
surplice. Many Puritan preachers regarded the hood and surplice as 'rags of
popery' and refused to wear them, and likewise resisted worshipping by the
Prayer Book. The apparent laxity of Marvell Sr in points of ceremony had
clearly attracted the attention of the Laudian bishop at York, Richard Neile.

These orders also reflect, however, the diocesan authorities' apparent confidence in the elder Marvell's conformability, and an attempt to get round the
curate at Hull, John Gouge, who at the time was leveraging Puritan sentiment
in the Hull Corporation to prevent the vicar of Holy Trinity from promoting
the Prayer Book (see Allison 1969, 97–98). Marvell's father was also distressed
by what he called 'some discourtesies, and injurious carriages' which he experienced at the hands of sectaries within his own congregation. In private meetings, they maligned his 'doctrine in the point of Christ's merit' and his
'doctrine concerning the lawful and profitable use of godfathers in baptism'.
More sinisterly, 'They have undertaken to inveigle others closely, and among
the rest one of mine own family'. Others 'played the informers, relating my
doctrine and manner of preaching to those who were more diligent to inquire
and seek narrowly into my ministry then charitable to advise me in anything,
or Christianly wise in their own courses to avoid scandal'. Like many middle-
of-the-road Anglicans in the 1630s, Marvell Sr was caught between Laudian

conformity and sectarian dissent. What dispirited him most was the spurning of his openness to tolerant debate, being subject rather to 'Whisperings and back-bitings' (see *Chronology*, 25–27).

Our picture of the Rev. Marvell is further clarified by the capsule biography supplied in Thomas Fuller's *The History of the Worthies of England* (1662). 'Bred a master of Arts ... in Cambridge', notes Fuller, 'He afterwards became Minister in Hull, where for his life time he was well beloved. Most facetious in his discourse, yet grave in his carriage, a most excellent preacher, who like a good husband never broached what he had new brewed, but preached what he had pre-studied some competent time before. Insomuch that he was wont to say, that he would cross the common proverb, which called Saturday the working day, and Monday the holy day of preachers' (159). The quality of being facetious yet grave cannot help but suggest the junior Marvell's disposition as well. Indeed, these are the very principles of Marvell's handling of Parker in their pamphlet controversy. Faulting the crabbed structure of Parker's earlier writings against the nonconformists, Marvell affirms, 'Yet I will not decline the pursuit, but plod on after him in his own way, through thick and thin, hill or dale, over hedge and ditch wherever he leads; till I have laid hands on him, and delivered him bound either to reason or laughter, to justice or pity. If at any turn he gives me the least opportunity to be serious I shall gladly take it: but where he prevaricates or is scurrilous (and where is he not?) I shall treat him betwixt jest and earnest' (*PW*, 1:267–268). Marvell's professed method of dealing with his rival—'betwixt jest and earnest'—was to prove influential among the Augustan satirists, especially Swift; for him Marvell was 'a great genius'.

Marvell also seems to have inherited his father's propensity to 'brew' his discourse carefully, but he had little of Rev. Marvell's excellence in public speaking. Marvell's works of satire and animadversion give the impression of extemporaneous verve and velocity, but these were studied qualities. As a Member of Parliament, he was not used to giving speeches, and when he did speak up, did so abruptly and indecorously. Following an incident on the floor of the House of Commons in 1677, in which Marvell appeared to give Sir Philip Harcourt a 'box on the ear', he was called upon to apologise for this breach of protocol, and in so doing gave further insult to the Speaker of the House, prompting Sir John Charlton to move for Marvell's being sent to the Tower. Having put himself in a tight spot, Marvell humbly submits 'He is sorry he gave an offence to the House. He seldom speaks to the House, and if he commit an error, in the manner of his speech, being not so well tuned, he hopes it is not an offence' (Grey 1769, 4:330).

In the 1670s, Marvell seems to have frequented London's coffeehouses, establishments which occupied an important place in the circulation of political talk in the emerging public sphere. But he is depicted (admittedly by his enemies) not as presiding over a circle of coffeehouse wits, or holding forth himself, but as a silent lurker, taking down notes for later use: 'Many secret intrigues were whispered too close to be heard', Samuel Butler (1673) writes, purporting to look in on a coffeehouse frequented by Marvell, 'but amongst all, none were so loud as a junto of wits, that had seated themselves near our author: while they were engaged in a very warm dispute, the man of observations draws out his table-book ('tis his most dangerous tool) ... pop, he slaps them down [the wits' opinions], and makes them his own' (36–37). Similar things were said about Marvell's erstwhile colleague and rival John Dryden, an arriviste at court and a mimic of his social betters, and it is interesting to compare the stress laid by their enemies on their personal awkwardness with the assured brilliance of Marvell's and Dryden's writings. In literary studies, it has become commonplace to construe the illocutionary force of texts within the public, political sphere. But writing is not simply a set of moves to be decoded against other moves within a shared discursive context. In the case of Marvell and Dryden, poetry and eloquence serve, among other things, as prosthetics of the self. The act of poesis, of poetic making, compensates for what these writers experienced, and were at times bracingly confronted with, as a personal lack. To understand them well is perforce to try to grasp this dialectic of strength and vulnerability.

Though we have little direct knowledge of life in the Charterhouse from Marvell's time, vulnerability is a theme there as well. 'God's house in Hull', as it was known, the hospital was a place for poor folk, and its rhythms were fundamentally religious. Its original grant was for the provision of 'thirteen poor men and thirteen poor women', and while the number of residents rose and fell in relation to how well the endowment was managed, by the early 1620s it appears that the hospital was operating at or near capacity (see Page 1974). It has usually been thought that young Andrew and his family lived in the Master's house, separate from the Charterhouse, and indeed the historical plaque on the listed building informs visitors 'Here, from 1624 until 1640 while his father was Master of the Charterhouse, lived Andrew Marvell (1621–1678), poet, public servant, and Member of Parliament for Kingston-upon-Hull'. But the evidence is ambiguous. The original hospital buildings were destroyed in the Siege of Hull in 1642. The current Master's house likely dates to the rebuilding of the hospital in the 1640s. It is unclear whether a separate Master's house was part of the old grounds. This raises the possibility that the Master and his family once lived more closely with the other residents of the Charterhouse than would be the case after 1642. This gives us the image of a slightly humbler and more intimate ministry than we might otherwise have and invites us to consider the basis of the mature Marvell's intolerance for high-handedness in matters of church and state. Marvell's defence of causes that were not entirely his own speaks to his empathy and his devotion to ideals that perhaps had less to do with political theology than with the humane values Anne and Andrew Marvell nurtured in their children.

The young Andrew Marvell would have had many occasions to hear his father preach; indeed, the voice of that 'most excellent preacher' must have long sounded in the echoing vault of the poet's imagination. We can get a sense for the Rev. Marvell's style, and what's more, for his 'brewing materials', from the sermons which survive in a manuscript book Marvell Sr kept, now in the Hull History Centre (Reference No. C DIAM/1). Especially telling for our purposes is an undated sermon titled 'Galatians: 6, 15. For in Christ Jesus, neither circumcision availeth anything, nor uncircumcision: but a new creature', a meditation on Christian reason. 'Do not the Stoics desire a blessed man to be one that lives according unto reason?', the reverend asks, rhetorically.

> Paul tells us of unreasonable men. Peter tells us of unreasonable beasts. These perhaps are Paul's beasts after the manner of men. Our doctrine lets us see the world peopled with beasts. The furious is a bear robbed of her whelps. The lecher a goat or a horseleech not leaving till she be full, nor full till she burst. The drunkard a swine or a poisoned rat, that drinks as long as it can stand. The subtle a fox. The malicious a mad dog. The envious a dog in a manger. The idle a dormouse. The swaggerer a colt unbridled. The ignorant an ass. The impatient a resty jade that seeks to cast his burden. (manuscript sig. 137ʳ⁻ᵛ)

In 2 Thessalonians, Paul prays 'that we may be delivered from unreasonable and wicked men: for all *men* have not faith' (3:2). Elsewhere he alludes to fighting wild beasts at Ephesus, a phrase which appears to refer to cruel opponents there (1 Corinthians 15:32). Peter, in his turn, likens sinners and blasphemers to 'brute beasts, made to be taken and destroyed, [who] speak evil of the things that they understand not; and shall utterly perish in their own corruption' (2 Peter 2:12). In homilizing these passages, however, Marvell Sr turns insistently to extra-scriptural materials, namely Aesop. The moralised beasts of Aesopian fable presented types of human defined by animal appetite: as such, they are perfect illustrations of 'unreasonable and wicked men'.

At the conclusion of his Aesopian cavalcade, Marvell Sr doubles back to his original theme and doubles down on humanist exegesis:

So that the world is a wilderness full of beasts; Circe's island where all are turned into beasts which have not Moly that is reason for a counter-charm. Hence Pythagoras his transmigration of men's souls into beasts when men for want of reason are turned bestial. The whole world is a Bedlam or Fooliana.

In Homer's *Odyssey*, the magician Circe tempts sailors into her palace, where she feeds them a potion 'mixed with baneful drugs' which turns the men to swine. The wise Pythagoras held that only the acquisition of 'true philosophy' could prevent the soul from being reincarnated as an animal. Pythagoras's *mathematica* here becomes Homer's Moly, the magic herb given by Hermes to Odysseus and his crew, and the antidote to ignorance, unreason, and bestiality. As impressive as the daisy chain of glosses is the naturalness with which Rev. Marvell works recursively up to his conclusion: the whole world is 'Bedlam or Fooliana', and our only means of escape the charm of Christian reason. The last line savours of Marvell's facetious wit. Was he thinking of his father's sermon when he wrote of the unreasonable Samuel Parker, 'Had he no friends to have given him good counsel before his understanding were quite unsettled? or if there were none near, why did men not call in the neighbours, and send for the parson of the parish to persuade with him in time, but let it run on like this till he is fit for nothing but Bedlam or Hogsdon?' (*PW*, 1:74). The likelihood that Marvell was in possession of his father's sermon book to the end of his life, as Stewart Mottram (2021) has recently found, only deepens our sense of Marvell Sr's influence on his son's mental world.

Not for nothing did Marvell make a point of his father's reputation for piety and learning. The sermon book moves fluently between English and Latin and is in places also studded with passages of Greek and Hebrew. Marginal glosses locate passages from Aesop, Aristotle, and Seneca as readily as they do passages from the Bible. And indeed, one of Marvell Sr's lasting legacies to the Charterhouse was the establishment, in 1626, of a 'perpetual library for the master of the hospital and any other about the town upon due caution', a project that admittedly catered to his own interests, but one which he justified on the grounds that it would be a boon to the godly and learned of Hull and a credit to the institution and the town (*Chronology*, 18–19). Marvell would depend on access to the libraries of aristocratic patrons for the writing of his pungent and exuberantly referential prose works. Growing up in the Charterhouse, his early studies were likely fostered in the library his father founded. A list of titles in the sermon book suggests the wide range of Marvell Sr's grounding in theology and theological controversy, and his son may have gotten a taste of this, if at a certain remove. Clearly, the reading of

Scripture was a fixture of everyday life. As the sermon on *recta ratio* makes clear, however, the Rev. Marvell's godliness was hardly incompatible with an appreciation for poetry and fable; indeed, the two went hand in hand in him, an inheritance that would be writ large in his son.

Hull Grammar School and the Origins of Marvell's 'Echoing Song'

Having been first tutored at home in his English ABC, Marvell is likely to have entered grammar school around the age of eight, in 1629, near the time Milton was composing his first great poem. It is possible he began earlier; while we don't know for sure when Marvell matriculated at Hull Grammar School, we do know that he went down to Cambridge in late 1633 and was by then 'very well educated in grammar learning' (Wood 1691, 2:619). Four years is not much time 'to make a scholar each way fit for the University', and some pedagogues, like the Jacobean schoolmaster John Brinsley (1612), opined 'that the child if he be of any ordinary towardness and capacity, should begin at five year old at the uttermost, or sooner rather' (7, 9). We cannot doubt Marvell's towardness and capacity for education, as his precocious entrance to university attests: though there was no 'standard' age of admission at this time, sixteen or seventeen was more usual, twelve young by any measure. Then again, we know that Marvell's father first set out on a career as a school teacher, so he may have taken his son's tuition in hand until young Andrew was suitably advanced in his catechism and in his English and Latin grammar.

The grammar school represented a major development in English education. In mediaeval England, school governance was largely a function of the Church. At the dissolution of the monasteries, many schools which had been maintained under the auspices of religious institutions were re-founded by private benefactors or corporations, and a raft of new letters patent issued under Edward VI and Elizabeth I further expanded the reach of humanist education. From 1542, the Latin accidence prescribed in such schools, commonly known as Lily's Grammar, was one developed at the direction of James I from the works of John Colet and William Lily, its uniform adoption secured by royal decree. So too was the licensing of schoolmasters to be prescribed and regulated. According to Elizabethan statutes of 1559, 'No man shall teach either in public school, or private house, but such as shall be allowed by the Bishop of the diocese, or Ordinary of the place, under his hand and seal, being found meet as well for his learning and dexterity in teaching, as for sober and honest conversation, and also for right understanding of God's true religion'. The grammar school thus stood at the dual front of humanism and Protestantism in the cultural landscape of early modern England. (See Charlton 1965; Simon 1966; Green 2009).

'The run-of-the-mill grammar school', Peter Mack (2016) writes, 'had three main aims: to teach the reading, writing, and speaking of Latin; to read portions of the best authors in the major genres of Latin literature; and to practise Latin composition' (201). Its remit was the renovation of manners, morals, and religion, an ideal rooted in the Ciceronian notion that 'eloquence and wisdom are one'. The grammar school pupil's endeavours thus revolved around the discipline of imitation (*imitatio* in Latin). Such discipline was in the first instance vocal and manual, as preceptual knowledge—'the reason of the rules'—gradually encrusted itself on the habitual reproduction of oral and written exempla. To quote Colet's advice in his *Grammatices rudimentis* of 1527, 'busy imitation with tongue and pen more availeth shortly to get the true eloquent speech than all the traditions, rules, and precepts of masters (sig. D7ᵛ).

The grammar school syllabus was remarkably consistent across early modern England: in the lower forms, students began with Cato's distichs (moral sayings) and Aesop's fables, supplemented by simple conversation books, such as Erasmus's *Colloquies*. They then went on, in the more advanced forms, to the works of Terence, Cicero's letters, Virgil's eclogues, Cicero's *De officiis*, Caesar, Sallust, Ovid, Horace, and the *Aeneid* (see Mack 2002, 2016). The *progymnasmata* or rhetorical exercises set for pupils (named after a textbook by the Greek rhetorician Aphthonius) were likewise organised along a sliding scale, from the copying and imitating of fables and familiar letters to more complex exercises in the various genres of oratory and poetry. Taking the long view of the method he employed as a schoolmaster in Plymouth, William Kempe put it thus: 'first the scholar shall learn the precepts; secondly, he shall learn to note the examples of the precepts in unfolding other men's works; thirdly, to imitate in some work of his own; fourthly and lastly, to make somewhat alone without an example' (Kempe 1588, sig. F2ʳ).

Marvell's juvenilia provide us a good example of imitation of this kind. Though it dates to his time at Cambridge, Marvell was still just a boy of fifteen when he wrote the Latin verses 'Ad Regem Carolum Parodia', which appeared in a collection of poetry by Cambridge academics published in honour of the birth of Anne Stuart, daughter of Charles I and Queen Henrietta Maria, in March 1637. Marvell's 'parody' takes its model from the first book of Horace's *Odes*. Horace's poem celebrates Augustus Caesar as Rome's deliverer from civil war, the disturbances of which are symbolised by the violent flooding of the Tiber. Marvell's poem looks to Charles as a saviour from the plague, which had carried off more than a thousand people in London between April and July 1636 and caused the university to close. The 'yellow Tiber, its waves hurled back from the Tuscan bank' (*Odes*, 1.2.13–14) finds its analogue in the Cam, 'his waves violently cast back from his right-hand shore' (ll. 13–14), and the Granta, 'straying over his left bank' (ll. 17–19). Within these modulations of theme and occasion, Marvell replays Horace's script quite closely; the wit of the Renaissance *parodia* consisted in preserving as much of the exemplar as possible while refashioning its purpose (see Haan 2003, 26–27). Thus, parents' crimes said by Horace to have whetted the sword of the gods against the young which might 'rather have slain the deadly Parthians' (*Odes*, 1.2.21–24) become in Marvell 'vices' that 'have sharpened a sword by which the oppressive Turks should better have perished' ('Parodia', ll. 21–24). Prayers of vestal virgins intended to expiate guilt (ll. 26–28) are transformed into the murmurs of a 'learned gathering' ('Parodia', ll. 26–28). In the close of his poem, Marvell glances at the 'sweet image' of Charles and Henrietta Maria's offspring (ll. 40–44), lines which have no precedent in Horace, but ends by hailing Charles as 'Caesar, our father' (l. 52), just slightly varying Horace's tribute to 'Caesar, our leader' (l. 52). 'Ad Regem Carolum Parodia' remains very much Horace's poem; Marvell's more famous Horatian ode is, of course, another story.

Imitative exercise, then, was a form of conditioning that imprinted itself on Marvell as it did to some extent on all early modern poets. As Jeff Dolven (2007) observes of Marlowe, Shakespeare, and Milton, 'The rhetorical discipline and virtuosity cultivated in the classrooms where they labored over Lily's *Grammar* and Aphthonius's exercises make an unmistakable contribution to their literary art' (9). And indeed, it is fair to say that Marvell's 'echoing song' has its origins in the felicity of *imitatio*. But it is just as important to recognise how humanist *imitatio*—for all of its promise to form and regulate the subject of its discipline—also produces a set of inverse qualities: wayward variety, self-reflexive play, creative subversion.

Sir Philip Sidney touches on this paradoxical dynamic in the *Apology for Poetry* (1580/1595). Addressed to those who 'inveigh against Poetry', the *Apology* insists above all on poetry's capacity for promoting virtue (Sidney 2002, 82). Sidney maintains that the teaching of poets is at once *truer* than that of the historian, who, being constrained by 'what men have done', teaches not what men should do (85); and *more forceful* than that of the moral philosopher, who teaches virtue, but only 'by certain abstract considerations' (89). Whereas the peerless poet, Sidney avers, 'yieldeth to the powers of the mind an image of that whereof the philosopher bestoweth but a wordish description, which doth neither strike, pierce, nor possess the sight of the soul so much as that other doth' (90). On this account, the Sidneyan reader is imagined as being seized or arrested and moreover possessed by the moral force of poetic fictions. He or she (though it is always 'he' in Sidney) cannot help but be moved to 'take … goodness in hand' and to 'know that goodness whereunto they are moved' (87). Poesy, in other words, serves 'not only to make a Cyrus, which had been but a particular excellency as Nature might have done, but to bestow a Cyrus upon the world to make many Cyruses, if they will learn aright why and how that maker made him' (85).

But if poetry accomplishes its ends so ravishingly, so resistlessly, what need is there for the schoolmaster? As the humanist Sidney well knew, the whole system of grammar school education was designed to inculcate 'right reading', binding the pupil, through an unremitting diet of imitative exercise, to demonstrating that he understands what he has read (see Dolven 2007). That such understanding was not to be taken for granted is the motivating premise of humanist pedagogy, as Sidney obliquely acknowledges in that conditional phrase, '*if* they will learn aright why and how that maker made him'. And to be sure, as Shakespeare's comic travesties of school Latin so brilliantly suggest, the busy tongue and pen were not always wed to the powers of the mind. Hence Marvell's quip that Parker has 'searched every corner in the Bible, and *Don Quixot*' for ammunition to use against the nonconformists, but to very little use; 'So that', Marvell gibes, 'except the manufacture and labour of your periods, you have done no more than any schoolboy could have done on the same terms' (*PW*, 1:172). The very type of the uncomprehending pupil, Parker produces only busy nonsense. But neither does a student's adeptness guarantee sound doctrine or univocal meaning ('right reading'): virtuosic imitation is distinguished by the quality of *serio ludere*, serious play, which tends not to limit or constrain but rather to multiply possible meanings. Some of the Renaissance texts which most fully embody this spirit include Erasmus's *Praise of Folly*, Rabelais's *Gargantua and Pantagruel*, and Cervantes's *Don Quixote*, all masterpieces of irony, paradox, and uncertainty.

To put this a little more philosophically, we might say that humanist pedagogy is rooted in an appeal to universal truth: to read the ancients 'aright' was to see into nature itself. At the same time, the rhetorical habits cultivated by humanist pedagogy tend to promote an exuberant multiplicity of sense. What emerges under these conditions is the perception, not of the naturalness of signs and values, but rather of their contingency and malleability. This can be shown of even the simplest kinds of texts and exercises. The classical *progymnasmata*, for instance, begins with the composing of fables. Thus Richard

Rainolde (1563), a kind of English Aphthonius, prescribes the following steps for making an oration by a fable:

1. First, ye shall recite the fable, as the author telleth it.
2. There in the second place you shall praise the author who made the fable, which praise may soon be got of any studious scholar, if he read the author's life and acts therein, or the godly precepts in his fables, shall give abundant praise.
3. Then thirdly place the moral, which is the interpretation annexed to the Fable, for the fable was invented for the moral's sake.
4. Then orderly in the fourth place, declare the nature of things, contained in the Fable, either of man, fish, foul, beast, plant, trees, stones, or whatsoever it be. There is no man of wit so dull, or of so gross capacity, but either by his natural wit, or by reading, or senses, he is able to say somewhat in the nature of anything.
5. In the fifth place…. (sig. A2ᵛ–A4ᵛ)

As is clear, this exercise requires the student to retell a fable of Aesop already committed to memory and then expound upon its meaning. More advanced students might be asked to produce their own fables after the fashion of Aesop, often as a way of digesting and commenting upon other texts, for instance, stories out of Ovid or Virgil. Fables could also be used, as Erasmus teaches, to give point to propositions or enliven longer works.

Here, as in Sidney, we have the image of an almost effortless moral education, as the schoolboy, however callow, reads Aesop in order to see into 'the nature of things'. The exercise of writing serves to materialise, to make visible and useful, the fruits of such reading. Hence, the ubiquitous humanist practice of commonplacing, in which especially pithy or memorable passages were extracted and organised into a notebook for later use. But how are we meant to take Rainolde's assurance, 'There is no man of wit so dull, or of so gross capacity, but either by his natural wit, or by reading, or senses, he is able to say somewhat in the nature of anything'? Clearly, Rainolde thinks all his students *ought* to have sufficient wit to complete this exercise in fabling; just as clearly, his experience is that they often do not, or at least, that the results vary widely. And what else would we expect? Aesopian fables do not in fact write themselves, nor do they produce automatic or self-evident (i.e. 'natural') interpretations. Indeed, we might say that truth is irretrievably bound up in the transits of fabling, of imitation, insofar as virtuosity and deficiency in the performance alike evince the waywardness, the plasticity of writing.

To stress-test the truth value of fables and fabling, we can do no better than turn to Marvell's enigmatic lyric 'Mourning'. The poem begins with a sort of didactic challenge, to moralise or state the nature of Chlora's tears: 'What mean these infants which of late / Spring from the stars of Chlora's eyes' (ll. 3–4). To that end, the speaker observes Chlora carefully:

> II
> Her eyes confused and doubled o'er,
> With tears suspended ere they flow,
> Seem bending upwards, to restore
> To heaven, whence it came, their woe.
>   III
> When, moulding of the wat'ry spheres,
> Slow drops untie themselves away;
> As if she with those precious tears,
> Would strow the ground where Strephon lay.
> (ll. 5–12)

Chlora looks up to the heavens, and down at her beloved Strephon; her tears seem at once to flow upward (like those of Crashaw's Weeper) and to strew the ground as flowers strew the funeral hearse (as in Milton's 'Lycidas'). According to the poet's wit, his reading, and his senses, Chlora's tears appear—almost redundantly, as it were—emblematic of female grief.

Before the moral of this feigned scene can be fully articulated, however, the poem introduces contrary opinion into its midst, what 'some affirm' (l. 13), and what 'others, bolder' say (l. 21): that Chlora's tears are false, that they only serve to soften her heart for another lover (Stanza IV); that they're a form of self-gratification ('Herself both Danaë and the shower') (Stanza V); that the joy of a new lover causes her to throw 'whatsoever does but seem / Like grief' from her 'windows' (Stanza VI); that her tears are not tribute to a dead lover but gifts to a new one (Stanza VII). In two concluding stanzas, the speaker thus seeks to contain or defuse these unruly glosses and to reassert his own interpretation; on both accounts, he deploys the resources of fabling:

> VIII
> How wide they dream! The Indian slaves
> That dive for pearl through seas profound,
> Would find her tears yet deeper waves,
> And not of one the bottom sound.
>   IX
> I yet my silent judgement keep,

Disputing not what they believe:
But sure as oft as women weep,
It is to be supposed they grieve.
(ll. 29–36)

Here the misogyny of those bold 'others' is answered first by one, then another moral commonplace: women's tears are unfathomable; and, 'as oft as women weep, / It is to be supposed they grieve'. But the hesitance of the speaker's final judgement continues to reflect the instability which entered the poem with the contrary voices of Stanzas IV-VII; we possess but cannot be wholly satisfied with the self-evident reading of Chlora's tears. 'Herself both Danaë and the shower': it is the brilliance of 'Mourning' to reflect and enact both sides of humanist pedagogy, fabling to reveal universal truth, fabling to reveal the artifice, the constructedness, of fabling.

Coda: The Master's Birch

Taking care not to be led too far into abstraction, it bears restating that the schoolroom was not merely a 'space of writing', a là Roland Barthes, but a physical space defined by strict conditions of bodily discipline. The ethos of humanist education is well attested by its prescribed textbook: Lily's Grammar deemed Latin a lesson 'well-beaten into a student'. In the satirical literature of the sixteenth and seventeenth centuries, the master's rod or birch was almost proverbially connected to the mending of rhetorical exercises. Marvell complains of persecuting clergy, 'they seem to have contracted no idea of wisdom, but what they learnt at school, the pedantry of whipping' (*PW*, 1:162), while schoolboys know they must 'down with their breaches as oft as [their master] wants the prospect of a more pleasing nudity (1:82). Clearly, 'correction' often went well beyond its official use. In early modern literary culture, an association thus arose, as recent scholars of the humanist schoolroom have shown, between the arts of eloquence and the pain and humiliation of sexualized violence (see Stewart 1997; Enterline 2006). Marvell's compassing of schoolroom abuse is suggestive enough, but it is far outgone, for instance, by this scabrous prolusion written by a late seventeenth-century student at Merchant Taylors' in the voice of the master's birch:

'Tis true I used like tortured Martyrs
And laid about your hinder quarters,
When finding an unlucky urchin,

(Whose bum's in cue for putting birch in
Down went his breeches, up his jerking,
And straight the whipster fell to forking)
Be sworn I'll soundly make you smart it,
And suffer too, as many have done.
The laying of a whipping on,
Whipping that's Virtue's Governess
Tutress [Tutoress] of Arts and Sciences;
That mends the gross mistakes of Nature
And puts new life into dull matter;
That lays foundation for renown
And all the honours of the gown:
(qtd. in Enterline 2006, 180)

Marvell's masters at Hull Grammar School, James Burnett, and, briefly, his successor Mr Stevenson, do not seem to have had a particular reputation for their zeal in whipping. But then only the most unusual cruelty tended to make itself visible within this deeply engrained culture of bodily correction (see Hirst 2018). Marvell's echoing song may reverberate with *imitatio*; but so too does it echo with traces of the verger's wand and pedant's lash, however difficult it may be to apprehend the precise history of the body to which such traces point.

References

Brinsley, John. 1612. *Ludus Literarius: Or, the Grammar School*. London.
Butler, Samuel. 1673. *The Transproser Rehears'd*. London.
Charlton, Kenneth. 1965. *Education in Renaissance England*. London: Routledge and Kegan Paul.
Colet, John. 1527. *Ioannis Coleti theologi … Grammatices rudimentis*. London.
Dolven, Jeff. 2007. *Scenes of Instruction in Renaissance Romance*. Chicago: University of Chicago Press.
Enterline, Lynn. 2006. Rhetoric, Discipline, and the Theatricality of Everyday Life in Elizabethan Grammar Schools. In *From Performance to Print in Shakespeare's England*, ed. Peter Holland and Stephen Orgel, 173–190. Basingstoke: Palgrave Macmillan.
Fuller, Thomas. 1662. *The History of the Worthies of England*. London.
Green, Ian. 2009. *Humanism and Protestantism in Early Modern English Education*. Farnham: Ashgate.

Grey, Anchitell. 1769. *Debates of the House of Commons, from the Year 1667 to the Year 1694*. 10 vols. London.

Haan, Estelle. 2003. *Andrew Marvell's Latin Poetry: From Text to Context*. Brussels: Latomus.

Hirst, Derek. 2018. Understanding Experience: Subjectivity, Sex, and Suffering in Early Modern England. In *Texts and Readers in the Age of Marvell*, ed. Christopher D'Addario and Matthew C. Augustine, 113–130. Manchester: Manchester University Press.

Horace. 2004. *Odes and Epodes*. Ed. and trans. Niall Rudd. Loeb Classical Library 33. Cambridge, MA: Harvard University Press.

Kempe, William. 1588. *The Education of Children in Learning*. London.

Mack, Peter. 2002. *Elizabethan Rhetoric: Theory and Practice*. Cambridge: Cambridge University Press.

———. 2016. Rhetorical Training in the Elizabethan Grammar School. In *The Oxford Handbook of the Age of Shakespeare*, ed. Malcolm Smuts, 200–212. Oxford: Oxford University Press.

Marvell, Andrew. 2003. *Prose Works of Andrew Marvell*. Ed. Annabel Patterson, Martin Dzelzainis, Nicholas von Maltzahn, and N. H. Keeble. 2 vols. New Haven: Yale University Press.

———. 2007. *Poems of Andrew Marvell*. Ed. Nigel Smith. Rev. ed. London: Longman.

Marvell, Andrew, Sr. *Sermons & c. of the Rev. Andrew Marvell*. Hull City Archives. C DIAM/1.

Mottram, Stewart. 2021 (forthcoming). "A Most Excellent Medicine": Malaria, Mithridate, and the Death of Andrew Marvell. *SC*.

Page, William. 1974. *A History of the County of York: Volume 3*. London: Victoria County History.

Parker, Samuel. 1673. *A Reproof to the Rehearsal Transprosed*. London.

Rainolde, Richard. 1563. *A Book Called the Foundation of Rhetoric*. London.

Roth, Frederic H., Jr. 1972. Marvell's "Upon Appleton House": A Study in Perspective. *Texas Studies in Language and Literature* 14 (2): 269–281.

Sidney, Sir Philip. 2002. *An Apology for Poetry*. Ed. R. W. Maslen. 3rd ed. Manchester: Manchester University Press.

Simon, Joan. 1966. *Education and Society in Tudor England*. Cambridge: Cambridge University Press.

Sistermans, Paul, and Odelinde Nieuwenhuis. 2013. *Eurosian Case Study: Holderness Coast (United Kingdom)*. Amersfoort: DHV [ebook].

Smith, Nigel. 2010. *Andrew Marvell: The Chameleon*. New Haven: Yale University Press.

Stewart, Alan. 1997. *Close Readers: Humanism and Sodomy in Early Modern England*. Princeton: Princeton University Press.

von Maltzahn, Nicholas. 2005. *An Andrew Marvell Chronology*. New York: Palgrave Macmillan.

Wood, Anthony. 1691. *Athenae Oxonienses*. 2 vols. London.

3

In loco parentis: Cambridge, 1633–1641

Marvell's years as a university student in Cambridge are relatively bare of biographical detail. The record of his father's ministry in Hull is substantial enough, but we know little of this period in the poet's life that comes from direct testimony. His sisters marry, making connections that will be important to Marvell later in life. And towards the end of this time, Marvell loses first his mother, in April 1638, and then his father, in a boating accident of January 1641. Unmoored, perhaps, by the grief of these experiences, Marvell seems to have drifted away from his studies and from the destiny they likely augured as a cleric in the Church of England. He was rusticated from Cambridge for non-attendance in September 1641, and it is thus in a triple sense that we might think of Marvell as 'the orphan of the hurricane' seen through a glass darkly in 'The Unfortunate Lover'—dispossessed of mother, father, and alma mater and thrust into the 'storms and wars' of revolutionary England.

No less than Marvell's education at Hull Grammar School, his training at Trinity College, Cambridge, is surely part of a literary life: the diet of reading and intellectual exercise to which Marvell was subject over seven years at Cambridge at once consolidated and extended into new areas the play of mind fostered in Marvell's precocious youth. We have probably underestimated the degree to which Marvell was impressed by the study of mathematics and astronomy in the university which would precipitate the discoveries of Isaac Newton a few decades hence. But these years also represent a crucial stage of Marvell's development: they see him enter the university as a boy of twelve and leave as a young man of twenty who would make his way in the world as a tutor to 'noblemen's sons'—youths not unlike some of the more privileged students Marvell would have met in his time at Cambridge.

© The Author(s), under exclusive license to Springer Nature Switzerland AG 2021
M. C. Augustine, *Andrew Marvell*, Literary Lives,
https://doi.org/10.1007/978-3-030-59287-5_3

Going Down to Cambridge

From the matriculation books, we know Marvell officially entered the university on 14 December 1633, a Saturday. The trip from the East Riding would have been long and slow, especially in winter: from Hull south across the Humber to Barton, then south and west along the trunk road towards Elsham and Wrawby to the Glamford Bridge at Brigg; from there the road ran mostly due south to Lincoln, then on through Sleaford, Morton, Born, and Market Deeping until reaching Peterborough; from Peterborough south again to Stilton, Buckden, and St Neots before turning east to Cambridge (see Ogilby 1733). At a distance of over 100 miles altogether, the journey would have taken the better part of a week. Old Hobson the Carrier, eulogised by Milton just two years previously, regularly made the forty-mile trip from London to Cambridge in three days and two nights (Fletcher 1961, 9). Young Andrew likely would have come by horse-drawn wagon, rumbling along with the goods of some Hull merchant. Did he travel alone? Or was he accompanied by his father? The liturgical season of advent was presumably a busy one for the minister, perhaps he could ill afford to neglect his duties for two weeks at this time of year. It is also curious that Marvell should have matriculated just before Christmas, especially with the wedding of his sister Anne to James Blaydes due to be celebrated at the Charterhouse on December 29. The young scholar's first few weeks at the college were undoubtedly lonely ones.

Marvell entered Cambridge as a subsizar, the lowest rank of student. The greatest proportion entered as pensioners, mostly sons of the clergy and small landowners; fellow-commoners, so-called because they sat at table with the fellows and tutors, paid higher fees and were typically offspring of the upper gentry and nobility. Sizars were poorer students who were granted fee relief and a meagre allowance in return for performing menial tasks for fellows of the college. Once he had arrived and entered his name on the rolls, Marvell would have been assigned quarters within the college, rooms shared with two or three other boys and sometimes a tutor. Roommates were also bedfellows, a locus of physical, affective, and intellectual intimacy often warmly recalled by university graduates of the period. Edmund Spenser (1580) enjoyed just such a close relationship with his Cambridge tutor, the renowned scholar Gabriel Harvey, asking Harvey, in *Three Proper and Witty Familiar Letters, Lately Passed between Two University Men*, whether he remembered those verses 'which I translated you *ex tempore* in bed, the last time we lay together in Westminster?' (6). Reformers and satirists, on the other hand, tended to see in the propinquity of school ties the spectre of sexual deviance: 'the greatest corruption, in our land', wrote the English Benedictine Father Augustine Baker (1933), 'as to such abominable vice … cometh from the two universities of England' (34).

The Cambridge of Marvell's day was a university of some three thousand members, and it is worth noting, with that great Victorian compiler of Cantabrigiana John Venn (1897), 'the commanding position which had then been attained by [Oxford and Cambridge]. Absolutely—not relatively merely—the number of graduates in the years 1625–30 was never attained again till within living memory [i.e. until the late nineteenth century]' (xxi). By the 1630s, Trinity had overtaken Marvell's father's college, Emmanuel, as the largest in the university, 'wherein is a Master, 60 Fellows, 67 scholars, 4 conducts [conduct priests or chaplains], 3 public professors, 13 poor scholars, a Master of the Choristers, 6 clerks, 10 choristers, 20 almsmen, besides officers and servants of the foundation, with many other students, being in all 440'. Marvell's near contemporary Gerard Langbaine the Elder (1651) praised Trinity as 'one of the most goodly and uniform colleges in Europe' (15).

While it may be true that 'Cambridge was the engine house of English Puritanism' (*Chameleon*, 31), the constituent colleges were doctrinally diverse, and Trinity was ranged in the middle of the spectrum, between the reformist zeal of Emmanuel and the Laudian orthodoxy of Peterhouse. In Trinity Chapel, Marvell would have heard the preaching of John Sherman, whose conviction that 'truths supernatural are not contradicted by reason' (1641, 1) would be echoed in the works of the so-called 'Cambridge Platonists'—Benjamin Whichcote, Nathaniel Culverwell, John Smith, Henry More, Ralph Cudworth—to which Marvell's poetry and later tolerationism owe a meaningful debt. Given that the choice of college likely lay with Marvell Sr rather than his son, it is notable that the boy of twelve was steered away from Emmanuel's insurgent brand of godliness: targeted by Laudian authorities for nonconformity, 'no less than eleven of the seventeen Heads of Colleges during the Commonwealth Period came from [Emmanuel's] walls' (Cunningham 1916, 73).

Dialectic Teaching and the Cambridge Arts Course

Trinity College was founded by Henry VIII in 1546, combining what had been Michaelhouse and King's Hall. Though the famous Wren Library was not completed until 1695, the grounds of the college as they stand today would have been largely recognisable to Marvell: Trinity College Chapel dates to the 1550s and anchors the north-east corner of the Great Court constructed by the college's Master and benefactor Thomas Nevile in the early seventeenth century, with its main hall, Master's Lodge, fountain, clock tower, and Great Gate. So much for the fabric of the College; what, then, were the course and manner of Marvell's studies at Cambridge, and what were the effects of such study on his writing and thinking? The first of these questions appears straightforward enough. However, unlike teaching in the grammar school, which was highly regulated and for which we possess detailed curricula, what was taught and the methods of teaching at Oxford and Cambridge in the sixteenth and early seventeenth century are less than certain. This is owing to the slow but steady transformation of these mediaeval institutions under the influence of the Reformation and Renaissance and in response to the widening purposes for which higher education was being reimagined in early modernity. University teaching was also in large part a function of individual tutors, who exercised wide authority over their pupils and prescribed their course of study. University and college statutes, together with tutorial account books and contemporary statements about academic work, give us some insight into this relatively closed world.

Joseph Mede was a fellow of Christ's College, Cambridge and from 1618 until his premature death in 1638 Mildmay Lecturer in Greek, 'a great philologer, a master of many languages, and a good proficient in the studies of history and chronology' (Worthington 1677, 1:ii). From Mede's biographer comes this intimate portrait of both life in the college and of the Cambridge arts course in the early seventeenth century:

> being a Fellow of the College, he esteemed it a part of his Duty to further the education of young scholars; which made him undertake the careful charge of a tutor: and this he managed with great prudence and equal diligence. After he had by daily lectures well grounded his pupils in Humanity, Logic and Philosophy, and by frequent converse understood to what particular studies their parts might be most profitably applied, he gave them his advice accordingly: and when they were able to go alone, he chose rather to set every one his daily task, then constantly to confine himself and them to precise hours for lectures. In the evening they all came to his chamber to satisfy him that they had performed the task he had set them. [...] And then, having by prayer commended them and their studies to God's protection and blessing, he dismissed them to their lodgings. (Worthington 1677, 1:iv)

Mede clearly took pains to tailor his pedagogy to each student on the basis of their interests and abilities. At the same time, the course had a general outline, 'Humanity, Logic, and Philosophy', or what we would call 'classical literature, philosophy and the natural sciences, led by mathematics and astronomy; or in other words, most of the seven liberal arts of the medieval university' (Morgan and Brooke 2004, 437). Not unreasonably then have Marvell's biographers suggested the consonance of his university training with the mediaeval trivium and quadrivium.

Such apparent continuity, however, belies important intellectual and pedagogic shifts which took hold in the Cambridge arts course in the latter half of the sixteenth century. The argument for continuity maintains that the early modern universities were insulated by tradition and inertia from the humanist transformation of intellectual life in the wider culture. Oxford and Cambridge on this view represent the rear-guard of mediaeval scholasticism (see Costello 1958). Alternatively, some argue that humanism did indeed penetrate the universities, but had a vitiating effect on logic as a discipline, replacing a formidable Aristotelian analytics with a superficial emphasis on rhetoric, in which 'boys were not taught to pay attention to an author's argument or technique, but simply to collect uncommon idioms, pithy sayings, colourful anecdotes, anything that might one day serve to pad out a limping paragraph of their own' (Bolgar 1973, 11). I am persuaded, however, by Lisa Jardine's work on this question, which makes the case that humanism did transform the curricula of early modern Oxford and Cambridge, and in ways that were at once intellectually robust and consequential (see Jardine 1974, 1975).

Jardine began by studying inventories of decease for those who died in residence at Cambridge in the later sixteenth century. From the surviving books of these unfortunate scholars, we glean an unvarnished insight into the texts which comprised, as it were, the common intellectual property of Cambridge fellows and pupils at this time. Unsurprisingly, Virgil, Ovid, Terence, and Cicero appear most frequently among classical authors. But by far the most commonly owned books were dialectic manuals. Moreover, these were humanist refashionings of Aristotelian dialectic along neo-Ciceronian lines, written by the likes of Lorenzo Valla, Rudolph Agricola, Philip Melanchthon, Johannes Caesarius, and John Seton (to which we should add the name of Peter Ramus, the seventeenth-century heir to Valla and Agricola). The force of these manuals lay in the emphasis they placed on 'aptness' of argument as opposed to formal validity and on natural discourse as opposed to the specialised terms of scholastic logic. The net effect is an opening out of dialectic from the narrow compass of the professional logician into the public, political sphere Aristotle had identified as the precincts of rhetoric. Thus Agricola—whose *De Inventione Dialectica* (1479) was the text owned by the greatest number of scholars in Jardine's sample—argues that his system of reformed dialectic 'is of particular advantage to those who deal with matters which lie *outside* [my emphasis] the bounds of academic instruction … who must often produce belief in the senate and the people in regard to war, peace, and other pressing civil matters' (McNally 1967, 396). In their resistance to what they regarded as scholastic dogmatism, the humanist dialecticians also dealt more in probable truth and practical persuasion than did their traditional counterparts (see Jardine 1977, 1988; cf. Spranzi 2011, 65–98). As Peter Mack (1993) memorably puts it, Agricola's textbook is a manual for 'how to think about what to say' on any subject (120).

In our own time, the humanities have come under fire as useless or impractical in a technicalized society: it is salutary to be reminded that the liberal arts were expressly conceived by Renaissance theorists as training for everyday life. Students' capacities for discoursing plausibly in 'each art and science' and for creating belief through eloquent speech were cultivated at Cambridge through regular disputations which required candidates to argue *in utramque partem* or on both sides of the question. At Trinity, disputations were held in the chapel thrice weekly during term time, while the tutorial group provided a near-daily context for practising *inventione* (the discovery of plausible arguments) and honing *eloquentia*. 1681) he was encouraged and in due time required to engage in dialectical disputation, 'And once begun, the wrangling never ceased' (Fletcher 1961, 66). (See 'Early Statutes of Trinity College', Stat. 18).

In the course of his potted biography of Samuel Parker in the *Rehearsal Transpros'd*, Marvell writes of his opponent's education at Wadham College, Oxford, 'there he studied hard, and in a short time became a competent rhetorician, and no ill disputant. He had learnt how to erect a *Thesis*, and to defend it *Pro* or *Con* with a serviceable distinction: while the Truth (as his comrade Mr. Bayes hath it on another occasion) … *Was here with a Whoop and gone with a Holla*' (1:74). It is possible to see in this burlesque a reflection on Marvell's own collegiate experience, but it is too simple to regard such remarks as merely derisory of university training. Marvell is playing up Parker's relish for disputation and his flexible attitude towards the truth as a rhetorician, but at the same time Marvell is himself engaging in point-by-point refutation of an opponent and flaunting rhetorical and dialectical skills of the kind he would have learned at Cambridge. I have dwelt at some length on what may seem the minutiae of ancient syllabi because I think it matters that Marvell's university course stressed the adequacy of natural discourse in the conduct of academic debate; that the dialectic manuals he likely read allowed for the provisional and contingent nature of truth within the human sciences; and that the procedure for clarifying controversial subjects, to recall Agricola, required 'the encounters of disputants' *pro et contra* (McNally 1967, 396), and hence, to recall T. S. Eliot (1975), the capacity for recognising 'in the expression of every experience … other kinds of experience which are possible' (170).

Dialogues and Debates

The counterposing of arguments, what we might think of as a dialectical approach to the competing claims of life and art, takes us to the heart of Marvell's poetry. Such an approach is most obvious in the small handful of poems which are formally structured as dialogues or debates. These include pastoral dialogues spoken by stock characters which owe much to the influence of Spenser—'A Dialogue between Thyrsis and Dorinda', 'Clorinda and Damon', 'Daphnis and Chloe', 'Ametas and Thestylis Making Hay-Ropes'— as well as the more abstract, philosophical dialogues 'Between the Resolved Soul, and Created Pleasure' and 'Between the Soul and Body'. Though these poems are generally of uncertain date, commentators have tended to view them—especially the slighter pastorals—as having been written relatively early, anticipating in various respects Marvell's more mature lyric achievements. Perspectival friction, the tension of differing viewpoints, is not just internally thematic to these poems but also relational, that is, the apparent outcome of one debate is implicitly called into question by that of another. We should be cautious of prizing one or another of these poems as a badge of Marvell's identity, for such epithets as they invite—'Puritan', 'Platonist', '*libertin*'—are but one aspect, as it were, of a wider dialogue.

'Thyrsis and Dorinda' occupies a curious place in Marvell's canon, in that it was widely copied and circulated in manuscript, and yet its authorship remains murky. The earliest version comes from a verse miscellany of the 1630s, a stretch for Marvell, compounded by the fact of its attribution in the miscellany to an Oxford poet. The dialogue was published under Marvell's name in the 1681 folio, a volume of high authority, though the text appears out of sequence there, inserted between some political verses of the Cromwell era, and was deleted from the copy ostensibly owned by Marvell's nephew. But I do not agree that the poem jars with Marvell's oeuvre, and if he did not write the original air, the prospect that he was involved in its later manuscript revision, as John Klause has hypothesised, prompts us to consider the hints it may have given to the developing poet, and to gauge the effects of his presumed rewriting (it is worth taking note that Dorinda's dialogue from line 27ff. of the text given in *Poems* is the product of secondary revision).

In '*My Echoing Song*', Rosalie Colie (1970) identified the Marvellian device of 'unmetaphor', by which she meant the way Marvell renovates overused tropes by taking them literally (111). The stormy sighs and tears of the conventional Petrarchan lover thus become, in 'The Unfortunate Lover', the elements in which he lives: 'The sea him lent those bitter tears / Which at his eyes he always wears: / And from the winds the sighs he bore, / Which through his surging breast do roar' (ll. 17–20). 'Thyrsis and Dorinda' is at once a Christian pastoral and a Christianizing of pastoral; its drama, like that of 'Clorinda and Damon', is one of conversion, as Dorinda becomes persuaded of Thyrsis's higher 'truth'. This apparent victory of Christian piety over classical nature, however, is unsettled in at least two ways. The first is through a strategy akin to 'unmetaphor' in that one of the speakers (Dorinda) insists on interpreting figurative language as literal. Her naïve questioning of Thyrsis's pastoral commonplaces works on one level as a sort of rustic catechism; but her literal-mindedness also threatens to deflate Thyrsis's good news by unclothing his rhetorical promises. When Dorinda bids Thyrsis to tell her where they shall go when Death parts them from this world, Thyrsis replies, 'To the Elysium' (ll. 1–5). This little comforts Dorinda, who knows 'no way but to our home' and fears she won't be able to find the place (ll. 5–8). Thyrsis advises, 'Turn thine eye to yonder sky, / There the milky way doth lie; / 'Tis a sure but rugged way, / That leads to everlasting day' (ll. 9–12). Dorinda sensibly points out that she has no wings and cannot fly (ll. 13–14). No sooner is she assured by Thyrsis that her soul will climb to heaven as fire reaches to the sky (ll. 15–18), Dorinda wants to know what people do there for eternity (ll. 19–20). If this were a different kind of poem, and Thyrsis were complaining of burning and melting away inside, like the speaker of Petrarch's eighteenth *canzone*, Dorinda might hand him a bucket of water. The first half of the dialogue wonderfully destabilises the speakers' roles: who is the shepherd and who the sheep, who the pupil, who the teacher.

The second half of the poem unsettles through the zeal of the newly converted. A version of 'unmetaphor' continues to play a part in this, as Dorinda insists on moving from rhetoric to action. Here the functional trope is that of *contemptus mundi*, the deprecation of the material world for the spiritual, this life for the life to come. Evidently pierced by Christian conviction following Thyrsis's description of Elysium as a place beyond hope or fear (the literal hinge of the poem, occupying lines 21–6 of a total 48), Dorinda cries, 'Oh sweet! Oh sweet! How I my future state / By silent thinking antedate: / I prethee let us spend our time to come / In talking of Elysium' (ll. 27–30). While Thyrsis is thus content to pipe his 'heavenly pastoral' (so-called by Smith, lines 31–8), Dorinda presses to know if his Christian vision is mere poetry, mere metaphor: 'Convince me now, that this is true; / By bidding, with me, all adieu' (ll. 41–2). When Thyrsis avers 'I cannot live, without thee' (l. 43), Dorinda promptly suggests they give their sheep into the care of another shepherd and seek a smooth death in the sleep of poppies (ll. 45–8). The pastoral fiction makes this affecting, but the pedagogy of unmetaphor should make us think twice about Thyrsis and Dorinda's—and the poem's—resolution. A true Christian ethic and hermeneutic surely require more 'silent thinking'. Dorinda's lines following Thyrsis's vision, as we have seen, do not appear in the earliest manuscript witnesses—in other words, the poem we call 'Marvell's' becomes so by virtue of a dialectical sally that answers, and in answering rewrites, its precursor. If in a less arresting way, we also have here that element of surprise which Eliot so admired in 'Coy Mistress', an effect not merely of formal ingenuity, but of generic and intertextual innovation as well.

'Clorinda and Damon' follows a pattern very similar to that of 'Thyrsis and Dorinda', as Damon seeks to convert Clorinda, and in turn, the dialogue they share, from pagan to Christian pastoral. Clorinda is a more sophisticated figure than Dorinda, however, and Marvell allows her to assume the role of carpe diem persuasion usually reserved for the male speaker in the context of pastoral lyric. The poem works, again, through a self-conscious interrogation of poetic language. Clorinda's initial solicitation invokes *The Faerie Queene* (see *Poems*, ll. 3–4n) while also importing the devices of courtly verse and translating them into pastoral terms: 'I have a grassy scutcheon spied, / Where Flora blazons all her pride. / The grass I aim to feast thy sheep: / The flowers I for thy temples keep' (ll. 3–6). Clorinda here naturalises the heraldic escutcheon—a shield decorated with the symbolic figures of a noble house or family—which becomes the grassy clearing dotted with bursts of flowers, a prospect she identifies with the handiwork of Flora. 'Blazon' refers both to the heraldic arts and to the familiar Petrarchan cataloguing of female attributes. Clorinda thus underlines her own fluency in the conventions of classical pastoral and in love poetry derived from courtly and Continental models.

Against these, Damon poses the idiom of Christianized pastoral, 'Grass withers; and the flowers too fade' (l. 7), recalling the famous passage from Isaiah, 'All flesh is grass, / And all its loveliness is like the flower of the field. / The grass withers, the flower fades' (40:5–7). Clorinda, whose ear is not attuned to the gospel, seizes this as an opening to articulate that fundamental argument of all carpe diem verse, from Horace to Herrick to Marvell's 'Coy Mistress': 'Seize the short joys then, ere they vade [i.e. fade, disappear]' (l. 8), she implores Damon, directing him towards an 'unfrequented cave' (l. 9). But Damon's hermeneutic is calibrated to heaven, not to this world, so that what follows is a punctuated set of exchanges which unmask and transvalue Clorinda's pastoral blandishments. 'That den?,' Damon retorts sceptically. 'Love's shrine', Clorinda insists. D: 'But virtue's grave' (l. 10). Undeterred, Clorinda suggests they can lie there (a double entendre) 'Safe from the sun'; heaven's eye sees all, is Damon's stern reply (ll. 11–12). Finally, exasperated by talk of all-seeing eyes and thirsty souls, Clorinda demands, 'What is't you mean' (l. 16). Damon explains that he of late met 'great Pan' (l. 20) while driving his flock and has since undergone a 'change', a change registered—as befits the lyrical context in which it takes place—as an essential retuning: the pastures, caves, and springs no longer hold meaning for Damon in and of themselves, as bearers and sites of pastoral significance and pastoral pleasure, but insofar as they 'sing', 'echo', and 'ring' of Pan (ll. 27–30). To that universal choir of praise Damon now tunes his 'slender oat' (l. 23), and so too Clorinda her voice: the four-line hymn with which the poem ends is spoken by a Chorus in which the previously distinct identities of Clorinda and Damon are merged.

Like Dorinda's, Clorinda's conversion is precipitous, but she and Damon are left where Thyrsis was before Dorinda's newfound contempt for the world ('I'm sick, I'm sick, and fain would die') and epistemological anxiety ('Convince me now, that this is true') led to Thyrsis and Dorinda's 'suicide pact' (Rees 1989, 63), that is, hymning a pastoral vision of heaven without abandoning earthly responsibility. The two poems thus partly complement and partly complicate each other. If we take Clorinda and Damon to be images of a more apt pupil and teacher, the Christian moral framework of 'Thyrsis and Dorinda' is thereby improved. At the same time, the way Damon resists Clorinda's inducements to pleasure by virtue of possessing a 'truer' set of figures ('D. That den? C. Love's shrine. D. But virtue's grave') is qualified by the comic undercutting of Thyrsis's Christian metaphorics by Dorinda's naturalism. The movement of the dialectic in these poems is obviously towards transcendence—of pagan mythos, of pastoral ease—but their Christian resolve is also overlaid with a touch of artificiality and uncertainty.

Body and Soul

Marvell's philosophical dialogues enact a similar conflict between nature and grace, body and soul, matter and spirit, only shifted into a different set of languages—Hellenistic philosophy, Puritan divinity, and Neo-Platonism of the kind which was beginning to take root in Cambridge while Marvell was a student there. 'A Dialogue, Between the Resolved Soul, and Created Pleasure' opens *Miscellaneous Poems*, and is perhaps the most unambiguous of Marvell's dialectics in that the Resolved Soul comes through its test seemingly without yielding anything to Created Pleasure. The battery of sensual, material, and intellectual temptations that confronts the Resolved Soul loosely mirrors the temptation of Christ in the wilderness, while the image of the Soul arming itself for battle (ll. 1–10) places the poem within the ambit of the 'Christian warfare' genre of Puritan literature inspired by the Pauline exhortation to put on 'the whole armour of God' (see Luttmer 2000, 44n; Friedman 1970, 74). Body and soul debates are common in Latin and vernacular poetry of the middle ages; the genre withers in the fifteenth and sixteenth century, then briefly revives, only to 'disappear … completely' by the middle of the seventeenth century, as the topos is absorbed into more prosaic modes of moral and religious discourse (see Osmond 1974, esp. 400ff; Bossy 1976).

What, then, are we to make of J. B. Leishman's claim (1966, 31–2n) that 'A Dialogue, Between the Resolved Soul, and Created Pleasure' bears echoes of *Paradise Lost* such that Marvell's poem could only have been written after 1667, in spite of its obvious affinities with poems belonging to the period c. 1646–52? Looking ahead, this question has implications for how we should think about the case for re-dating the composition of 'The Garden' to the Restoration. The Marvellian lines which resonated for Leishman are these: 'All this fair, and soft, and sweet, / Which scatt'ringly doth shine, / Shall within one beauty meet, / And she be only thine' (ll. 51–4). Their alleged source, the serpent's overpraising of Eve in Book IX of *Paradise Lost*:

> I turned my thoughts, and with capacious mind
> Considered all things visible in heaven,
> Or earth, or middle, all things fair and good;
> But all that fair and good in thy divine
> Semblance, and in thy beauties heavenly ray
> United I beheld …
> (9.603–8)

Cautiously accepting Leishman's suggestion for the date of 'A Dialogue' ('?After August 1667'), Smith (*Poems*, ll. 23–4n) ventures a further Miltonic parallel. Of Marvell's couplet, 'My gentler rest is on a thought, / Conscious of doing what I ought' (ll. 23–4), he notes: 'appears to echo verbally the temptation to learning in Milton, *Paradise Regained* (1671)', quoting from Book IV the lines, 'Think not but that I know these things, or think / I know them not; not therefore am I short / Of knowing what I ought'. To hear in Marvell this 'echo' of Milton would seem to require pushing the composition of the dialogue later still, that is, sometime after September 1670, when Milton's book was entered into the Stationer's Register.

The case for re-dating 'A Dialogue' and other of Marvell's lyrics from the earlier to the later part of his career thus rests on the strength of supposed parallels in Marvell's verse with print sources published after 1660. On the whole, however, those advancing such arguments have little theorised the forensic value of what James Loxley calls 'echoes as evidence', putting down to conscious allusion what may just as well be attributed to the 'molding force' of poetic language, literary form, and generic constraint within the compositional process, in other words, to non-deliberate structures of causation (see Loxley 2012, esp. 169–70). How far to seek, one might ask, are the rhymes 'thought/ought' or 'ought/not'? Moreover, we have a reasonably good sense of the occasions Marvell had for writing Christian-Platonic dialogues in the 1640s; and indeed, where 'The Garden' is concerned, for meditating on the respective merits of the *vita activa* and *vita contemplativa* in the early 1650s. Marvell's biography has so far provided no comparably strong sense of occasion for the composition of 'A Dialogue, Between the Resolved Soul, and Created Pleasure' around the same time as he was writing 'The Last Instructions to a Painter'. The prospect of making 'a whole man out of this poet with too many personae' can fairly be called the holy grail of modern criticism of Marvell. This helps to understand the desire to find the Whig politician singing in a Restoration garden, but no less the prudence of insisting on a high bar of proof.

If we might circle back, then, to the poetry, we can explore a little further Marvell's body and soul dialogues and how they speak to each other. The give and take of 'A Dialogue, Between the Resolved Soul, and Created Pleasure' is characterised by an escalating series of temptations, centred first on the five senses, then on 'worldly things' and 'alluring baits' (John Downame's 1632 *The Christian Warfare* may be a source; qtd. at 359). Superb dialectician that the Soul is, its victory consists in a Bartlebyesque immovability which the Soul maintains by categorically denying the premises of its interlocutor. This strategy becomes increasingly clear in the second round of proffers, as the Resolved Soul debunks earthly definitions of beauty ('If things of sight such heavens be, / What heav'ns are those we cannot see', ll. 55–6); of wealth ('Were't not a price who'd value gold? / And that's worth nought that can be sold', ll. 61–2); of glory ('What friends, if to myself untrue? / What slaves, unless I captive you?', ll. 67–8); and of knowledge ('None thither mounts by the degree / Of knowledge, but humility', ll. 73–4). With nothing left to offer, Created Pleasure is utterly defeated, as is declared in a final choral stanza:

'Triumph, triumph, victorious Soul; / The world has not one pleasure more: / The rest does lie beyond the pole, / And is thine everlasting store' (ll. 75–8).

'Pole', as Smith suggests (l. 77n), may be a metonym for 'sky', but it is also the case that the Resolved Soul and Created Pleasure are in this dialogue two 'poles', standing at a total remove from each other (cp. 'The Definition of Love', 'And therefore her [Fate's] decrees of steel / Us as the distant poles have placed', ll. 17–18). This distance stands as a measure of how faithfully the poem articulates a traditional Platonic dualism, in which body and soul are understood to be ontologically distinct, the soul a 'captive' to the body and to the senses, which veil the soul's perception of the absolute Good. Thus is the soul counselled, in the *Phaedo*, 'that inquiry through the eyes is full of deception, as also is that through the ears and the other senses', and so 'to retreat from these senses except where it is necessary to use them', and *'to gather and collect itself together and trust nothing else but itself in itself'* (*Phaedo*, 83b, my emphasis).

The sense of opposition and dis-implication achieved in 'A Dialogue, Between the Resolved Soul, and Created Pleasure' is effectively collapsed in 'A Dialogue between the Soul and Body', though both poems are rooted in the same Platonic source. Their point of contact, or dialectical hinge, I want to suggest, may be found in the Resolved Soul's response to the final temptation of sense. Our attention is drawn here, first, by the fact that hearing supersedes sight within the poem's sensual schema, overturning the assumption of sight's pre-eminence among the faculties. Moreover, the Resolved Soul's rejection of 'charming airs; / Which the posting winds recall' (ll. 38–9) is the only stanza of nine spoken by the Soul not in the form of a single octosyllabic couplet, and, significantly, the only to concede the attractiveness of that which is refused: 'Had I but any time to lose', the Soul confides, 'On this [i.e. on music] I would it all dispose. / Cease tempter. None can chain a mind / Whom this sweet chordage cannot bind' (ll. 37–40). 'Chordage' is of course a pun, referring to the nets or cords Created Pleasure would throw over the Resolved Soul, but also to the musical chords of 'charming airs'. Having wavered for half a moment—and what sensitive intelligence does not feel the attractions of music—the Soul duly gathers itself and, flexing its resolve, declares its impervious self-sovereignty ('Cease tempter. None can chain a mind…'). Having been sensitised to Miltonic echoes, we might hear in these words an allusion to the Lady's defiance of Comus, 'Fool do not boast, / Thou canst not touch the freedom of my mind / With all thy charms…' (ll. 662–4). Unable to resist the culminating play on words, however, the Resolved Soul is fleetingly betrayed by and into the substance of language, with its ambiguities and double-meanings, its puns and paradoxes, its endless malleability. In 'A

Dialogue between the Soul and Body', language holds out little hope of allowing the Soul to cleave to itself, and the Soul cannot get free of the Body or its arguments.

Suggestively following 'Clorinda and Damon' in *Miscellaneous Poems*, 'A Dialogue between the Soul and Body' exemplifies 'unmetaphor' in its fully creative aspect. Marvell here recurs to the trope of the body as 'prison-house' house of the soul, only this poem, in contrast to the 'Dialogue, Between the Resolved Soul and Created Pleasure', appears to illustrate not the success but rather the failure of Platonic philosophy. Once again, Milton's Lady provides a local accent, in her scorn of Comus's charms, 'although this corporal rind / Thou hast *immanacled*, while heaven sees good' (ll. 664–5, my emphasis). Thus Marvell's Soul:

> Oh who shall, from this dungeon, raise
> A soul inslaved so many ways?
> With bolts of bones, that fettered stands
> In feet; and manacled in hands.
> Here blinded with an eye; and there
> Deaf with the drumming of an ear.
> A soul hung up, as 'twere, in chains
> Of nerves, and arteries, and veins.
> Tortured, besides, each other part,
> In a vain head, and double heart.
> (ll. 1–10)

Taking the prison-house metaphor literally, the body is here anatomised as an elaborate torture trap; pun and paradox brilliantly rewrite sensibility and motility—the capacity to feel and to move—as forms of deprivation and unfreedom. 'Fetter' is etymologically related to 'foot', as 'manacle' is to 'hand', thus underscoring the carceral nature of embodiment. To be blinded *with* an eye and deaf *with* 'the drumming of an ear' likewise restate emblematically the teaching of Plato's Socrates that the soul 'is utterly bound up in the body and fastened to it and forced to examine reality through it, as if through prison bars, but not by itself on its own' (*Phaedo*, 82d). The threads of the nervous and circulatory systems readily suggest themselves, on this paradigm, as a mesh in which the soul is caught, perhaps evoking as well the strings of a marionette. (Donald J. Millus [1973] has argued for the influence of Andreas Vesalius's anatomy textbook *De humani corporis fabrica* in these lines, but the hint also lay nearer to hand, in the middle stanza of Donne's 'The Funeral'). Philosophy, on the standard Platonic account given in 'A Dialogue Between the Resolved Soul, and Created Pleasure', promises to liberate the soul from its prison; hopelessly bound up with the Body, thought, according to the Soul of 'A Dialogue between the Soul and Body', amounts to little more than vain delusion.

Too right! is the Body's apt response. In a witty inversion of the Platonic doctrine of the tripartite soul, the Body insists on the preferability of insentient creaturely life and, indeed, vegetable being, to what we might call the tyranny of consciousness. Typifying the 'boomerang' device of Milton's and Marvell's polemical writing, whereby the animadverter 'quotes and slants a phrase to retort it upon the sender's head' (*CPW*, 4:692), the Body outgoes the Soul's 'bolts of bones' in making the Soul a spike on which the Body is hoist:

> O who shall me deliver whole,
> From bonds of this tyrannic soul?
> Which, stretched upright, impales me so,
> That mine own precipice I go;
> And warms and moves this needless frame:
> (A fever could but do the same).
> And, wanting where its spite to try,
> Has made me live to let me die.
> (ll. 11–18)

Smith's comment here is very fine: '*OED* v. 4 b quotes this line in the sense of "to transfix upon, or pierce through with, anything pointed; fig. to torment or render helpless as if transfixed", but [Marvell] is making an image out of the literal meaning of the previous entry', that is, *OED* v. 4 a 'To thrust a pointed stake through the body of, as a form of torture or capital punishment; to fix upon a stake thrust up through the body' (*Poems*, l. 13n, *impales*). 'Besoulment', on this view, is an existentially painful proposition, and corresponds to a circumstance of perpetual vertigo; much better to be a creeping thing or beast of the earth (in the language of Genesis) than upright, 'rational' man (cf. Smith, *Poems*, l. 13n, *That mine*). It is doubtful whether Rochester could have read this lyric in manuscript—it is well established that he read Marvell's satires in prose and verse and with no little interest—but we might nonetheless be reminded of Rochester's 'thinking fool' in 'A Satire against Reason and Mankind', climbing 'with pain / Mountains of whimsies heaped in his own brain, / Stumbling from thought to thought', only to fall 'headlong down / Into Doubt's boundless sea…' (ll. 16–19).

Paradox begets paradox in Marvell's dialogue: to the Body, besoulment is both a life sentence and a death sentence (the Soul, it chides, 'Has made me live to let me die'); in turn, the Soul complains of its share in the Body's griefs, and of its felt duty to preserve that 'which me destroys', that is, the Body, an experience the Soul compares to being 'shipwracked into health' just when it hopes to gain the port of death (ll. 29–30). Movingly, the Body argues that such pangs as the Soul complains of are nothing next to the peculiar maladies of sentience—Love, Hatred, Joy, Sorrow, all of which 'Knowledge forces me to know / And Memory will not forgo' (ll. 35–40).

At this point, Soul and Body stand equal, each having spoken twenty lines; the balance is thus tilted by the last four lines Marvell allows to the Body:

> What but a soul could have the wit
> To build me up for sin so fit?
> So architects do square and hew
> Green trees that in the forest grew.
> (ll. 41–4)

We know something of the special value Marvell placed on the green world and too of the way 'green' seems to function in Marvell's poetry as a private shibboleth of sorts. In 'The Garden', green trees serve as emblems of an existence apart from the heats and toils of human endeavour (see stanzas II–III), as they serve here for the Body in contrast to the heedless contrivance of the builder. As 'The Garden' progresses, however, green life comes to represent the ideal vector of (duly sublimated) human drives, at once the object of aesthetic communion and a self-reflexive simile for the product of such communion: 'Apollo hunted Daphne so, / Only that she might laurel grow; / And Pan did after Syrinx speed, / Not as a nymph, but for a reed' (ll. 27–32). Following another turn of perspective, greenness famously asserts itself as the gnomic adjective of pure mind, 'Annihilating all that's made / To a green thought in a green shade (ll. 47–8). The way these contradictions are folded together in the greenness of 'The Garden' helps us appreciate the opposed but mutually imbricated nature of Soul and Body in the 'Dialogue'. The resulting ironies are thoroughly Marvellian: through the contrivance of the poet-maker, the Body is given extra scope to reproach all that the Soul grafts onto insentient nature; in so doing, the Body completes a sonnet.

Maturity and Loss

The figure of shipwrack prompts us to turn our attention back to Marvell's lived experience, the progress of his Cambridge career, and its eventual foundering in circumstances of personal disaster. Though Henrician reform had officially severed the ties between England's religious houses and its universities, monasticism remained a defining feature of university life long after the 1540s. On a typical day, undergraduates were expected to rise at 4.30 in the morning, engaging in private prayer before attending Chapel service at 5.00. Even breakfast revolved around Scripture being read and homilised. Following breakfast, students recited their lessons in the College; morning and afternoon, they attended lectures or disputations in the public schools. From 3.00 to 6.00 students undertook their private studies, followed by evening chapel and dinner. The gates were closed at 9.00 or 10.00 at night depending on the time of year. According to statute, students were only permitted to go into town by special permission and novice bachelors only under the supervision of their tutor or a Master of Arts. College regulations prohibited visiting taverns or lodging-houses, attending boxing matches, bear-baitings, or cockfights, or generally loitering about the town; they forbade owning irreligious books, keeping dogs or 'fierce birds', gambling, or playing at dice; and so on. The comprehensiveness of the regulations suggests how far the University sought to extend its discipline, though the laundry-list of potential offences perhaps speaks to a reality somewhat looser than the prescription. (See Masson 1859–80, 1:96; Ball and Rouse 1906, 51–2).

Though Marvell's indirect reflections on his time at university are hardly nostalgic, he nevertheless did well. In April 1638, a few weeks after his seventeenth birthday, he was elected to a scholarship by the Fellows of Trinity College, an acknowledgment of academic merit and promise, but moreover the award more than doubled the meagre stipend Marvell received as a subsizar. In February of the following year, 1639, Marvell subscribed for his BA, duly acknowledging the authority of the king, the Book of Common Prayer, and the Thirty-Nine Articles. So too had Milton done, in taking his BA in 1629 and his MA in 1632, though he gives a rather different impression in *The Reason of Church Government* (1642), where he speaks of 'coming to some maturity of years and perceiving what tyranny had invaded the Church, [such] that he who would take orders must subscribe slave, and take an oath withal, which unless he took with a conscience that would retch, he must either straight perjure, or split his faith' (*CPW*, 1:822–3). If the mature Marvell had any inward reservations about taking the Oaths of Supremacy and Allegiance as a Restoration MP, they were evidently not sufficient to make his conscience 'retch'. His decision to advance towards the MA degree argues a steady view to preferment in church or university, and Marvell continued to enjoy collegiate support in the form of a Lady Bromley scholarship.

For all his apparent academic success, interruptions more than once threatened to derail Marvell's studies. The first and most puzzling of these is young Andrew's brush with Roman Catholicism. This anecdote first appears in the Life of Marvell written by Thomas 'Hesiod' Cooke for his 1726 edition of Marvell's *Works*, gets repeated by Marvell's later eighteenth-century editor Capt. Edward Thompson, and thus becomes part of the permanent biographical record. As Thompson (1776) has it, Marvell's 'genius and parts brought him forward with more brilliancy and rapidity than is usual in youth of that age', even to the attention of some sedulous Jesuits who were then trawling the universities for young men of ability who might be made 'great and useful supporter[s] of their cause'. 'In their attention to him', says Thompson, 'they so far succeeded as to inveigle him to London, where his father pursued him, and met with him by accident in a bookseller's shop, and there prevailed upon him to return to college' (438–9).

In its details, the story stretches belief: an absence of 'some months' (per Cooke) would have run afoul of the College's residency requirements, and there is no record of Marvell having been disciplined as an undergraduate for such an offence. Marvell Sr's 'chance' discovery of his truant son in a London bookseller's shop seems the stuff of eighteenth-century novels. In early 1640, however, the vicar of a neighbouring village wrote Marvell's father seemingly in reference to young Andrew's seduction by the Jesuits. The vicar told Rev. Marvell of his own son's being tempted, while studying at St Catharine's Hall, with preferment in return for the son's conversion to popery. 'I perceive by Mr Breercliffe some such prank used towards your son', the vicar writes, and asks if he might 'know what you did therein' (Margoliouth 1922, 24). On the strength of this evidence, it seems likely that Marvell did indeed have some kind of run-in with Catholic agents while at Cambridge. Black-coated Jesuits might thus suggest themselves as candidates for the predatory cormorants who feed Marvell's Unfortunate Lover 'with hopes and air', famishing him while they feast, and so prepare 'Th'unfortunate and abject heir' for his bloody and traumatic destiny (see stanzas IV–V). But the biographical details do not readily fit with the poem's narrative of devastation subsequent to the Unfortunate Lover's 'orphaning': Marvell was nineteen by the time he lost his parents, and the episode with the Jesuits emphasises the role of Marvell's father in preventing their success. Was experimenting with Catholicism an act of adolescent rebellion directed *at* the Rev. Marvell? No doubt we should at the least be reminded that religious identity was not a fixed thing, even—perhaps especially—in the polarising years before the outbreak of civil war. Later in life, Marvell would of course become the scourge of 'popery and arbitrary government'. But his anti-popery has little of the visceral disgust for Catholic spirituality so often found in Puritan polemic. An air of indefeasible mystery hangs about the story.

There is however nothing mysterious about the spectre of disease and loss which troubled Marvell's Cambridge years. Plague visited the town in 1636–7, causing the University to close, as witnessed by Marvell's poem 'Ad Regem Carolum Parodia'. Marvell's hometown of Hull, a port city, was even harder hit, being infected 'for upwards of three years' from 1635–8, to the extinction of 'all commerce'. In December 1637, Marvell Sr risked his own health to preach at the funeral of John Ramsden, Mayor of Hull, and see to his Christian burial. The following April, Marvell's mother died, of causes unknown. In November 1638, his father remarried, taking as his wife the twice-widowed Lucy Alured. She would soon be widowed a third time: on 23 January 1641 Marvell's father drowned 'crossing Humber in a Barrow-boat', that is, from Barrow Haven to Hull. 'The same was sand-warped, and he drowned therein, by the carelessness, not to say drunkenness of the boat-men, to the great grief of all good men' (Fuller 1662, 159).

Marvell had lost his patron and guide. Ever unforthcoming where we would most like him to reveal himself, Marvell's feelings about the untimely death of his father only become legible, as Marvell's inwardness most often becomes legible, through displacement. Though childless himself, Marvell nonetheless writes with surpassing sympathy in August 1667 to his friend John Trott, following the loss of Trott's son. Marvell begins by acknowledging his incapacity to supply any true consolation. 'Only having a great esteem and affection for you', he continues, 'and the grateful memory of him that is departed being still green and fresh upon my spirit, I cannot forbear to inquire how you have stood the second shock at your meeting of friends in the country. I know that the very sight of those who have been witnesses of our better fortune, doth but serve to reinforce a calamity. I know the contagion of grief, and infection of tears', the poet writes, 'and especially when it runs in a blood' (*1681*, 67). Marvell would have made the trip from Cambridge to Hull for his father's funeral; his studies, and whatever hopes for a career were wrapped up in them, also found their end in the calamity. In September 1641 Marvell's name appears in the record book of Trinity College along with some others who 'in regard that some of them are reported to be married and the other look not after their days nor acts, shall receive no more benefits of the College, and shall be out of their places unless they show just cause to the College for the contrary in 3 months' (*Chronology*, 29). 'Andrew's Son', *Andreae Filiae*, as he would later sign certain of his poems, was on his own.

References

Baker, Fr Augustine. 1933. *Memorials of Father Augustine Baker and Other Documents Relating to the English Benedictines*. Ed. Dom Justin McCann and Dom Hugh Connolly. Leeds: Privately Printed.

Ball, W., and W. Rouse. 1906. *Trinity College Cambridge*. London: Dent.

Bolgar, R.R. 1973. From Humanism to the Humanities. *Twentieth Century Studies* 9: 8–21.

Bossy, Michel-André. 1976. Medieval Debates of Body and Soul. *Comparative Literature* 28 (2): 144–163.

Costello, William. 1958. *The Scholastic Curriculum at Early Seventeenth-Century Cambridge*. Cambridge, MA: Harvard University Press.

Cunningham, William. 1916. *English Influence on the United States*. Cambridge: Cambridge University Press.

Downame, John. 1633. *The Christian Warfare against the Devil, World, and Flesh*. London.

'Early Statutes of Trinity College' (1560). In *The University of Cambridge from the Royal Injunctions of 1535 to the Accession of Charles I*, by J. B. Mullinger, Appendix A. Cambridge: Cambridge University Press.

Eliot, T.S. 1975. Andrew Marvell. In *Selected Prose of T. S. Eliot*, ed. Frank Kermode, 161–171. London: Faber.

Fletcher, Harris Francis. 1961. *The Intellectual Development of John Milton*. Vol. 2. Urbana: University of Illinois Press.

Friedman, Donald. 1970. *Marvell's Pastoral Art*. London: Routledge.

Fuller, Thomas. 1662. *The History of the Worthies of England*. London.

Jardine, Lisa. 1974. The Place of Dialectic Teaching in Sixteenth-Century Cambridge. *Studies in the Renaissance* 21: 31–62.

———. 1975. Humanism and the Sixteenth-Century Cambridge Arts Course. *History of Education* 4 (1): 16–31.

———. 1977. Lorenzo Valla and the Intellectual Origins of Humanist Dialectic. *Journal of the History of Philosophy* 15 (2): 143–164.

———. 1988. Language and Logic: Humanistic Logic. In *The Cambridge History of Renaissance Philosophy*, ed. C.B. Schmitt, Quentin Skinner, Eckhard Kessler, and Jill Kraye, 173–198. Cambridge: Cambridge University Press.

Langbaine, Gerard Sr. 1651. *The Foundation of the University of Cambridge*. London.

Leishman, J.B. 1966. *The Art of Marvell's Poetry*. London: Hutchinson.

Loxley, James. 2012. Echoes as Evidence in the Poetry of Andrew Marvell. *SEL* 52 (1): 165–85.

Luttmer, Frank. 2000. Persecutors, Tempters and Vassals of the Devil: The Unregenerate in Puritan Practical Divinity. *Journal of Ecclesiastical History* 51 (1): 37–68.

Mack, Peter. 1993. *Renaissance Argument: Valla and Agricola in the Traditions of Rhetoric and Dialectic*. Leiden: Brill.

Margoliouth, H.M. 1922. Andrew Marvell: Some Biographical Points. *Modern Language Review* 17 (4): 351–361.

Marvell, Andrew. 1681. *Miscellaneous Poems by Andrew Marvell, Esq*. London.

———. 2003. *Prose Works of Andrew Marvell*. Ed. Annabel Patterson, Martin Dzelzainis, Nicholas von Maltzahn, and N.H. Keeble. 2 vols. New Haven: Yale University Press.

———. 2007. *Poems of Andrew Marvell*. Ed. Nigel Smith. Rev. ed. London: Longman.

Masson, David. 1859–80. *The Life of John Milton: Narrated in Connexion with the Political, Ecclesiastical, and Literary History of His Time*. 6 vols. Cambridge and London: Macmillan.

McNally, J.R. 1967. Rudolph Agricola's *De Inventione Dialectica Libri Tres*: A Translation of Selected Chapters. *Speech Monographs* 34 (4): 393–422.

Millus, Donald J. 1973. Andrew Marvell, Andreas Vesalius, and a Medieval Tradition. *Yale University Library Gazette* 47 (4): 216–223.

Milton, John. 1953–82. *Complete Prose Works of John Milton*. Ed. Don M. Wolfe et al. New Haven: Yale University Press.

———. 2008. *The Major Works*. Ed. Stephen Orgel and Jonathan Goldberg. Oxford World's Classics. Oxford: Oxford University Press.

Morgan, Victor, and Christopher Brooke. 2004. *A History of the University of Cambridge: Volume II: 1546–1750*. Cambridge: Cambridge University Press.

Ogilby, John. 1733. *Britannia Depicta or Ogilby Improved: Being a Correct Copy of Mr Ogilby's Actual Survey of All Direct & Principal Cross-Roads in England and Wales*. 4th ed. London.

Osmond, Rosalie. 1974. Body and Soul Dialogues in the Seventeenth Century. *ELR* 4 (3): 364–403.

Plato. 2017. *Euthyphro. Apology. Crito. Phaedo*. Ed. and trans. Christopher Emlyn-Jones and William Preddy. Loeb Classical Library 36. Cambridge, MA: Harvard University Press.

Rees, Christine. 1989. *The Judgment of Marvell*. London: Pinter.

Sherman, John. 1641. *A Greek in the Temple: Some Common-places Delivered in Trinity College Chapel in Cambridge*. Cambridge.

Smith, Nigel. 2010. *Andrew Marvell: The Chameleon*. New Haven: Yale University Press.

Spenser, Edmund. 1580. *Three Proper and Witty Familiar Letters, Lately Passed between Two University Men*. London.

Spranzi, Marta. 2011. *The Art of Dialectic between Dialogue and Rhetoric*. Amsterdam and Philadelphia: John Benjamins.

Thompson, Edward. 1776. The Life of Andrew Marvell. In *The Works of Andrew Marvell, Esq.*, ed. Edward Thompson, vol. 3, 435–493. London.

Venn, John. 1897. *Biographical History of Gonville and Caius College, 1349–1897*. Vol. 1. Cambridge: Cambridge University Press.

Wilmot, John, Earl of Rochester. 2013. *Rochester: Selected Poems*. Ed. Paul Davis. Oxford: Oxford University Press.

Worthington, John. 1677. The Life of the Reverend and Most Learned Joseph Mede, B. D. In *The Works of the Pious and Profoundly Learned Joseph Mede, B. D.* 4th ed. London.

4

'Our wits have drawn th'infection of our times': London and the Continent, 1641–1650

This chapter tracks Marvell's movements and activities following the loss of his place at Cambridge, taking us first to London (c. 1641–1642), then to the Continent (c. 1642–1647), where Marvell spent the war years as a tutor to 'noblemen's sons'. At the conclusion of his charges' grand tour, Marvell makes his way back to England no later than November 1647 and seems to have taken up residence in or near the Inns of Court, where he associated with a circle of poets under the patronage of Thomas Stanley, an ardent royalist. To the late 1640s and to these connections we can trace Marvell's triptych of royalist poems, 'An Elegy Upon the Death of My Lord Francis Villiers', 'To His Noble Friend Mr Richard Lovelace, upon His Poems', and 'Upon the Death of Lord Hastings', as well as some of his most famous lyrics, including 'To His Coy Mistress', 'The Nymph Complaining for the Death of Her Fawn', and 'An Horatian Ode upon Cromwell's Return from Ireland'. In the last of these, the royalist sentiments of the Stanley circle are balanced against the providential force of Cromwell's 'active star' (l. 12), and Marvell appears to pivot towards the contingent and uncertain republican future. In 1650 he finds new employment in the household of Thomas Lord Fairfax, late Captain General of the parliamentary armies, and so entered his astonishingly creative residence at Nun Appleton. Marvell's trajectory from Cambridge back to Yorkshire is of course inescapably shadowed by the events of the English civil war, and attention will be renewed in this chapter to the background of politics and political upheaval against which Marvell's literary life began to take shape in this decade.

© The Author(s), under exclusive license to Springer Nature Switzerland AG 2021
M. C. Augustine, *Andrew Marvell*, Literary Lives,
https://doi.org/10.1007/978-3-030-59287-5_4

In Want of Employment

From the Trinity College Conclusion Book, where the orders of the Master and Seniors were entered, we saw that Marvell was given notice in September 1641 that he must show cause for not keeping his days or else lose his benefits and place 'in three months'. This allows for the possibility that he hung around Cambridge until late in the year. If he did not mean to resume his studies, however, there would have been little point, and probably he had already left, since that is the reason for his admonition. Marvell's second sister Mary wed the Hull merchant Edmund Popple in 1636, and it has been thought that Marvell may have gone to clerk for his brother-in-law; in due time, Edmund Popple was to become the chief backer of Marvell's political career. Business dealings, however, put Marvell in London by February 1642, and we already have some indication of his attraction to the capital—he likely went there soon after mortgaging some Meldreth property he had inherited in July 1641. He may have been a student at one of the Inns of Court: Marvell's name appears as a witness to three deeds representing transactions of property between the Yorkshire grandees Sir William Savile of Thornhill and Thomas, Viscount Savile of Pontefract. The deeds' principal witnesses were Yorkshire-connected lawyers, and the transaction may have served to introduce young Marvell to men of influence. He was living at this time in Cowcross, half a mile or so from the Inns, and the same distance, or a little more, north of St Paul's. On 17 February 1642 he subscribed to the Protestation Oath in Clerkenwell; the oath was an instrument of the Long Parliament meant to flush out recusant Catholics and was framed by a preamble denouncing 'the exercise of an arbitrary and tyrannical government by most pernicious and wicked counsels, practices, plots, and conspiracies' (see Burdon 1978; Kelliher 1978; Kelliher 2008).

Almost as soon as Marvell shows up on the documentary radar, he disappears again, though we have a good idea where he goes—to the Continent, in the role of travelling tutor or governor, presumably to some young gentleman of means. In a letter of February 1653, recommending Marvell as a candidate to replace his late assistant George Weckherlin, Milton relates that Marvell's 'father was the Minister of Hull and he hath spent four years abroad in Holland, France, Italy, and Spain, to very good purpose, as I believe, and the gaining of those four languages; besides, he is a scholar and well-read in Latin and Greek authors, and no doubt of an approved conversation, for he comes now lately out of the house of the Lord Fairfax who was General, where he was intrusted to give some instructions in the languages to the lady his daughter' (*CPW*, 4:859–860). In 1655, Marvell is brought to the attention of the intelligencer Samuel Hartlib as one 'who hath spent all his time in traveling abroad with noblemen's sons who is skilled in several languages, who is now to go again with one's son of eight thousand [pounds] a year' (*Hartlib Papers* 2013). The first of these stints must have been from 1642/3 to 1647—a span of time that corresponds more or less exactly with the hottest part of the conflict between king and Parliament.

The Coming of War: England in the 1640s

In Chap. 2 we glanced at the religious policies of Charles I in the context of religious difference in England and across the three British kingdoms. Neither those policies nor those differences may be thought sufficient to account for the outbreak of armed conflict between king and Parliament in 1642, but they are nevertheless the most salient features of the crisis and political breakdown which led to it. The pressure came from Scotland, where Charles had in 1636–1637 imposed English church canons and the Laudian Book of Common Prayer on the basis of his ecclesiastical supremacy. There were riots in Edinburgh: when that 'black popish superstitious service book' was urged upon the congregation of old St Giles Church, according to a contemporary report, 'a wonderful confused tumult arose'. 'Many mouths' there opined 'to the bishop's public disgrace', calling him 'false anti-Christian wolf, beastly belly-god, and crafty fox' ('The Stoneyfield Sabbath Day' 1637). A widespread petitioning campaign led to the drafting of a National Covenant to uphold the doctrine and discipline of the kirk and to detest and refuse 'the usurped authority of that Roman Antichrist upon the scriptures of God, upon the kirk, the civil magistrate, and consciences of men' (*ConstDoc*, 125). The king's innovations were declared unlawful, and the Scottish episcopacy was dissolved.

Faced with rebellion in his northern kingdom, Charles prepared for war. Without the benefit of parliamentary supply, however, and confronted with a superior Scots army mustered just behind the northern border, Charles was forced to accept a temporary truce, referring disputed questions of kirk and state to sessions of the General Assembly and Scottish Parliament. Illustrating the bad faith he would exercise in all his negotiations with those who defied him, Charles meanwhile determined on another military campaign to subdue the Scots. New levies were raised, and the king's forces were mustered in Yorkshire and Northumberland in the summer of 1640. But the Covenanter army struck first, pushing across the border and within days taking Newcastle, a demoralising defeat for the underpaid and undertrained English troops.

Again, the king had no choice but to capitulate and, on humiliating terms, agree to the Scottish occupation of Northumberland and Durham, and to an indemnity of £850 a day while the occupation lasted. The Bishops' Wars were over, and Charles had lost; he was paying to maintain an invading army in the north of England; and his only remedy was the calling of Parliament, and an accounting for 11 years of personal rule.

Writs were issued in September 1640 for a Parliament to be convened on 3 November. Several points bear emphasis here, the first being the sense of optimism that attended the assembly of the Long Parliament. Thus the Yorkshire MP Sir Henry Slingsby (1836) wrote in his diary, 'great expectation there is of a happy Parliament where the subject may have a total redress of all his grievances' (64). Inevitable as the English civil war has appeared to later historians, it hardly seemed so to contemporaries. But Slingsby's comment, coming from a future royalist officer who would be executed in 1658 for conspiracy against the Commonwealth, also underscores the resistance Charles was facing at the start of the Long Parliament: his subjects' grievances were many, and their redress found support even among those who would fight for the king. But fight they did; and the fact that the eventual military contest between king and Parliament would be conducted on a more or less equal footing alerts us to a key dynamic of England's revolutionary decades: expressions of political and religious radicalism tended to push more moderate sorts into positions of conservative reaction.

The opening session of the Long Parliament shows a monarch backed into a corner, forced to accept the scapegoating of 'evil councillors' and the passage of reform bills that undid the king's prerogative rule. In a speech to both houses at the Whitehall banqueting house, the king signified his intention 'to reduce all matters of religion and government to what they were in the purest time of Queen Elizabeth'. 'I must tell you, however', the king continued, 'that I make a great difference betwixt reformation and alteration of government; though I am for the first, I cannot give way to the latter' (Parry 1839, 346). The difference between *reformation* and *alteration* of government—terms just as easily applied to the Church—would provide the nexus of debate in the struggle to come and, when push came to shove, served to define the shifting coordinates of side-taking. This is to be reminded that the taking of sides was not for most a singular moment of choice but rather plural and provisional: those who supported Parliament usually did so because they wanted 'reformation' in church and state, but when they thought the leaders of the opposition, whether in Parliament or the army, meant to go beyond that point, they frequently shifted their allegiance back to the king. The English 'revolution'— the purging of bishops from the Church of England, the trial and execution of the king, the abolition of monarchy, the dissolution of the House of Lords—was accomplished by a narrow political and religious minority, a fact which made the English Commonwealth vulnerable from the beginning and ultimately led to its demise.

If Charles's plan was to ride out the parliamentary storm and then try to reassert his authority once its energies abated, this was not a strategy without hope of success. Following the flurry of legislation in 1640–1641, attendance in the House of Commons thinned once the machinery of the personal rule appeared to be dismantled. Reversion to traditional norms was disrupted, however, by a pair of events in Charles's other kingdoms which deepened mistrust of the king at home and enflamed popular fears of popish conspiracy to undermine English Protestantism. In August 1641, the king journeyed north to treat with the Scottish Parliament and, by conciliating with the Covenanters, hoped to weaken the leverage of Presbyterian opposition in his English Parliament. While there, a coup against the Covenanter leaders by Scottish royalists was exposed and thwarted; despite the king's protestations of innocence, 'the Incident', as it was called, cost the king in his negotiations with the Scots and set Westminster on edge. More problematic still for Charles, a rebellion then broke out in Ireland, which began in the attempt of some Old Irish landowners to seize control of the government in Dublin and so force concessions for Irish Catholics but quickly spiralled into a chaotic confrontation between the native Irish and English Protestant settlers. Sensationally reported in newsbooks and in Parliament, the Irish rebellion electrified divisions in the Commons and set king and Parliament on a collision course.

A series of escalations followed. In November 1641, Puritan leaders in the House of Commons succeeded in passing the Grand Remonstrance, an extensive list of grievances which encompassed the whole of Charles's rule. In January 1642, Charles sought to have the opposition leaders John Hampden, Arthur Haselrig, Denzil Holles, John Pym, and William Strode arrested for treason, under suspicion of conspiring with the Scots and stirring up riots against the king in London. The five members escaped, and as tension in the capital mounted, with rumours circulating of an imminent clash between crown soldiers and the City trained bands, the king withdrew to Hampton Court. The next time he entered London, in January 1649, it would be Charles who stood trial for treason. In March 1642, Parliament passed an ordinance placing control of the county militias under its own authority and asserted its right to act 'for the safety and defence of the kingdom' without royal consent. Royal levies were raised in June, putting county loyalties to the test *A True and Exact Relation* (1642). On 22 August 1642, on a hill called

Derry Mount north of the main gateway of Nottingham Castle, the king raised his royal standard, declaring as his ground and cause the suppression of the 'pretended rebellion … against him', for which 'he required the aid and assistance of all his loving subjects' (*A True and Exact Relation* 1642, sig. A4ʳ). Charles I was at war with his own people.

The Grand Tour

Marvell's allegiances have been the subject of much scrutiny and debate. It is thus well worth observing, in the light of the pressures of engagement noted above, that Trinity was for the king, as were most Cambridge colleges; Hull went for Parliament; while Marvell escaped the fighting by virtue of employment that prudently took him abroad. Smith maintains that 'Marvell clearly did not leave the country primarily to avoid the war', 'He took a gamble with his limited means … in order to fund travel and gain the experience of foreign lands and languages that would make him indispensable as a secretary' (*Chameleon*, 45). Nevertheless, strategic absence was the upshot of his decision to go abroad, and so he escaped the forcing of conscience. Thirty years later, reflecting on the causes and the justice of the civil war in the *Rehearsal Transpros'd*, Marvell persisted in a posture of indeterminacy: 'Whether it were a war of religion, or of liberty, is not worth the labour to enquire', he writes. 'Whichsoever was at the top, the other was at the bottom; but upon considering all, I think the cause was too good to have been fought for' (1:192). According to the Marxist historian Christopher Hill (2001), Marvell's remark 'does not mean what those who cite it out of its proper context appear to think—that Marvell was disavowing "the Good Old Cause". He meant, on the contrary, that the war *should* not have been fought because it *need* not have been fought, because the victory of Parliament was inevitable, war or no war' (305). It is indeed possible to see Marvell articulating here a Whiggish faith in the inexorable triumph of liberty: 'The king himself being of so accurate and piercing a judgment, would soon have felt where it stuck. For men may spare their pains where Nature is at work, and the world will not go faster for our driving' (1:192). But Marvell's careful phrasing thus casts Parliament as unduly belligerent, muddying the waters as to how far the conflict might be thought to reflect a split over principle as opposed to 'a split in the governing class', as Conrad Russell (1973) has described the crisis of 1641–1642 (2). Being too good a cause to fight for as well as to fight against also obliquely justifies Marvell's response to the outbreak of war: to sidestep the question altogether by removing to the Continent.

No doubt he saw the opportunity to gain experience of foreign lands and languages as a potential means of self-advancement, though in later life he would disguise the fact that such experience was the by-product of 'work of service'. What exactly was the gentleman abroad meant to acquire from his travels? Management of the horse and skill with weapons were among the most desirable attainments, usually complemented by instruction in dancing and music. Ability in arithmetic, geometry, and drawing found practical application in the art and science of fortification and siege-craft. 'But tutors and parents, no doubt', John Stoye (1989) observes, 'were more concerned about the staple fare of French, Latin, and history, for many of the young men abroad were hardly more than boys and often they were boys' (40–41). To these concerns we should also add piety and religion, which were always thought to be at risk for English Protestants sojourning in papist countries. And indeed, in the Restoration Marvell helped identify sufficiently 'principled' tutors for clients like the Puritan Earl of Clare, who was sending his eldest son abroad (see Coster 2018).

Marvell's linguistic gifts, his university training, and perhaps too his father's reputation for godliness well recommended him for the role of tutor, and it was one he would intermittently perform until entering state employment in 1657. Such a position was not without its possibilities; Timothy Raylor (2018) notes the careers of several contemporaries of modest background for whom the role of tutor led to appointments at court or, in the case of Joseph Williamson (with whom Marvell was acquainted), as Secretary of State. Milton clearly has as much in mind in presenting Marvell as 'one who, I believe, in a short time would be able to do [the Council of State] as much service as Mr. Ascan', that is, Anthony Ascham, the murdered diplomat who had been tutor to the Duke of York (*CPW*, 4:860). But while Marvell's poetry of the 1650s touts the patronage of great men, like Fairfax and Cromwell, he has comparatively little to tell us of the youths he served as governor or tutor, especially at this time. He certainly does not seem to relish the identity of 'schoolmaster' (a term frequently used in derision of Milton). Marvell's later years are inflected by rumours of poverty and what has seemed to some a bitterness and a shortness of temper born of frustrated ambition. It was not only within the precincts of love and desire that Marvell felt the cruel pinch of fate's iron wedges, crowding themselves betwixt and between will and possibility (see 'The Definition of Love', ll. 9–12).

We know, then, that Marvell's grand tour saw him honing his language skills and remotely auditioning, or so he had reason to hope, for preferment by or through the noble family which had engaged him. But what else in Marvell's literary life can we connect to his experience of Europe? The Estates

General of Holland would of course command a good deal of Marvell's attention in the 1650s and 1660s in his satires 'The Character of Holland' and the
'Instructions to a Painter', both artefacts of the Anglo-Dutch Wars. To an
extent these poems, in particular 'The Character of Holland', recirculate
nationalist stereotypes of the Dutch as part of the propaganda battle that
attended this intense seventeenth-century naval and economic rivalry ever so
thinly mediated by the English Channel. It did not require all the resources of
Marvell's art to depict the mercantile and maritime Dutch as reeking of fish,
'flaming with brand [brandy] wine' (l. 115), and worshipping Mammon:
'Hence Amsterdam, Turk-Christian-Pagan-Jew, / Staple of sects and mint of
schism grew; / That bank of conscience, where not one so strange / Opinion
but finds credit, and exchange' (ll. 71–74). Conventional to the point of being
pastiche, 'Nearly every line in the poem', Smith observes, 'has a source or an
echo in anti-Dutch writing from the previous twelve years' (*Poems*, 247).

In 'The Last Instructions', however, the Dutch other comes to occupy a
derelict English national and sexual identity in the figure of the Dutch admiral Michel de Ruyter:

> … the while, that had our ocean curbed,
> Sailed now among our rivers undisturbed,
> Surveyed their crystal streams and banks so green
> And beauties ere this never naked seen.
> Through the vain sedge, the bashful nymphs he eyed:
> Bosoms, and all which from themselves they hide.
> He finds the air and all things sweeter here.
> The sudden change, and such a tempting sight
> Swells his old veins with fresh blood, fresh delight.
> Like am'rous victors he begins to shave,
> And his new face looks in the English wave.
> (ll. 523–534)

Sailing up the Thames on his way to sack the flaccid, 'unrigged' English
fleet (l. 573), the admiral's 'old veins' are swelled with 'fresh blood' raised by
English nymphs, his bluff Dutch face turned into a spruce English reflection
by the crystal stream. Thus, despite their stereotypical elements, Marvell's
poems touching on Anglo-Dutch relations are informed by a strategic double
consciousness that allows him to move between, and indeed to blur, domestic
and foreign perspectives, a consciousness facilitated by his familiarity with
Dutch and with Dutch satire as well as with anti-Dutch English writing. But
this is also a broader strategy in Marvell's poetry: objects of satire and derision

frequently double or 'boomerang' to reveal, perhaps even to Marvell's surprise, images of the self (see Smith 2010b; Zwicker 2018).

Marvell's lifelong fascination with the visual arts, observable in the play of perspectives so characteristic of his verse, and above all in the ekphrasis of the Painter poems, points to the power and precision of Dutch painting, then in its golden age. 'As for the art of painting and the affection of the people to pictures', the English traveller Peter Mundy (1925) records of his visit to Amsterdam in 1640, 'I think none other go beyond them, there having been in this country many excellent men in that faculty, some at present, as Rembrandt, etc., all in general striving to adorn their houses, especially the outer or street room, with costly pieces, butchers and bakers not much inferior in their shops, which are fairly set forth, yea many times blacksmiths, cobblers, etc., will have some picture or other by their forge or in their stall' (70). Marvell's later poetry makes direct reference to works by Peter Lely and Peter Paul Rubens, and he may even have had his own portrait painted by Dutch masters: the antiquary George Vertue (d. 1756) mentions a painting of Marvell by Lely in the possession of the Ashley family; while one of the lesser-known extant portraits of the poet is said to be by Bartholomeus van der Helst, a rival of Rembrandt's, though the identity of both sitter and artist are open to doubt.

Though no specific anecdote or poetic composition has been linked to the French stage of Marvell's tour, this was the most familiarly plotted terrain for English travellers. As tutor to Cromwell's ward William Dutton, Marvell, we know, spent part of the years 1655–1656 at the Protestant *académie* in Saumur, which 'offered a safe place to stay to reformed students from abroad and to young aristocrats who stopped there on the way to Geneva' (Pittion 2018, 3). That Marvell's first tour culminated in residencies at Rome and Madrid, however, argues a more fashionably cosmopolitan itinerary; from Amsterdam the tutor and his pupil would have gone to Paris. In and around the Parisian court, Marvell would have encountered a surfeit of English travellers and exiles: the queen, Henrietta Maria, had retreated to France in late 1644, and following major royalist defeats at Marston Moor (June 1644) and Naseby (June 1645) and his father's eventual surrender to the Scots (May 1646), Prince Charles and his court would be forced to join her there at St Germain. Thomas Hobbes had fled to France at the start of the Long Parliament, and the poets Edmund Waller and Abraham Cowley, the dramatist William Davenant, and the courtier and virtuoso Sir Kenelm Digby were all part of the circle of exiled royalists in Paris by the mid-1640s. Cowley's *The Mistress*, first published in London in 1647, was 'fated to become one of the most admired books of the age' (Gosse 1913, 207). Having returned to

England sometime that year, Marvell could have soon acquired a copy, and echoes of Cowley's 'love-verses' have been variously heard in Marvell's poetry by his editors and critics (see *Chameleon*, 64–66; Scott-Baumann 2013, 81–112).

Underlying both Marvell's and Cowley's poetry is the French *libertin* tradition represented by Antoine Girard de Saint-Amant, Théophile de Viau, and others, whose sceptical, epicurean writings enjoyed wide currency amongst Parisian wits and beaux esprits and in transvernacular poetry networks. More than 60 editions of Théophile's works appeared in the course of the seventeenth century; Cowley translated Saint-Amant's 'La Solitude' in *The Mistress*; so did Lord Fairfax, likely in conversation with Marvell at Nun Appleton; so too did Katherine Philips, in her *Poems* (1667). In his 1651 *Poems and Translations*, Thomas Stanley published a reworked digest of Théophile's *La Maison de Sylvie*, while Charles Cotton, another figure linked to Stanley's circle, translated the French poet's 'Chère Isis' as 'Ode de Théophile'. In the last chapter, we considered some of the arguments for re-dating certain of Marvell's lyrics to the Restoration on the basis that they 'echo' works published in the 1660s. Most prominently, as Allan Pritchard (1983) was the first to suggest, 'The Garden' has been thought to bear the mark of works published by Philips and Cowley in 1667 and 1668, respectively. A book of this sort is not the place for rehearsing the nitty gritty of print and manuscript circulation in this world, but I share with Derek Hirst and Steven Zwicker (2012, 'Chronology') a decided scepticism towards the idea that 'The Garden' issued from the influence of works printed in the late 1660s, and not just because the poetry of Cowley and Philips was circulating in manuscript long before it reached print (it indisputably was) or because the influence may have run in the other direction if perhaps Marvell's verse had a wider circulation than we have thought (it may have). But rather, because all three of these poets were reading, translating, and imitating French *libertin* poetry much earlier. Nicholas McDowell (2008, 35) highlights the 'shared literary interest, collaboration, and even competition' among the poets gathered around Stanley in the late 1640s, interests which firmly embraced the *libertin* tradition Susan A. Clarke (2010). Susan A. Clarke adds important further detail to this picture in a 2010 essay, reaching the conclusion that 'Pritchard's arguments in relation to the references in poems by Philips and Cowley do not take sufficient account of the dominance of the literature of retirement of the Civil War years and the Interregnum'. Victoria Moul (2018), one of the foremost authorities on Marvell's Latin poetry, attending closely to the style and content of Marvell's 'Hortus', the Latin companion poem to 'The Garden', likewise identifies 'a clustering of parallels with Latin poetry either dating from, or particularly popular during, the later 1640s and early 1650s' (330). In subsequent work, McDowell (2017) has suggested that Cavalier poetics as a whole might be redefined in terms of 'imitation and translation of continental lyric forms' (425), a proposal reinforced by Nigel Smith's (2017) contribution to the same special issue of the *Seventeenth Century*, in which he argues that 'Cavalier verse was indebted to continental poetry in one or another of the European vernacular languages, defined by continental culture and recognised by contemporaries for these qualities (433). Marvell's reading of European poetry probably began at Cambridge; it was surely deepened by his extended stay on the Continent in the 1640s; and when he returned to England in 1647, European verse served as the lingua franca of the poets with whom he associated. In Saint-Amant and Théophile, Marvell also found an impressive 'eco-poetics', which he would expound most richly in 'Appleton House'—even as his patron translated 'La Solitude' (see Pertile 2013). The seeds of Marvell's poetic gardens came from France in the 1640s.

Our clearest view of Marvell abroad is in Rome, where he arrived probably in late 1645. That December he dined in the English College at Rome in the company of George and Francis Villiers. The latter Marvell would eulogise in his poem of 1648, following Lord Francis's death in the second civil war, a performance that reflects Marvell's traffic in royalist circles at the time, but which nonetheless bespeaks personal familiarity and personal grief. George, the second Duke of Buckingham, later wed Mary Fairfax, daughter of Lord Fairfax and Marvell's pupil at Nun Appleton, and after the Restoration became Marvell's patron. Anatomising the scribal community from which arose an important miscellany of Restoration verse, Harold Love (1989) deems Rochester the faction's 'star writer', Buckingham 'the political leader of the group', 'and their ideologue, Buckingham's long-term adviser, Andrew Marvell' (225). It was Buckingham and his coterie of wits who composed *The Rehearsal*, which provided the template for Marvell's satire on Samuel Parker and his 'posse Archdiaconatus'. One of the play's co-authors and Buckingham's secretary, Martin Clifford, was a younger contemporary of Marvell's at Trinity College (matric. 1640). The Villiers brothers had themselves been sent there in 1641, and depending on when Marvell left the university, his association with them may have begun then, though the young nobles would have been just 12 and 13.

Another English exile with whom Marvell dined at the English College was Richard Flecknoe, a Catholic lay priest, a go-between for Catholic patrons, a poet, and a musician. Marvell's satire 'Flecknoe, an English Priest at Rome' was likely written in March 1646, judging from its jokes about Lenten fasting, its allusion to 'frequent visits of this man' (l. 1), and its general sense of being set within a Roman *regime de vivre*. Though it has not garnered a great deal of sustained attention from critics, the poem is in many ways the lynchpin of Marvell's literary life to this point. It is the first securely dateable poem of Marvell's mature achievement. One is immediately struck by its assured manner, its erudition lightly worn, its witty dispatch of its victim, all light years from the laboured preciosity of student exercises. Indeed, in order to write 'Flecknoe', Marvell must have composed a good deal of verse which he chose not to preserve or which has not survived—the author of this poem is clearly a practised hand. 'Flecknoe' well captures the 'facetious yet grave' quality Fuller attributed to Marvell Sr and which would become Marvell's calling card as a writer of satire and prose polemic; it is also an example of *serio ludere*, the 'serious play' associated with humanist learning. Marvell's representativeness as a writer of 'baroque' or 'metaphysical' verse has often been overstated, but in 'Flecknoe', such influences are readily discernible, a fact no doubt owing to Marvell's exposure to continental poetry in the course of his tour. But we must also read 'An English Priest at Rome' in the light of Marvell's own supposed experimentation with Roman Catholicism and his abandoned path towards a career in the church.

In keeping with the principle of 'aptness' or decorum, Marvell's sources seem to be primarily Roman, with intimations of Horatian and Juvenalian satire and of Trimalchio's dinner party in the *Satyricon*, though Marvell does not tie himself to any one model as he did in his earlier parody of Horace. The poem's antithetic or dialectical strategy is brilliantly realised through the poem's sources: Roman satire and comedy rely extensively on types, but the conventionality of Flecknoe as a satirical persona—a parasite, a boor, a wretched poetaster—is offset by a vivid sense of individuality rooted in the poet's intimacy with his subject. Satiric laughter also betrays a strain of wonder at Flecknoe's absurdities, and the poem depends upon a certain ironic perspective: Flecknoe was not in fact altogether inconsiderable, 'a man made much of by elegant ladies, entertained by the nobility and in contact with cardinals' (Burdon 1972, 16). Approaching 25, uncertain of his prospects, in search of patronage, and very evidently composing verse, Marvell must have glimpsed a possible future which bent towards the 40-year-old Flecknoe.

Led by a broad notion of the baroque that stresses 'the disorienting, ecstatic, dazzling implications of the age's visual practices' (Jay 1993, 47), and which might thus embrace a heterogeneous group of writers—from Góngora, Marino, Vondel, and Théophile to Donne, Crashaw, Cowley, Cleveland, and Katherine Philips—we can productively read 'Flecknoe' in terms of its striking sequence of images and imaginative conceits. The speaker visits Flecknoe in his chamber, 'as 'twas said, / But seemed a coffin set on the stairs' head' (ll.

9–10), such that the door, which opens inward, 'wainscot[s] half the room' (l. 14)—a metaphor that depends on a blurring or confusion of depth perception (wainscot is wooden wall panelling), but which also thematises hallucinatory effects. And what could be more appropriate to this chamber, which sees Flecknoe transform into a hollow lute, the taut strings of his 'hungry guts' (l. 43) sympathetically tuning themselves to the catgut strings of his instrument; into the likeness of a frog or toad, darting his tongue at 'passing flies' (l. 50); into the '*basso relievo* of a man', so thin he stands (l. 63); and into a suit of clothes made up of papers of verses (ll. 69–72), which he covers with his cassock and 'an antique cloak, / Torn at the first Council of Antioch' (ll. 75–76). 'Were he not in this black habit decked', the speaker tells us, 'This half-transparent man would soon reflect / Each colour that he passed by; and be seen, / As the chamelion, yellow, blue, or green' (ll. 79–82). But trompe l'oeil is not just Flecknoe's signature quality, it is the poet's as well, the two figures tuned by 'hidden sympathies' (l. 40) like Flecknoe and his lute. (The germ of Smith's biography—Marvell as 'the chameleon'—comes from this poem).

In addition to the baroque characteristics of 'Flecknoe', there are also attributes which seem to point towards what used to be called 'Augustan' satire, specifically in the technique whereby 'a hyperbole of insult is wedded to a malicious realism' (Rogers 1978, 171). We know Swift admired Marvell, though Swift's interest has usually been confined to Marvell's prose, to which Swift alludes in the 'Apology' to *A Tale of a Tub*. But there is no reason to think that Swift—a poet himself, despite Dryden's taunt—would not have been familiar with Marvell's verse, and he would have found much in 'Flecknoe' to his purpose. Like Swift's *Tale of a Tub*, Marvell's poem brings together religious satire, religious toleration, and religious scepticism in a way that blurs their attitudinal or illocutionary force, and so challenges the taste and discernment of his audience.

After being subjected to Flecknoe's reading and playing, and noticing the rumbling of Flecknoe's guts, Marvell's speaker ironically queries his host's Lenten preparations: 'I, that perceived now what his music meant, / Asked civilly if he had eat this Lent' (ll. 45–46). Flecknoe's answer shows up (as no doubt the speaker means) his dependency and social pretension; he eats only in company because he dines at others' expense, circumstances of garrulity and plenitude which starkly contrast with the image of Flecknoe in his coffin-like chamber darting his tongue at flies (ll. 47–50). His laxity about fasting before mass, feigning illness while also claiming 'th'ordinance was only politic' (l. 54), is the more amusing for Flecknoe's willingness to break his fast for fly meat ('I asked if he eat flesh', l. 51). But despite the speaker's evident satiric purpose, 'civility' nonetheless prevails here. We recall that the speaker feels himself 'obliged' to Flecknoe 'by frequent visits of this man', an obligation the speaker makes good; the Protestant guest shows himself well versed in Roman Catholic observance; and while Flecknoe's shallow devotion is played for laughs, it also signifies an undogmatic spirit amenable to mixing with his reformed brethren. The speaker's initial question, 'if he had eat this Lent', promises an invitation to dinner: 'Nor was I longer to invite him scant: / Happy at once to make him Protestant, / And silent' (ll. 55–57).

'Nothing now our dinner stayed', the speaker continues:

> But till he had himself a body made.
> I mean till he were dressed: for else so thin
> He stands, as if he only fed had been
> With consecrated wafers: and the Host
> Had sure more flesh and blood than he can boast.
> This *basso relievo* of a man,
> Who as a camel tall, yet eas'ly can
> The needle's eye thread without any stitch.
> (ll. 57–65)

Flecknoe's spectral thinness is one of the poem's running jokes, and Marvell cannot resist the beckoning pun on 'host', which unites priest and wafer aurally as well as visually, the wafer being so thin as to show light through. The irony tilts heavily here towards Protestant satire of transubstantiation: 'the Host / Had sure more flesh and blood than he can boast' is literally true for one who believes in the Catholic doctrine of real presence.

Enlisting Scripture in the withering fun this poem has with Flecknoe, however, flirts with an impiety and a facetiousness that arguably overflow the poem's circumscribed aims and may remind us of the way both the *Rehearsal Transpros'd* and *A Tale of a Tub* were characterised as works which threatened *all* religion with 'a mastery in fooling'. This sense only increases as the speaker and his host descend the narrow staircase from Flecknoe's chamber to the commons of the inn where Flecknoe resides. As the speaker goes down, another visitor is coming up who insists on his right of way, prompting a ridiculous confrontation in the cramped space of the stair:

> He gathr'ing fury still made sign to draw;
> But himself there closed in a scabbard saw
> As narrow as his sword's; and I, that was
> Delightful, said, 'There can no body pass
> Except by penetration hither, where
> Two make a crowd, nor can three persons here

Consist but in one substance.' Then, to fit
Our peace, the priest said I too had some wit:
To prov't, I said, 'the place doth us invite
By its own narrowness, Sir, to unite.'
He asked me pardon; and to make me way
Went down, as I him followed to obey.
(ll. 95–106)

Demurring to give way, Marvell's 'delightful' persona suggests that only by miraculously combining into 'one substance' can three persons inhabit this close space, thus parodying the doctrine of the trinity. The homoerotic overtones of the scene—the brisk newcomer's move to take out his 'sword', the reference to 'penetration', to inviting 'narrowness'-es, to male 'union'—gesture satirically to the proverbial (for English Protestants) buggery of 'Romish Jesuits and priests'. But the trinity was a touchstone of orthodoxy for Protestant as well as Catholic (witness the debate surrounding Milton's supposed antitrinitarian 'heresies'), and the sexual innuendoes at once force Father, Son, and Holy Ghost into a rather unseemly conjunction and serve (as it were) as a kind of social lubricant which leads to the kiss of peace and the breaking of bread. A mastery in fooling, indeed.

After they have supped, Flecknoe resumes his torture of the speaker by reciting his verses, which he peels from beneath his cassock 'Like white flakes rising from a leper's skin!' (l. 134). The 'waxen youth' encountered in the stairwell eagerly collects every scrap of paper Flecknoe lets fall, kissing each one as a priest reverences the Bible (ll. 138–139). He then proceeds to read some of Flecknoe's poetry himself, but with such ill accent that the English priest 'swelled, with anger full' (recalling the image of the frog, now in full throat), and so retires 'Home, his most furious satire to have fired / Against the rebel' (ll. 160–161). Meanwhile,

I, finding myself free,
As one 'scaped strangely from captivity,
Have made the chance be painted; and go now
To hang it in St Peter's for a vow.
(ll. 167–170)

The poem thus ends in a prospect of further aesthetic transformations: the scene will be re-narrated by Flecknoe, who turns from object to author of satire, while Marvell will have his fortunate delivery made into a votive painting, which he will hang in St Peter's. The device of translating an image of the poem or part of the poem into other media takes us close to 'The Unfortunate Lover', whose final lines sublime into perfume and music, and to 'The Nymph Complaining', which closes with the image of the nymph and fawn made into statuary. We are, to borrow a phrase, 'deep into Marvell land' (Zwicker 2018, 7).

Return to England and the Second Civil War

The final stage of Marvell's grand tour (c. 1646–1647) took him from Italy to Spain, likely sailing around the European coast to the port of Barcelona or Valencia and then travelling overland to Madrid. We have already heard of Marvell's fencing lessons there, and further traces of the poet's Spanish experience may be found in 'Appleton House', with its allusions to 'Aranjuèz' and the 'Bel-Retiro' (ll. 755–756), palace complexes near the Spanish capital. Poetry societies were known to meet in the palaces' extensive gardens, and it may be in such a context that Marvell read the Spanish poet Luis de Góngora y Argote, whose brilliant, bewildering *Soledades* (1613) has lately been put forward as an overlooked touchstone of Marvell's verse (see Smith 2018, 176–185). But time now points us back to England, where Marvell returned sometime in 1647, not later than November and probably some months before. He seems to have gone first to Hull, to see his sisters and perhaps to consult with his brothers-in-law, Edmund Popple and James Blaydes, with whom he had entrusted some of his financial interests. In November and December (12th and 23rd, respectively) we find him in Cambridgeshire, selling the rest of the Meldreth property he had inherited in 1641. With the £80 from the sale of his modest estate, along with whatever remained of the wages from his grand tour, Marvell thus embarked, at the start of 1648, on a career in London. The nature of Marvell's business in these years remains unclear, but it's possible he returned to Gray's Inn, and he was in any case 'moving in Inns of Court circles' (Kelliher 1978, 37).

This was a heady time in the capital. The first civil war had ended in May 1646 with the surrender of Charles I to the Scottish army at Newark; in January 1647 he was handed over to Parliament for an indemnity of £400,000 and held at Holdenby House in Northamptonshire. As in 1640 at the calling of the Long Parliament, most English people seem to have favoured a well-grounded settlement to the constitutional and religious questions which had enflamed the nation. But settlement on what terms? For the king's opponents were now splintered by divisions of interest and opinion, both against one another and within their own ranks. Among MPs, a 'Presbyterian' faction were willing to accept the king's return with few pre-conditions, placing their faith in the king to honour the reforms of 1640–1641 and the ordinances of the Long Parliament restructuring the Church along moderately Presbyterian lines with the proviso that it remain subordinate to Parliament. An 'Independent' faction wanted drastic concessions from the king before agreeing to disband the army and generally supported a wider toleration of Protestant worship. The Scots sought a religious covenant establishing a Britannic Presbyterianism directed by the kirk. To muddy the picture further, 1647–1648 saw the parliamentary New Model Army become politicised in its own right and threatening to act independently of parliamentary control. Facing disbandment while still owed millions of pounds in back pay, and fearful of reprisals once the king was restored, army officers and soldiers demanded satisfaction of their grievances and a voice in how the conflict they had won was settled. But the army, too, split along ideological lines: its leading officers, Fairfax, Cromwell, Cromwell's son-in-law Henry Ireton, and John Lambert, were socially conservative Puritans, not republican firebrands, while the rank and file were increasingly influenced by London radical movements calling for true representative government and religious freedom.

By May 1647, an agreement between the king and the ascendant 'Presbyterian' faction seemed imminent. The army, perceiving their petitions to fall on deaf ears, responded on 3 June by seizing the king from his parliamentary guards and marching on London. But a rift soon emerged between the army grandees and the radicalised troops, leading to rival constitutional proposals, neither of which were acceptable to MPs. In November, with no deal having been reached, the army in disorder and at odds with Parliament, the king slipped his gaolers at Hampton Court and made his way to Carisbrooke Castle on the Isle of Wight. Still captive but no longer in the army's power, the king sent fresh representations to Parliament. Meanwhile, he received commissioners from Scotland, who offered their own terms of engagement: pledge provisional support for the establishment of Presbyterianism in England, and in return the Covenanting army would fight to restore Charles to his just rights.

The king took the Scottish Engagement. The royalist risings and Scottish invasion of 1648, however, are belied by their retrospective billing as a 'second civil war', rapidly crushed as they were by the New Model Army. Moreover, the renewal of fighting and destruction drove a wedge between the political nation and the de facto power of the army: most MPs and their county constituents desired a treaty with the king perhaps now more than ever; but to the army leaders and their Independent allies, Charles could no longer be trusted to abide by any agreement, and he was increasingly reviled as 'that man of blood'. Thus did Thomas Brook remind members of the House of Commons on their monthly fast day in December 1648, 'So ye shall not pollute the land wherein ye *are*: for blood it defileth the land: and the land cannot be cleansed of the blood that is shed therein, but by the blood of him that shed it' (Numbers 35:33). Regicide and the declaration of a commonwealth were soon to follow.

Royalist Verse and the Stanley Circle

Lord Francis Villiers was killed on 7 July 1648 at the close of the royalist rising in Surrey, a vain attempt to free the king from his imprisonment in Carisbrooke. The 19-year-old Villiers had apparently sent his company ahead of him the night before while he paid court to his mistress Mary Kirke, the married daughter of the Cavalier poet and courtier Aurelian Townshend (*The Parliament-Kite* 1648). Accosted by parliamentary soldiers, he refused to surrender himself and 'fought with 8 or 9 of the stoutest butchers of the army', who after he was dead, according to a royalist report, 'cut off his nose, and then run him through and through the neck and cut and mangled his body in a most barbarous and inhumane manner' (*The Parliament-Kite* 8, 44–45). Marvell's elegy upon Villiers's death was published in an unsigned quarto pamphlet that may have been privately printed; its grace notes of personal and familial intimacy, and its overtly royalist sentiments give it the appearance of having been written for a coterie audience rather than the print public. The circulation of the elegy and knowledge of its author must have been sufficiently restricted to give Marvell confidence that he would not be embarrassed by its revelation to his future patrons, who are referred to invidiously in the poem as 'heavy Cromwell' (l. 14) and 'long-deceivèd Fairfax' (l. 16). Likely more unpalatable still to such patrons would have been the elegy's praise for the 'pyramid / Of vulgar bodies' young Villiers 'erected high' as a most fitting obsequy to the fallen royalist (ll. 115–120) and its promise to turn from writing epitaphs to taking up the sword: 'And we hereafter to his honour will / Not write so many, but so many kill' (ll. 125–126).

The exclusion of the Villiers elegy from the 1681 folio and its somewhat distant attribution to Marvell have been used by some to call his authorship of the poem into question, an exclusion that helps smooth out Marvell's conversion to commonwealth principles or what Derek Hirst (2004) has called 'liberalism *avant la lettre*' (698). But Marvell's political 'contradictions' have perhaps been overstated. The Horatian Ode of 1650 adopts a stance that mingles emotional royalism with political realism; and despite his increasingly firm support for Cromwell in the 1650s, Marvell has no qualms, in his satires and pamphlets of the Restoration, taking the part of an aggrieved Stuart loyalist, devolving blame on corrupt advisers and paying homage to his majesty's 'most happy and miraculous Restoration' (*PW*, 1:90). Whiggish critics would be quick to call this 'lip service', but as I have argued elsewhere, the whole political-rhetorical strategy of the *Rehearsal Transpros'd* depends on the force of such expressions being taken at face value. It is only in *An Account of the Growth of Popery and Arbitrary Government* (1677) that Marvell seems to have 'lost all faith in the government and its direction' and may be seen moving 'between faith in petitioning a Godly Prince and the lack of faith that promises resistance once more' (Condren 1990, 177).

With most of the doubt now removed about the authorship of the Villiers elegy, we stand to gain a fuller appreciation of the poem as an exceptionally fertile incubator of ideas Marvell would return to and rework in later compositions. There is a fine sense of private irony in the fact that several of these moments of déjà vu come in poems on Cromwell. 'The forward youth that would appear' (l. 1) at the start of the Horatian Ode, for instance, mirrors the poet at the end of 'An Elegy Upon the Death of My Lord Francis Villiers' only with his allegiances presumably flipped: the youth 'Must now forsake his Muses dear, / Nor in the shadows sing / His numbers languishing' (ll. 2–4), trading his books for armour. The Villiers of Marvell's elegy, 'Scorning without a sepulchre to die', 'did whole troops divide', and 'cut his epitaph on either side' (ll. 118–120). In the Ode, Cromwell 'Did thorough his own side / His fiery way divide' (ll. 15–16), not only recalling the figure of division but repeating the rhyme 'divide/side' and the auxiliary verb construction ('did … divide'). The most arresting line of 'A Poem upon the Death of his Late Highness the Lord Protector', the four consecutively stressed monosyllables 'I saw him dead' (l. 247), leadens the iambic formula with which the Villiers's poem opens, ''Tis true that he is dead'. Harold Love (1993) has commented that those who find it hard to credit Marvell's authorship of the elegy in the light of his praise for Fairfax and Cromwell 'display a naïve attitude towards the politics of patronage as they affected the scribal medium' (63), an observation all the more acute for recognising the shared DNA of these speech acts.

The Villiers poem also opens onto erotic territory that feels characteristically Marvellian. As Smith observes, the love elegy and the funeral elegy were still in the process of defining themselves as distinct genres in the earlier seventeenth century (*Poems*, 12), and the poem's Ovidian linking of Villiers in particular to the figure of Adonis serves to transform Villiers's death 'into the stuff of Caroline romance' (Cousins 2016, 151). His 'unimitable handsomeness' (l. 45), for which Villiers was almost universally remembered, 'Made him indeed be more than man, not less' (l. 46), Marvell insists, and the morally compromising and ultimately fatal circumstance of his dalliance with Kirke is redeemed by rendering it platonically chaste and by displacing the topical with the mythical: Villiers's parliamentarian 'butchers' are turned into the wild boar who gored Venus's lover. But though we can see the poetic strategy in this, eros nonetheless asserts itself in the poem in ways that confound heterosexual romance narrative. The circuits of desire and of looking and longing in the elegy include the narcissistic, the homoerotic, and the fantastically liminal—the beginnings of a figural map of Marvellian sexuality.

Two passages deserve brief consideration in this regard. The first comes where the poet seeks to make martial Villiers's handsome image, which had served to conjure up Adam-like perfection and to identify the king's cause with Cavalier beauty. 'Lovely and admirable as he was', Marvell writes, signalling a shift in his theme:

> Yet was his sword or armour all his glass.
> Nor in his mistress' eyes that joy he took,
> As in an enemy's himself to look.
> I know how well he did, with what delight
> Those serious imitations of fight.
> Still in the trials of strong exercise
> His was the first, and his the second prize.
> (ll. 51–58)

So far does Villiers embody chivalric ideals his greatest joy is said to come from the reflection of his own image in his sword or armour or in the eyes of martial opponents. But if Villiers takes the first prize for his excellent mimesis of combat in 'trials of strong exercise' and the second for his delight in that excellence, the third prize must surely be taken by the poet who looks and delights in looking at Villiers. Should the poet's first-person testimony to Villiers's manly grace be thought to imply not merely spectation but the intimate knowledge of a sparring partner (for which, as we have seen, there is biographical scope), the admiring poet also becomes an intermediary object in Villiers's self-seeking gaze. That gaze is itself mirrored in 'Damon the Mower', where Damon, stung by love of Juliana, consoles himself by observing, "'Nor am I so deformed to sight, / If in my scythe I lookèd right; / In which I see my picture done, / As in a crescent moon the sun'" (ll. 57–60). In both poems, an 'all-male circuit of vision' contrasts the gaze of a lover or mistress, whose look promises death (the phrase is Paul Hammond's, 1996, 108).

Further erotic touches which may seem 'superfluous to the occasion' appear in Marvell's description of Villiers's death: 'Such fell young Villiers in the cheerful heat / Of youth: his locks entangled all with sweat / And those eyes which the Sentinel did keep / Of Love closed up in an eternal sleep' (ll. 105–108). Here a note in the Longman edition directs our attention to 'another simultaneous association of sweat with amorous soldiery' in 'Appleton House', 'Where every mower's wholesome heat / Smells like an Alexander's sweat' (ll. 427–428); the same pair of rhyme words is also used by Damon the Mower, who boasts, 'And, if at noon my toil me heat, / The sun himself licks off my sweat' (ll. 45–46). Yet more programmatically, Villiers's eroticised fall previews the self-sacrificing death of Archibald Douglas in 'The Last Instructions', another conjoining in Marvell's oeuvre of love elegy and funeral elegy:

> Like a glad lover, the fierce flames he meets,
> And tries his first embraces in their sheets.
> His shape exact, which the bright flames enfold,
> Like the sun's statue stands of burnished gold.
> Round the transparent fire about him glows,
> As the clear amber on the bee does close,
> And, as on angels' heads their glories shine,
> His burning locks adorn his face divine.
> (ll. 677–684)

The married Douglas and the gallant Villiers are both apotheosised as chaste virgins and indeed as emblems of unripe gender; Douglas has but 'early down' upon his chin, while Villiers, whose good looks were earlier said to make him 'more than man', is at the moment of his death twice styled 'young' or 'youthful'. The doomed soldiers' dishevelled hair captivates Marvell's gaze—his imagination—in both instances, the 'cheerful heat' which entangles Villiers's locks with sweat being transformed in 'The Last Instructions' into an actual blaze (Douglas went down with his burning ship) which enwraps the 'glad lover' and furnishes his bright halo of hair. These poems have much to teach us about the way in which elements of history, biography, genre, and fantasy combine to such brilliant and complex effect in Marvell's verse.

Thomas Stanley, the eldest son of a substantial gentry family in Hertfordshire, matriculated at Pembroke College, Cambridge, in December 1639, aged 14; it is possible that he met Marvell at university before Marvell abandoned his studies after the death of his father. Like Marvell, Stanley went abroad during the first civil war, returning shortly after the cessation of violence with the king's surrender to the Scots in May 1646. On his return to London, 'Stanley quickly gathered around him some of the most talented writers of the day: some were established poets and playwrights in need of support; others were, like Stanley himself, younger men embarking on a literary career in difficult times. Two of the central members of the coterie, [Edward] Sherburne and [Richard] Lovelace, were connected to Stanley by blood; the political background of several of the members was strongly royalist' (McDowell 2008, 18). Writers with links to the Stanley circle include Richard Brome, Thomas Carew, Robert Herrick, Thomas May, and James Shirley. Among the unproven young men who seem to have benefited from Stanley's patronage or who participated in the society which gathered in Stanley's Middle Temple rooms are Alexander Brome, John Davies, William Fairfax, John Hall, and our poet, Andrew Marvell.

The circle's project was political as well as literary. At first eschewing the stigma of print in order to preserve the tradition of English verse in 'untunable times', 'Stanley, Lovelace, Hall, Shirley, Sherburne, and Herrick all published volumes of their lyric poetry between 1646 and 1651' (McDowell 2008, 6), the very monuments of what has been called 'a resurgent Cavalier literary culture' (*Chronology*, 32) *Mercurius Elencticus* (1647–1649). But an allegiance to wit could also transcend political differences and the vagaries of what may appear to the eyes of a less ideologically fluid age as time-serving, opportunism, or self-interest: having enjoyed Stanley's support since he was a boy, at the outbreak of the second civil war John Hall turned his hand to writing parliamentarian propaganda, yet does not appear to have fallen out with those 'friends, who so much detest the Parliament', such 'ingenious and candid souls as Col. Lovelace, Captain Sherburne, Mr Shirley, or Mr Stanley', contrary to the prediction of a rival newsbook writer (*Mercurius Elencticus* 27, 206). Hall appeared among the commenders of Lovelace's *Lucasta* when it was published in May 1649 (it was licensed in February 1648), and among the weepers for Henry Lord Hastings in *Lachrymae Musarum*, collected by Richard Brome and published in June or July. On both occasions, Hall's poem follows one by Marvell (see McDowell 2008, 29–30).

Marvell is thought to have become acquainted with Lovelace at Cambridge in the late 1630s, and Lovelace may well have been his entrée to the Stanley circle. Having fought for the king in the Bishops' Wars and then against Parliament, the dashing Cavalier was twice arrested and imprisoned, in 1642 and in 1648–1649, and it was in the latter interval that he finished assembling his fugitive verse into the *Lucasta* volume. Written in the form of a verse epistle, 'To His Noble Friend Mr Richard Lovelace, upon his Poems' superbly articulates the sense that the civil wars had shattered not just shields and lances but the pre-war cultural order, a prototypically royalist argument, and not incidentally the same view taken by T. S. Eliot in his reactionary account of English literary history. 'Our times are much degenerate from those / Which your sweet Muse with your fair fortune chose', Marvell's poem begins, 'And as complexions alter with the climes, / Our wits have drawn th'infection of the times' (ll. 1–4). Critics have noted the careful juxtaposition of possessive pronouns, 'your' and 'our', a grammar which signifies the stark contrast between 'then' and 'now', the sweetness of Lovelace's muse and the degeneracy of Marvell's, despite the fact that the *Lucasta* poems were mainly products of the war decade—as signalled by titles like 'To Althea, from Prison' or 'To Lucasta, Going to the Wars'—and the contemporaneity of the two poets (Lovelace was four years older than Marvell). Such was the wounding shock of civil war to English poesy: a few years could have the impact of an age.

Moreover, the degeneracy of literary art is said to go hand in hand with an epidemic moral confusion:

> That candid age no other way could tell
> To be ingenious, but by speaking well.
> Who best could praise, had then the greatest praise,
> 'Twas more esteemed to give, than wear the bays:
> Modest Ambition studied only then,
> To honour not herself, but worthy men.
> These virtues now are banished out of town,
> Our civil wars have lost the civic crown.
> (ll. 5–12)

The most appropriate gloss on these lines is perhaps Dryden's famous statement, at a later moment of seventeenth-century political crisis, that 'wit and fool, are consequents of Whig and Tory: and every man is a knave or an ass to the contrary side' (*Works*, 2:3). Some commentators have seen Marvell's eulogy of 'the town'—the milieu evoked by Jonson's epigrams and verse epistles, one centred on 'theatres and literary circles; not the court' (*Poems*, l. 11n)—as a form of politic distancing; there is no mention of the king. But the passage is thus complexly ironised: if Jonson's name stands for honest praise, his was hardly a 'modest ambition', and he of course *did* in a manner wear the bays as poet laureate, fashioning in his masques the very iconography of Stuart kingship. The theatres were closed by order of Parliament.

In contrast to that 'candid age' of Jonson, with which Marvell associates Lovelace, now partisan worms have infested civic virtue and public discourse, while a new government censorship threatens to stifle the intellectual offspring of honest men, to recall Milton's protestation of the 1643 Licensing Act in *Areopagitica*. 'The air's already tainted with the swarms / Of insects which against you rise in arms', the poet avers:

> Word-peckers, paper-rats, book-scorpions,
> Of wit corrupted, the unfashioned sons.
> The barbèd censurers begin to look
> Like the grim consistory on thy book;
> And on each line cast a reforming eye,
> Severer than the young Presbytery.
> (ll. 17–24)

One point on which Marvell, John Hall, and John Milton could agree was the obtrusive and strangling effect of Presbyterian control of the press. A number of the commendatory poems which prefaced *Lucasta* refer to difficulty with parliamentary licensers, and the 15-month gap between its receipt of a licence in February 1648 and its entry in the Stationer's Register in May 1649, during which time Lovelace was imprisoned and his estates sequestered, suggests further political interference with the volume's publication. Lovelace continued to rework *Lucasta* while in prison, at once deepening and disguising the collection's royalist agenda; the commendatory apparatus it acquired meanwhile 'endeavors to construct a fragile, papier-mâché consensus' of royalists and Independents around high culture, deploring 'Presbyterian philistines' (Robertson 2006, 478).

Poetically what is of most interest here is Marvell's unpoetic diction, 'Word-peckers, paper-rats, book-scorpions', language which he borrows or adapts from contemporary newsbooks (see *Poems*, l. 15n, ll. 19–20n). On the one hand, this would appear to symbolise the infection of the poet's wits by the factious times, and yet the line is ostentatiously memorable and fresh; and indeed, scholars have lately begun to appreciate the stimulating traffic between Marvell's poetry and 'the language of pamphlets, newspapers, and political discourse' (Raymond 2018, 33). Marvell's strongest points of contact here seem to be with Marchamont Nedham's *Mercurius Pragmaticus*, but are the newsbook and its author to be regarded as targets or sources (Worden 2007, 61)? Nedham had written journalism on behalf of Parliament during the first civil war, then turned coat for the king in undertaking *Pragmaticus*, which he published from September 1647 to May 1649. Locked up in Newgate Prison by the Rump Parliament, he would strike a deal with the Commonwealth to switch sides once more, becoming an energetic propagandist for the regime, 'a great crony of Milton', and an associate of Marvell. A university graduate and a poet, much the same age as Marvell, Nedham makes a suggestive foil, at once one of those 'degenerate' scribblers and yet a writer of some talent, capable of being viewed as a cynical trimmer or as a case of conscience in vertiginous political circumstances: 'If these the times, then this must be the man' ('The First Anniversary', l. 144). And could there be a more representative figure of the confusions and contradictions of seventeenth-century political identity than Nedham? The side-changing author of *Pragmaticus* thus provides a thematic link to the closing section of the poem, in which Marvell calls up the image of a troop of 'beauteous ladies' who rally to Lovelace's defence:

> And one, the loveliest that was yet e'er seen,
> Thinking that I too of the rout had been,
> Mine eyes invaded with a female spite,
> (She knew what pain 'twould be to lose that sight).
> 'O no mistake not,' I replied, 'for I
> In your defence, or in his cause would die'.
> (ll. 41–46)

'The rout' to which Marvell's importunate interlocutor thinks he belongs is that of the insects which rise against Lovelace in arms, the word peckers, the paper rats; her piercing glance takes him for a partisan scribbler, prompting Marvell's assurance that he would 'die' for Lovelace's cause.

In January 1650, the book collector George Thomason acquired a copy of the second edition of *Lachrymae Musarum*, lamentations on the late Henry, Lord Hastings, the only son of a prominent royalist family, dead of smallpox on the eve of his wedding. The volume was a covert—though not very hidden—act of mourning for the regicide, a message reinforced by its being published in a second edition to coincide with the anniversary of that 'sad disaster' (in the formula of one of Hastings's elegists). Marvell's poem 'On the Untimely Death of the Lord Hastings, Son to the Earl of Huntingdon' appears with his signature on both occasions. Six months later, Cromwell returned from Ireland; under Marvell's gimlet eye the formerly 'heavy' Cromwell is now deemed 'restless' (l. 9) and 'indefatigable' (l. 114), hailed as 'the War's and Fortune's son' (l. 113). Not for nothing do Marvell's poems of the late 1640s self-consciously thematise the possibility of the poet appearing other than he does at a given moment.

The Consolations of Art

While parliamentary commissioners continued to treat with the king at Carisbrooke on the Isle of Wight in the aftermath of the second civil war, the army moved to seize control of events *Remonstrance of the Army* (1648). In November 1648, the *Remonstrance of the Army* (1648) was published under the authority of Fairfax, concluding that 'this king hath been the author and contriver of an unjust war, and so is guilty of all the blood and mischief to the kingdom', and demanding 'how can the public justice of the kingdom be satisfied, the blood avenged, the wrath of God for the same appeased without judgment executed against him' (6). When Parliament persisted in debating the king's proposals, the army marched on London, occupying it by 2 December. Four days later, under the orders of a sub-committee of army officers and Independent MPs, Pride's Purge, the exclusion and arrest of MPs who supported the Newport treaty, was begun, clearing the way for the trial of the king on charges of treason. On 20 January 1649 the trial was convened by an ordinance of the purged 'Rump' Parliament. Scoffing at the 'illegality of this pretended Court' (*ConstDoc*, 374), the king refused to enter a plea, and on 27 January the sentence was proclaimed, 'that he, the said Charles Stuart, as a tyrant, traitor, murderer, and public enemy to the good people of this nation, shall be put to death by the severing of his head from his body' (*ConstDoc*, 379). At about 2.00 pm on Tuesday 30 January 1649, the king laid his head on the block 'as upon a bed' ('Horatian Ode', l. 64); with the swing of an executioner's axe, the English republic was born.

In the days and weeks following the regicide, the king's death was widely reported, polemicised, and lamented, both directly and indirectly, in manuscript and print, in verse and prose. The poems assembled in *Lachrymae Musarum* on the death of Lord Hastings very obviously double as commentary on the death of the king, and Marvell's participation in that volume, and in the Lovelace collection, at once provides evidence of his poetic sociability c. 1648–1649 and of the public, political nature of that sociability. The Stanley circle was not royalist to a person and indeed may have facilitated cultural bonds across political differences; nor was Marvell, so far as we can tell, situated at its centre. But in the news-saturated atmosphere of post-civil-war London, Marvell's complaint in 'Upon the Death of Lord Hastings', that he weeps 'without redress or law' (l. 58), not only has the colour of royalist response to the regicide, it can be heard in part as ventriloquising the king's indictment of the arbitrary and illegal nature of his trial, several accounts of which were published in the newsbooks.

Two further poems that seem to date from this period (c. 1649) also carry themes of blood, guilt, and sacrifice, and interpose the language of the topical and the political amidst their self-consciously poetic—and indeed deliberately obscure, deliberately unfathomable—idioms. But these two poems are far weirder and more inward-facing than the poems to Villiers, Lovelace, and Hastings. Though the game of source-hunting which they tantalisingly invite would seem tailored to the activities of a coterie, it is nonetheless hard to imagine a fit audience for these poems, and there is no clear evidence of their circulation. Indeed, these are perhaps the most indecipherable of all Marvell's lyrics, brooking little agreement amongst the many learned critics who have searched out their mysteries. In their beauty, their strangeness, and their striking openness to interpretation, 'The Unfortunate Lover' and 'The Nymph Complaining for the Death of her Fawn' may thus also be thought the most 'Marvellian' of Marvell's poems: for all that they echo classical and contemporary sources, there is little that truly compares with them.

It may sound trite to say that Marvell's poetry is polyvalent or multi-layered, but one of the chief difficulties critics have had with 'The Unfortunate Lover' and 'The Nymph Complaining' lies in a certain reductiveness of method, that is, in treating them as literary artefacts largely explicable in terms of other literary artefacts, and so becoming trapped in an endlessly recursive programme of *imitatio*; or in the making of them political or religious allegories which do violence to the poetry by forcing Petrarchan or pastoral narrative into the procrustean bed of 'context'. In these poems are to be found allegories of politics, of poetry, and perhaps of the self, but such stories are as apt to confuse and disrupt as to complement one another. Ellipsis and disjunction are this poet's element no less surely than flames and waves are the Unfortunate Lover's.

'The Unfortunate Lover' is a story of origins, of star-crossed birth and tragic fate, but whose story is it? ''Twas in a shipwrack, when the seas / Ruled, and the winds did what they please, / That my poor lover floating lay,' Marvell writes, with Coleridgean portent:

> And, ere brought forth, was cast away:
> Till at the last the master-wave
> Upon the rock his mother drave;
> And there she split against the stone,
> In a Caesarean sectiòn.
> (ll. 9–16)

What, we may wonder, is the force of the possessive pronoun, in what sense is the poor lover here said to be *my* lover? One possibility is that the poet is marking out the lover as his creation, *my* poor lover as opposed to those fashioned by other poets, thus conjuring a field of Unfortunate Lovers against whom the speaker's is to be read. Is Marvell referring to the raft of verse on the regicide, writing which commonly deployed veiled or allegorised figures for the royal martyr in his sufferings? If so, the poem offers itself as both a type of such verse and as a kind of meta-poetic commentary, the 'poetry of criticism', in Rosalie Colie's phrase. Given that the lover's destiny is one apart from those 'Sorted by pairs' (l. 3), to suffer Love's arrows while bound to his surging rock, the phrase 'my poor lover' does not seem to convey the simple meaning of 'my beloved'; in that case, the intimacy of 'my' perhaps becomes intelligible as a form of 'me', the lover as allegory of the self. Fittingly, this split subject is born at once through trauma—a caesarean operation—and into traumatic circumstances, a state of abandonment and extreme vulnerability to the elements.

That the Unfortunate Lover—that stock figure of Petrarchism—is literally formed, made out of seas and winds, which lend him his sighs and tears (ll. 17–20), earlier prompted our recognition of Marvellian 'unmetaphor', a technique whereby inert or cliché figures of speech are reanimated by being expressed in a concrete form. Donne's witty speakers frequently imagine being drowned in tears; Marvell's Unfortunate Lover lives in a tempest. The impression the poem can thus give of Marvell 'running quickly through the pages of an emblem book' or lyric anthology has occasioned much criticism which purports to tell us which pages of which books (for the phrase, see Lederer 1946, 194). But the tracing of analogues in Alciati, Petrarch, Virgil, and so on, has supplied a bevy of hypothetical parts with little purchase on the whole (see *Poems*, 'Sources and Allusions', 85–87).

More inventive criticism has tended to focus on stanzas IV and V, which obscurely narrate the Unfortunate Lover's macabre upbringing by rapacious surrogates who are entrusted with or who assume responsibility for the Unfortunate Lover's care:

> IV
> While Nature to his birth presents
> This masque of quarr'lling elements;
> A num'rous fleet of corm'rants black,
> That sailed insulting o'er the wrack,
> Received into their cruel care
> Th'unfortunate and abject heir:
> Guardians most fit to entertain
> The orphan of the hurricane.

V

They fed him up with hopes and air,
Which soon digested to despair;
And as one corm'rant fed him still
Another on his heart did bill.
And while they famish him, and feast,
He both consumed, and increased.
And languished with doubtful breath,
Th'amphibium of Life and Death.
(ll. 25–40)

Here topical clues cluster teasingly: 'masques' seems to allude to those spec-
tacles of poetry and pageantry which nourished ideals of Stuart kingship;
'abject heir' too rings with royal associations, especially in a regicidal world,
while 'cormorant' was a term polemically associated with black-coated clergy.
But what kind of story can thus be discerned within the lineaments of these
actions and figures? For Margarita Stocker (1986), the abject heir is Charles I,
deluded by the flattery of masques, preyed upon by Laudian clergy, and
'Forced to live in storms and wars' (l. 60). Robert Wilcher (2001) suggests
that these lines refer more convincingly 'to the years of captivity when [the
king] was literally an "Orphan of the *Hurricane*" of Civil War' and pressed by
black-coated presbyters to accept the Covenant (306). Other substitutions
and other stories have reached themselves into critics' hands: the abject heir as
Prince Charles, 'cast away' on the Isle of Scilly; or as the Duke of York, who
had been depicted as a 'Venus armata' in an epigram by Sir Richard Fanshawe
Marvell may have seen (see Davidson and Jones 1985).

Surely the critics are on to something here, but as with the literary parallels
which have been adduced for the poem, attempts to draw a set of external
identifications into a narrative which harmonises with the poem's 'masque of
quarrelling elements' strain the limits of plausibility. That the fate of the
Unfortunate Lover arcs towards a 'spectacle of blood' (l. 42) is evident, but the
poem seems to short-circuit as allegory, turning in on itself, at once pained
and pleased to relish in symbols for their own sake. We might thus regard the
poem as an allegory, yes, of political shipwreck, but moreover, of representa-
tional crisis. When in the masque Jove or his cognates dispel the forces of
misrule, the gesture's symbolic force is of course to enact the mystery of kingship, the power to order the commonwealth. But at its most potent, the
masque insists on more than this, insists that the relation between signifier
(the symbolic materials of the masque) and signified (the realm of politics) is
in fact 'real' and seamless. 'The Unfortunate Lover' has the look of a

post-traumatic masque, its generic and aesthetic elements hopelessly confused, its protagonist's consolatory triumph rendered pointedly fictitious:

> VIII
> This is the only banneret
> That ever Love created yet:
> Who though, by the malignant stars,
> Forced to live in storms and wars;
> Yet dying leaves a perfume here,
> And music within every ear;
> And he in story only rules,
> In a field sable a lover gules.
> (ll. 57–64)

The poem savours wounds because it can do nothing to salve them; it exults
in a superfluity of figure because its purview is limited to 'story' ('here',
'within'), an aesthetic realm uncoupled from that 'without', from political
reality. And it is in this sense, I suggest, that 'The Unfortunate Lover' relates
to 'the poetry of embattled royalism and eventual lament for the execution of
Charles I' (*Poems*, 88). We may recall that Milton, in *Eikonoklastes* (1649),
witheringly characterised the king's posthumously published spiritual autobiography, the *Eikon Basilike*, as a congeries of 'quaint emblems and devices,
begged from the old pageantry of some Twelfth-night's entertainment at
Whitehall' (*CPW*, 3:343). One of Thomas Stanley's projects in the wake of
the regicide was to transform the prose meditations which closed each chapter
of the king's book into a series of odes (McDowell 2008, 217). Elegy and
allegory, emblem and device, these were ways of mediating and of meditating
on political crisis, but one might nonetheless—with derision or with sympathy—see in this emerging discursive field the fragments of Caroline culture
being shored against a shattered centre.

The Villiers, Lovelace, and Hastings poems were all written with the antici-
pation of their being read, of their being 'public' in some sense, and they are
situated within a demonstrably social matrix. Perhaps 'The Unfortunate
Lover' was begun with similar expectation: noting strong parallels to *Lucasta*,
McDowell (2008) ventures 'the possibility that "The Unfortunate Lover" was
written for an audience of grieving royalist writers in the Stanley circle in the
months after the regicide, perhaps before Stanley left London, "the place
guilty of Royall Blood", or perhaps during a visit by Marvell to Cumberlow in
the summer of 1649, when Stanley had his work on the *Psalterium Carolinum*
performed for his guests from the city' (218). But I would emphasise 'begun':

unlike the personal elegies, 'The Unfortunate Lover' and 'The Nymph Complaining' do not echo back to us in the poetry of Marvell's known or likely interlocutors. Neither was published until 1681, and no manuscript witnesses of either poem predate their appearance in the folio. There is little to suggest they had a readership before Mary Palmer recovered Marvell's poems from his desk drawer after his death. And indeed, there is in both lyrics the sense of a starting subject or set of intentions becoming baffled by a discovered subject which is never fully disclosed, perhaps even to the poet himself.

That 'The Unfortunate Lover' may hold a private meaning for Marvell, that its allegory of public events (however veiled or obscure) may at once cover and express a yet more obscure story of trauma and futurity, that the speaker's 'poor lover' may double as a version of the self, has lately found eloquent expression in the work of Derek Hirst and Steven Zwicker (2007, 2012). For these critics, the cruel care of the fleet of cormorants for the 'orphan of the hurricane' is nothing less than a screen memory of sexual abuse. 'Eros in Marvell's texts has been read as same-sex desire', they write, 'but what is narrated in this stanza [V] is surely no conventional story of the hidden flames of homoerotic attachment. Something altogether different is here imagined. What we must acknowledge in the stanza and more largely in the poem is a narrative of abusive, sustained, and yet pleasurable and deeply guilty violation' (*Orphan*, 81–82). Marvell scholars initially responded to this thesis with scepticism at times verging on hostility, unusual in a field more disposed to 'moderate varieties and brotherly dissimilitudes' than civil strife. And as Hirst and Zwicker themselves admit, they cannot say just whom or what is represented by the cormorants apart from noting their association with the clergy, though we do not have far to seek for signs of Marvell's wariness of churchmen. Their approach also raises difficult questions about how far poetry may be thought to constitute historical evidence and about the relation between the 'imagined life' and what we are used to thinking of as biography or autobiography. Over time, however, critics have been increasingly inclined to grant the resonance of this thesis at various points in Marvell's writing and career; once seen, the prospect of elemental trauma cannot be easily unseen. We are familiar with Marvell the patriot; with Marvell the poet of gardens; with Marvell the ironist, and with his echoing verse; we are now faced with a new and newly challenging figure, the poet of wounds, in whose imagination are conjoined pain, perfume, and song.

It is under such an aegis that we are called to read 'The Nymph Complaining' as a companion poem to 'The Unfortunate Lover'. Even so, it is hard to know where to begin with this deceptively slight pastoral, a poem of puzzles and contradictions which manages at once to impress with the innocence and simplicity of its untutored narrator even as it has come to be seen as a fabulous locus of writing and allegory. A brief survey of alleged sources for the poem might include Catullus's *Carmina*, Ovid's *Metamorphoses*, Virgil's *Aeneid*, Calpurnius Siculus's *Bucolica*, the *Greek Anthology*, and the *Song of Songs*, among sacred and classical texts, as well as Guarini's *Il Pastor Fido* (1590), William Browne's *Britannia's Pastorals* (1614), and Rowland Watkyns's *Flamma sine Fumo* (1662), among the European vernaculars. No less dizzying than the range of literary references said to be present in 'The Nymph Complaining' is the range of ulterior meanings which have been attributed to it. The poem has been read as a 'psychological journey' through the nymph's or the poet's mind; as a fable of innocence and experience; as a pattern of the soul, or the life of Christ, or the Holy Ghost; as a commentary on the stricken Anglican church, or on the regicide, or both (see *Poems*, 'Modern Criticism', 68–69). Under the influence of postmodernism, we have learned to think about validity in literary interpretation as a function of rhetoric and social power, of which critical languages are sanctioned at a given moment and who is empowered to speak. The extensive secondary literature on 'The Nymph Complaining' illustrates such an economy of meaning all too well; little which has been written about the poem justifies belief. In their heterogeneity and confusion, what source study and allegorical interpretation *do* reveal, however, is a relatively stable conviction that the poem's mode must in some sense be ironic, that there is a gap between the words on the page and what the poem 'means'.

The story told in 'The Nymph Complaining' is one of love and loss, substitution and displacement. The nymph is in love with Sylvio, who abandons her, leaving the fawn as a token of his former affection; the nymph transfers her love for Sylvio to the fawn, and the two creatures enjoy a pastoral idyll together in the nymph's garden until some 'wanton troopers riding by' (l. 1) shoot the fawn, occasioning the nymph's complaint. Over the fawn's bleeding body, the nymph thus relates the pair's sad history and ends by imagining their transformation into living statues, the nymph's tears 'themselves engraving there' (l. 118), forever writing her sorrow in her alabaster breast. While we can follow this readily enough, we must also note that such a description neatly orders what is in the poem's telling a non-linear series of events: the 'inciting incident' comes near the end of the story. This is to begin to grapple with one of the poem's chief difficulties, namely, the way the nymph's psychological immediacy—registered in her pure diction and naturalistic tetrameter couplets—seems to contrast with the poem's narrative and generic artifice. The poem's initial 24 lines take place within a tremulous present, as the nymph recounts a seemingly random act of violence and tries to make sense of it, as it were, in real time. But then the poem skitters backwards chronologically, as if the nymph realises an audience is listening to her lament, and she needs to back up and explain about 'Unconstant Sylvio' (l. 25); we don't catch up to the present again until line 93 (of 122). This deformation of the poem's temporal horizons also has a generic dimension: the nymph's dilatory treatment of how she used to sport with the fawn in her garden embeds a lyric of pastoral otium within her complaint.

Other problems are familiar from 'The Unfortunate Lover'. Of the troopers, Stanley Fish (2000) has commented that it seems as if 'the characters from another poem have for a moment burst into this one and left behind something to decipher' (30). But is it a matter of characters bursting in from outside, or rather a matter of language? Where we had the politically redolent 'masque', 'cormorants', 'abject heir', and 'malignant' in 'The Unfortunate Lover', here we have 'troopers' and 'deodands'. 'Troopers' was a coinage of the 1640s used in connection with the Scottish Covenanting Army; 'deodand' is a term from Canon Law which designates something to be forfeited to God, specifically an animal or chattel which had caused the death of a human being. The presence of these public-political glyphs is all the more blatant in 'The Nymph Complaining', which is spoken not by a learned poet but by a young girl, and an inhabitant of the pastoral universe.

The 'out of place' is an ancient critical category, and as such these abrasions in Marvell's ventriloquising of the young nymph 'cry out for our interpretive efforts' (Coulter 1976, 66). 'Heaven's King / Keeps register of everything', the nymph avers, 'And nothing may we use in vain. / Ev'n beasts must be with justice slain; / Else men are made their deodands' (ll. 13–17). Thus is Smith inclined (for instance) to read the nymph's lines as reversing the charge of blood guilt put to the king following the second civil war: here it is the troopers who have blood on their hands and whose lives are said to be forfeit for the unjust death of the fawn (*Chameleon*, 79). So thick with symbolism is sacrificial blood that it seemingly has to be translated into something else, into a set of relations that signifies more than the death of a pet, an impulse deepened by the sense that the fawn is already a substitute or stand-in for the absent Sylvio, and hence a readymade plaything for allegory.

But high-flown allegory of this kind seems bound to be embarrassed by the poem. If the fawn is Christ, is the nymph's unfaithful lover supposed to be God? If the fawn is the Church, does the nymph's sport with the fawn convey a proper image of communion? If Charles I, how should we understand the nymph's surmise, 'Had it lived long, I do not know / Whether it too might have done so / As Sylvio did: his gifts might be / Perhaps as false or more than he' (ll. 47–50). The gap between the metaphorical and the actual, or between text and allegorical subtext, seemingly cannot be traversed without leaving much of the poem behind. Taken as itself, 'The Nymph Complaining' appears a somewhat overwrought pastoral elegy; taken 'beyond' itself in any systematic way, it falls to pieces. We are at an impasse, what the poststructuralists taught us to call an aporia, from the Greek for 'no way out'. Our only recourse, I would suggest, is to try to dwell within the poem's spaces of uncertainty, within the gaps and wounds of its textual body.

Most definitions of allegory stipulate that it is a 'complete narrative', and thus, when the allegorical content is topical, that the religious or political events shadowed in the work are themselves complete. But if 'The Nymph Complaining' was written 'in the early months of 1649', as Smith infers (*Chameleon*, 79), we may ask whether the regicide had the status of a completed action. Not long after the king was executed upon the scaffold, he sprang back to life in the pages of *Eikon Basilike*, the most brilliant piece of royalist propaganda the century produced. A controversy soon broke out over the government's forcing of loyalty oaths to the new republic. It is one thing to bring about a sudden political revolution; quite another to say what happens next. In the Horatian Ode, written some 18 months after the regicide, Marvell wonders at Cromwell's 'industrious valour', which led him to climb from his private gardens 'To ruin the great work of time, / And cast the kingdom old / Into another mould' (ll. 34–36). But giving the man 'his due' required a certain amount of distance: as Blair Worden (1984) observes, the writer of 'heartbroken elegies on Charles I, the passive martyr, the Christ figure, born to suffer', has in the Ode 'cleared and dried his eyes' (547). In 'The Nymph Complaining', tears flow copiously over the fawn's 'warm life-blood' (l. 19); yet if the poem fails to allegorise the regicide, in the sense of making a complete narrative, we may speculate that this reflects its being written within a gap in time during which the meaning of the regicide remained deeply inchoate.

The poem also seems to encode a regicidally inflected version of the arguments Marvell made in his poem to Lovelace, for example 'Our wits have drawn th'infection of our times' (l. 4), 'Our civil wars have lost the civic crown' (l. 12). We noted earlier Marvell's identification of Lovelace with the Tribe of Ben and with the literary community of the 1620s and 1630s. On Jonson's model, poetry was a quasi-autonomous sphere 'of imaginative and ethical reflection and reception' (Lowrance 2014, 714). Thus does Jonson write, in 'An Epistle Answering to One that Asked to be Sealed of the Tribe of Ben', 'What is't to me whether the French design / Be, or be not, to get the Valtelline' (ll. 31–32), that is to say, what's politics to Jonson, or Jonson to politics? In that poem the drawn sword defends not against political enemies but those 'That censure all the town, and all the affairs, / And know whose ignorance is more than theirs' (ll. 23–24). In the Lovelace poem, Jonson's would-wits and ignorant censurers are replaced by government censors, and politics infects the very air. Supposing 'The Nymph Complaining' to have been written after the regicide invites reimagining 'th'infection of our times' through the spilt blood of the fawn. The site of the wound is where politics leaks into the aesthetic: the death of Lesbia's sparrow in Catullus, of Cyparissus's stag in Ovid, of Silvia's deer in Virgil, all appear in the intertextual background of the poem, at once bleeding significance into the fawn's death, and being bled into by the death of the king. Source study and allegory pool together unfathomably.

But at the heart of 'The Nymph Complaining' there is also an ecstatic fantasy of erotic and ontological openness, of love wounds that dissolve the boundary between subject and object, and indeed blur the distinctions of gender, of species, even of flora and fauna. 'With sweetest milk, and sugar, first', the nymph recalls, 'I it at mine own fingers nursed. / And as it grew, so every day / It waxed more white and sweet than they' (ll. 55–58). Though critics until recently tended to treat the fawn as male, assigning to it the gender of its giver, the nymph without exception uses gender-neutral pronouns in referring to the fawn. This seems to have to do with the fact that the nymph and fawn are described as sharing a deeply pleasurable experience of 'undifference'. The nymph even blushes 'to see its foot more soft, / And white (shall I say than my hand? / Nay any lady's of the land)' (ll. 60–63). She feeds the fawn with milk-white fingers, and 'it' becomes like 'them'; indeed, so thoroughgoing is the fawn's metamorphosis under the nymph's feeding regimen, its 'foot' becomes more soft and white than hers.

This spectacular merging of identities is repeated and elaborated in the ensuing scene of pastoral diversion: 'I have a garden of my own', says the nymph:

> But so with roses overgrown,
> And lilies, that you would it guess
> To be a little wilderness.
> And all the springtime of the year
> It only lovèd to be there.
> Among the beds of lilies, I
> Have sought it oft, where it should lie;
> Yet could not, till itself would rise,
> Find it, although before mine eyes.
> For in the flaxen lilies' shade,

It like a bank of lilies laid.
Upon the roses it would feed,
Until its lips ev'n seemed to bleed:
And then to me, 'twould boldly trip,
And print those roses on my lip.
But all its chief delight was still
On roses thus itself to fill:
And its pure virgin limbs to fold
In whitest sheets of lilies cold.
Had it lived long, it would have been
Lilies without, roses within.
(ll. 71–92)

Under the spell of pastoral, the fawn's lips 'bleed' with rose petals, and it 'prints' itself on the nymph, kissing her lips rose-red. Where one begins and the other ends is wholly, deliciously uncertain; and indeed, the possibility of merging more largely with nature blooms yet more radically into view. To become 'Lilies without, roses within' is pastoral communion unmetaphored.

But the fawn is bleeding to death, has been bleeding to death this whole time; the poem began with the motiveless crime of the troopers, to which we are here jarringly recalled: 'O help! O help! I see it faint: / And die as calmly as a saint' (ll. 93–94). Pastoral idyll, the prospect of escaping time, of Ovidian transformation, are inevitably shadowed by the forces of history, which threaten to burst in at any moment, like those wanton troopers riding by. 'The Nymph Complaining' finds Marvell giving full play to the liminal imagination and to a liminal poetics; even the history it limns is of indefinite shape and porous boundary. The Horatian Ode, for all the fine discriminations of its politics, reintroduces us to a discernible matrix of time, place, and action, of illocutionary force. Who can say just what Marvell was doing in producing that unbelievably strange utterance, 'The Nymph Complaining for the Death of her Fawn'? Cromwell, Fairfax, and Nun Appleton await without, but the aporias of the nymph permit no easy transit there.

References

Abridgement of the Remonstrance of the Army, An. 1648. London.
Burdon, Pauline. 1972. Andrew Marvell and Richard Flecknoe in Rome. *N&Q* 19 (1): 16–18.
———. 1978. Marvell after Cambridge. *British Library Journal* 4: 42–48.

Clarke, Susan A. 2010. Marvell in Royalist Gardens. *Andrew Marvell Newsletter* 2 (2). Web: https://www.st-andrews.ac.uk/marvellsociety/newsletter/susan-a-clarke-marvell-in-royalist-gardens/.

Condren, Conal. 1990. Andrew Marvell as Polemicist: His Account of the Growth of Popery, and Arbitrary Government. In *The Political Identity of Andrew Marvell*, ed. Conal Condren and A.D. Cousins, 157–187. Aldershot: Scolar Press.

Coster, Steph. 2018. "Sending them beyond the Sea": Andrew Marvell, the Earl of Clare, and Tutoring in the Restoration. *Marvell Studies* 2 (1): 3.

Coulter, James A. 1976. *The Literary Microcosm: Theories of Interpretation of the Later Neoplatonists*. Leiden: Brill.

Cousins, A.D. 2016. *Andrew Marvell: Loss and Aspiration, Home and Homeland in 'Miscellaneous Poems'*. New York: Routledge.

Davidson, P.R.K., and A.K. Jones. 1985. New Light on Marvell's "The Unfortunate Lover"? *N&Q* 32 (1): 170–172.

Fish, Stanley. 2000. Marvell and the Art of Disappearance. In *Revenge of the Aesthetic*, ed. Michael P. Clarke, 25–44. Berkeley: University of California Press.

Gardiner, S.R., ed. 1906. *The Constitutional Documents of the Puritan Revolution*. 3rd ed. Oxford: Clarendon Press.

Gosse, Edmund. 1913. *Collected Essays of Edmund Gosse: Seventeenth-Century Studies*. London: William Heinemann.

Hammond, Paul. 1996. Marvell's Sexuality. *SC* 11 (1): 87–123.

Hill, Christopher. 2001. *Puritanism and Revolution: Studies in Interpretation of the English Revolution of the 17th Century* (1958). London: Pimlico.

Hirst, Derek. 2004. Review of *The Prose Works of Andrew Marvell*, ed. Annabel Patterson et al. *Albion* 36 (4): 697–700.

Hirst, Derek, and Steven N. Zwicker. 2007. Eros and Abuse: Imagining Andrew Marvell. *ELH* 74 (2): 371–395.

———. 2012. *Andrew Marvell, Orphan of the Hurricane*. Oxford: Oxford University Press.

Jay, Martin. 1993. *Downcast Eyes: The Denigration of Vision in Twentieth-Century French Thought*. Berkeley and Los Angeles: University of California Press.

Jonson, Ben. 1988. *Ben Jonson: The Complete Poems*. Ed. George Parfitt. Harmondsworth: Penguin.

Kelliher, Hilton. 1978. *Andrew Marvell: Poet & Politician*. London: British Library.

———. 2008. Marvell, Andrew (1621–1678), poet and politician. *ODNB*.

Lederer, Josef. 1946. John Donne and the Emblematic Practice. *RES* 22 (87): 182–200.

Love, Harold. 1989. Scribal Texts and Literary Communities: The Rochester Circle and Osborn b. 105. *Studies in Bibliography* 17: 219–235.

———. 1993. *Scribal Publication in Seventeenth-Century England*. Oxford: Clarendon Press.

Lowrance, Bryan. 2014. Marlowe's Wit: Power, Language, and the Literary in *Tamburlaine* and *Dr Faustus*. *MP* 111 (4): 711–732.

Marvell, Andrew. 2003. *Prose Works of Andrew Marvell*. Ed. Annabel Patterson, Martin Dzelzainis, Nicholas von Maltzahn, and N. H. Keeble. 2 vols. New Haven: Yale University Press.

———. 2007. *Poems of Andrew Marvell*. Ed. Nigel Smith. Rev. ed. London: Longman.

McDowell, Nicholas. 2008. *Poetry and Allegiance in the English Civil Wars: Marvell and the Cause of Wit*. Oxford: Oxford University Press.

———. 2017. Towards Redefinition of Cavalier Poetics. *SC* 32 (4): 413–431.

Mercurius Elencticus. 1647–1649. Newsbook. London.

Milton, John. 1953–1982. *Complete Prose Works of John Milton*. Ed. Don M. Wolfe et al. New Haven: Yale University Press.

Moul, Victoria. 2018. The Date of Marvell's *Hortus*. *SC* 34 (3): 329–351.

Mundy, Peter. 1925. *The Travels of Peter Mundy, Vol. IV*. Ed. Sir Richard Carnac Temple for the Hakluyt Society. London.

Parry, C.H., ed. 1839. *Parliaments and Councils of England, from the Reign of William I to The Revolution in 1688*. London: John Murray.

Pertile, Giulio. 2013. Marvell as *Libertin*: *Upon Appleton House* and the Legacy of Théophile de Viau. *SC* 28 (4): 395–418.

Pittion, Jean-Paul. 2018. Marvell and Protestant Saumur in the 1650s. *Marvell Studies* 3 (1): 5.

Pritchard, Allan. 1983. Marvell's "The Garden": A Restoration Poem? *SEL* 23 (3): 371–388.

Raylor, Timothy. 2018. Andrew Marvell: Traveling Tutor. *Marvell Studies* 2 (1): 2.

Raymond, Joad. 2018. "Small Portals": Marvell's *Horatian Ode*, Print Culture, and Literary History. In *Texts and Readers in the Age of Marvell*, ed. Christopher D'Addario and Matthew C. Augustine, 33–55. Manchester: Manchester University Press.

Robertson, Randy. 2006. Lovelace and the "Barbèd Censurers": *Lucasta* and Civil War Censorship. *SP* 103 (4): 465–498.

Rogers, Pat. 1978. *The Augustan Vision*. London: Methuen.

Russell, C.S.R., ed. 1973. *The Origins of the English Civil War*. London: Macmillan.

Scott-Baumann, Elizabeth. 2013. *Forms of Engagement: Women, Poetry and Culture, 1640–1680*. Oxford: Oxford University Press.

Slingsby, Sir Henry. 1836. *The Diary of Sir Henry Slingsby*. Ed. Daniel Parsons. London: Longman.

Smith, Nigel. 2010a. *Andrew Marvell: The Chameleon*. New Haven: Yale University Press.

———. 2010b. "Mirrored Doubles": Andrew Marvell, the Remaking of Poetry and the Poet's Career. In *Classical Literary Careers and Their Reception*, ed. Philip Hardie and Helen Moore, 226–240. Cambridge: Cambridge University Press.

———. 2017. Cross-channel Cavaliers. *SC* 32 (4): 433–453.

———. 2018. The European Marvell. In *Texts and Readers in the Age of Marvell*, ed. Christopher D'Addario and Matthew C. Augustine, 169–188. Manchester: Manchester University Press.

Stocker, Margarita. 1986. *Apocalyptic Marvell: The Second Coming in Seventeenth-Century Poetry*. Brighton: Harvester.

Stoye, John. 1989. *English Travellers Abroad, 1604–1667*. Rev. ed. New Haven: Yale University Press.

The Hartlib Papers. 2013. Ed. Mark Greengrass, Michael Leslie, and Michael Hannon. Published by The Digital Humanities Institute, University of Sheffield. https://www.dhi.ac.uk/hartlib.

The Parliament-Kite. 1648. Newsbook. London.

The Stonyfield Sabbath Day. 1637. NLS Adv. Ms. 33.2.32, pp. 47–48.

True and Exact Relation of the Manner of His Majesty's Setting up of His Standard at Nottingham, A. 1642. London.

von Maltzahn, Nicholas. 2005. *An Andrew Marvell Chronology*. New York: Palgrave Macmillan.

Wilcher, Robert. 2001. *The Writing of Royalism, 1628–1660*. Cambridge: Cambridge University Press.

Worden, Blair. 1984. The Politics of Marvell's Horatian Ode. *HJ* 27 (3): 525–547.

———. 2007. *Literature and Politics in Cromwellian England: John Milton, Andrew Marvell, Marchamont Nedham*. Oxford: Oxford University Press.

Zwicker, Steven N. 2018. What's the Problem with the Dutch? Andrew Marvell, the Trade Wars, Toleration, and the Dutch Republic. *Marvell Studies* 3 (1): 4.

5

'Some great prelate of the grove': London and Nun Appleton, Yorkshire, 1650–1652

In the weeks and months following the regicide of 30 January 1649—and as the political nation engaged in the work of mourning the death of Charles I—the Rump Parliament set about establishing a constitutional basis for the new commonwealth. On 13 February, an act was passed appointing a Council of State to fill the breach in government left by the fall of the monarchy. Vested with full military authority, the Council's most urgent order of business was to oppose the late king's heirs and to suppress 'tumults and insurrections', with a particular view to reducing Ireland (*ConstDoc*, 381–3). On 17 March, the Rump voted to abolish the office of king and two days later to abolish the House of Lords (*ConstDoc*, 384–8). In so doing, the act abolishing monarchy declared, 'a most happy way is made for this nation (if God see it good) to return to its just and ancient right, of being governed by its own representatives or national meetings in council'. The act thus included a resolution 'to put a period to the sitting of this present Parliament, and dissolve the same so soon as may possibly stand with the safety of the people that hath betrusted them, and with what is absolutely necessary for the preserving and upholding the Government now settled in the way of a Commonwealth'. In a defining act that nonetheless appears born out of irresolution or uncertainty, and more than three months after the regicide, on 19 May the House declared England 'to be a Commonwealth and Free State', from henceforth to be governed 'by the supreme authority of this nation, the representatives of the people in Parliament' (*ConstDoc*, 388).

The political realities faced by the Rump, however, were less than accommodating, caught as it was between the people, in whom was said to reside 'supreme authority', and the army, to which it owed its existence. Pride's Purge had reduced the 471 active members of the Long Parliament to a body of a little more than 200, and the number in attendance between 6 December 1648 and 7 February 1649 rarely exceeded seventy; 'Forty-three MPs, less than one in ten of the unpurged House, sat in judgement on the king and subscribed his death warrant, though three of these seem to have been bullied into signing, for they withdrew from parliament soon afterwards' (Woolrych 2002, 435–6). For all that they lacked a popular mandate, the Rump and its Council of State were deeply wary of army influence, and especially of the Levellers, who still hoped to see their proposals for reform—including a radically expanded franchise and the separation of church and state—ratified by the new government. The perception of the Commonwealth's backsliding on these reforms provoked unsparing criticism from Leveller leaders and a consequent wave of imprisonments meant to deter defections in the ranks at a time when the Commonwealth needed to defend itself against threats from Scotland and Ireland. Little wonder the government wanted to stop the mouth of John Lilburne (1649) from inveighing against Cromwell and Ireton as 'tyrants of Athens', declaring 'the Parliament indeed is no Parliament, but a representative class of the Council of War; and the Council of War but the representative of Cromwell, Ireton, and [Major-General Thomas] Harrison; and these are the all in all of this nation, which under these guises and names of Parliament, Army, General Council, High Court, and Council of State play all the strange pranks that are played' (9). That September, the Rump approved 'An Act against Unlicensed and Scandalous Books and Pamphlets, and for Better Regulating of Printing'; it appointed John Milton one of its licensers.

The Forward Youth That Would Appear

Perhaps the only thing not in dispute about Marvell's 'An Horatian Ode upon Cromwell's Return from Ireland' is its occasion. In May 1649, Cromwell was commissioned Lord Lieutenant in Ireland to be general of the army there, with the aim of breaking the alliance between English royalists under the command of James Butler, Marquess of Ormond, and the Irish Catholic Confederation. The Confederation had controlled most of Ireland since the rebellion of 1641, and, following a forty-week campaign—punctuated by the bloody sieges of Drogheda and Wexford—Cromwell acquiesced to Parliament's wish that he return to England, landing at Bristol on 29 May 1650 and arriving in London to a hero's welcome a few days later. With Ireland subdued, the Commonwealth turned its attention north, where Charles II had been proclaimed king days after the regicide. On 26 June, Thomas Lord Fairfax resigned his generalship of the army, refusing to lead the proposed invasion of Scotland, and Cromwell was appointed in his place; two days later, he marched north from London with a force of 16,000 men. The Horatian Ode was presumably written within the window between Cromwell's return from the Irish campaign and the launch of the Scottish offensive Horace (2004).

And there agreement about the poem more or less ends. Stephen Booth (1974) has wittily described *Hamlet* as 'the tragedy of an audience that cannot make up its mind' (294). In a similar way, we might think of the Horatian Ode as Marvell's *Hamlet*, perhaps as revealing of its readers as of the poem's author or protagonist. What is the import, many have asked, of the poem's self-advertised Horatianism? In the Odes, Horace lavishes special praise on Augustus Caesar, and we have seen how Marvell adapted such praise for the purposes of Stuart panegyric in 'Ad Regem Carolum Parodia'. Horatian themes pervade royalist writing of this period. But Horace, a veteran of Brutus's army who fought for the republic, also bitterly lamented the spilling of Latin blood, 'witness by its graves to our unholy battles' (*Odes*, 2.1); routinely he celebrated the virtues of old Rome; and extolled the integrity of the man who is not shaken 'by the frown of an oppressive despot' or by 'the mighty hand of thundering Jove' (*Odes*, 3.3). It has proven possible to decode the politics of Marvell's Horatian ode as pro-Cromwell or pro-republic, as loyalist or royalist, or as embracing that unfathomable space between these positions. Shaded by the possibility that Marvell may be writing against the grain of generic expectation, the poem's Horatianism may open many doors, but it remains unclear where we are to walk through.

A host of other questions wait upon the issue of the poem's loyalties. Whom if anyone was Marvell writing *for*? Some tenuous evidence has emerged of the Ode's 'tightly controlled, scribal circulation among other poets in the 1650s' (McDowell 2012, 482), but such evidence has recently been cast into doubt (Dzelzainis 2019, 320–6); the poem was cancelled from virtually all copies of *1681*. And we cannot take our bearings from the little that is known of Marvell's activities or associations in the early days of the Commonwealth. It has been observed that one of Thomas Stanley's translations of 1651 uses the same metrical form as the Horatian Ode, an observation made the more interesting in light of an earlier version of Stanley's poem dating to 1646 which uses a different metre, allowing the possibility that he revised it after seeing the Ode (Kelliher 1978, 34). But Stanley, we know, left London soon after the regicide, retiring to his family estate at Cumberlow Green with several members of his circle in tow. If poetry functions as a kind of currency within a patronage environment, what could Marvell have hoped for by circulating the Ode within a coterie of self-exiled royalists? He was clearly in need of a job in the summer of 1650, as his entry into Fairfax's service soon thereafter attests. Was the Horatian Ode a bid for Cromwell's attention? For the Council of State's? Perhaps it was meant to impress Fairfax himself, and indeed, there is much to recommend reading the Ode 'as a construction of the personalities and events of 1648–1650 from Lord Fairfax's point of view' (Hirst and Zwicker 1993, 264n).

But to imagine the poem as prelude to Marvell's retreat with the Fairfaxes to Nun Appleton is to steer directly into the irony and uncertainty instated in the poem's opening lines, irony which crowds into the space between the figure of the 'forward youth' invoked in those lines and the poet who (self-reflexively?) invokes him. 'The forward youth that would appear', this Horatian speaker urges, 'Must now forsake his Muses dear,'

> Nor in the shadows sing
> His numbers languishing:
> 'Tis time to leave the books in dust,
> And oil the unusèd armour's rust;
> Removing from the wall
> The corslet of the hall.
> (ll. 1–8)

The Longman editor annotates Marvell's 'now' thusly: 'suggests the urgency of the recruiting drive for the Scottish campaign; ironically echoes and inverts Horace, *Carmina*, I.xxxvii (*'nunc est bibendum'*); the first instance of Machiavellian vocabulary in the poem, with the injunction of *occasione*, seizing the moment' (*Poems*, 273n). *'Nunc Est Bibendum'*, 'Now is the time for drinking', celebrates Octavian's victory over Cleopatra at Actium and the extinction of a foreign threat to Rome. Marvell's 'now' ostensibly reverses the thrust of Horace's, calling on the forward youth to lay aside song for action. Perhaps Horace's retrospective telling of how Caesar pursued Cleopatra 'like a hawk after a gentle dove or a speedy hunter after a hare' is mirrored by Marvell's prospective telling of how 'The Pict no shelter *now* shall find', as Cromwell, the 'English hunter', prepares to lay his hounds in for the 'Caledonian deer' (ll. 105, 110–12). But the speaker of Marvell's ode can hardly be said to be forsaking the Muses; he continues to sing from the shadows. If the forward youth is called to seize the moment, the Machiavellian *occasione*, the speaker's occasion is, above all, poetry, specifically the poetry of Horace (hence 'An Horatian Ode'). The movement towards *actio* and out of the shade is enunciated from a position of abiding languor. And of course, so long as we dwell within the poet's little rooms, we're not enlisting for the wars (*stanza* is of course Italian for 'room', but we might think as well of Joad Raymond's 'small portals'; see Raymond 2018).

As this makes clear, the Cromwell of Marvell's ode occupies the same position as Caesar in the odes of Horace, but this is a decidedly odd fit in the context of a 'Commonwealth and Free State'. In the spring of 1650, as Westminster waited on Cromwell's return from Ireland, royalist newsbooks buzzed with speculation about the tyrannical ambitions of 'his Nose-ship', that he would root Fairfax out of his commission, that he would overthrow Parliament, that his faction 'work hard to make him Generalissimo', that he would become king (see, e.g., *Mercurius Pragmaticus* 37, 8–15 January 1650; Worden 1984, 528). A Caesarean Cromwell was the stuff of royalist conspiracy but no less of republican alarm. This is to insist on the uncertainty of how we are meant to take the comparison between Octavian and Cromwell, an uncertainty which is only deepened by the presence of an additional Caesarean frame, Lucan's great epic on the war between Julius Caesar and the Roman Senate, the *Pharsalia*. Thomas May—the subject of a satire by Marvell upon his death that November—had published a complete translation of the *Pharsalia* in 1627; it was reissued in a fourth edition in 1650. Marvell seizes in particular on the fateful moment of Caesar's crossing the Rubicon into Araminum. Like the forward youth of Marvell's poem, the citizens of Araminum have let their armour go to rust, and are thus unprepared to resist Caesar's charge:

> … Shrill trumpets flourished round,
> And the hoarse horns wicked alarums sound.
> With this sad noise the people's rest was broke:
> The young men rose, and from the temples took
> Their arms, now such as a long peace had marred,
> And their old bucklers now of leather's bared,
> Their blunted piles not of a long time used,
> And swords with th'eatings of black rust abus'd.
> (*Lucan's Pharsalia*, trans. May, 1.255–63)

The allusion gives Marvell's youth due warning: *now* is the time 'to leave the books in dust, / And oil the unusèd armour's rust', but who is the Caesar crossing the Rubicon? Is it Cromwell returning from Ireland? Or Charles II crossing the Tweed at the head of a Covenanting army, the threat Cromwell is going to meet?

Such confusions can only be deliberate, reflecting a strategy Marvell would use to more obviously self-conscious effect in his poem 'On *Paradise Lost*'.

There he begins by dramatising how Milton's 'vast design' at first 'Held me a while misdoubting his intent, / That he would ruin (for I saw him strong) / The sacred truths to fable and old song' (ll. 2, 6–8). 'Yet as I read', he continues, 'soon growing less severe, / I liked his project, the success did fear' (ll. 11–12); and by the midpoint of 'On *Paradise Lost*' the commender is forced to beg the mighty poet's pardon, convinced 'Thou hast not missed one thought that could be fit' (l. 27). Its misapprehensions thus corrected, the poem's argument can proceed untrammelled. From its very title, the Horatian Ode prompts its reader to consider the nature of Cromwell's identity through a mist of Caesarean parallels and allusions, only to reveal Cromwell as a kind of anti-Caesar, 'burning through the air', rending palaces and temples, and 'blasting' Caesar's laureled head (ll. 21–4). It is not through tendentious 'Roman-cast similitude[s]' (l. 44), for which Marvell chides May in 'Tom May's Death', that Cromwell is to be defined, but rather through an appeal to the law of nature, to the mechanics of force and vacuum.

Indeed, in a bravura display of wit, historical similitudes are actively exploded in the course of narrating Cromwell's career. Marvell's similes at first combine the natural and the Roman: incapable of resting 'In the inglorious arts of peace', Marvell writes, Cromwell 'through advent'rous war / Urgèd his active star':

> And like the three-forked lightning, first
> Breaking the clouds where it was nursed,
> Did thorough his own side
> His fiery way divide.
> (ll. 9–16)

The lightning bolt is an emblem of the natural sublime, but it also harks back to May's Lucan, in which Caesar, as he strides towards the Rubicon, is compared to 'lightning by the wind forced from a cloud', which 'Breaks through the wounded air with thunder loud, / Disturbs the day, the people terrifies, / And by a light oblique dazzles our eyes' (1.165–7). Cromwell's emergence out of the cloud (his 'own' parliamentary 'side') also hints at a Caesarean origin: the 'Caesarean sectiòn' Marvell refers to in 'The Unfortunate Lover'. But Cromwell's surging elementality soon exceeds the grasp of these allusions: in succeeding stanzas Marvell's Cromwell bursts forth, not as Caesar but as the apocalyptic force which blasts an anointed Caesar's head (ll. 21–4), not as an embodiment of precedent types but as a breaker of precedent who would 'ruin the great work of time, / And cast the kingdoms old / Into another mould' (ll. 33–5):

Though Justice against Fate complain,
And plead the ancient rights in vain;
But those do hold or break,
As men are strong or weak.
Nature that hateth emptiness,
Allows of penetration less:
And therefore must make room
Where greater spirits come.
(ll. 36–44)

Alert to such figural patternings, David Norbrook (1990) has read the Ode as 'a radical rethinking of the politics of poetry and of classical culture', unhitching itself from a royalist Horatianism to praise Cromwell as 'the bold architect of a new state' and effecting a 'republican sublime' (152–3, 156). Here Marvell does glance at new-making as well as breaking the 'mould' of state, though we can hardly call this republican theory in any principled sense. Indeed, while it may be possible to view the supersession of 'ancient rights'—a watchword for Stuart abuses of prerogative?—with equanimity, it is hard to get round Marvell's pitting of Cromwell and Fate against 'Justice'. At best, justice simply has no claim on a pneumatical engine, such as is the Cromwellian republic.

''Tis madness to resist or blame / The force of angry's heaven's flame' (ll. 25–6). The question of resistance to which Marvell gives point in this couplet, as John M. Wallace (1968) noted long ago, situates the Horatian Ode within the controversy over 'engagement', which was at its height in the winter and spring of 1650. Shortly after the regicide, members of the newly created Council of State were obliged to take an Oath of Engagement, promising 'That I will be true and faith to the Commonwealth of England, as it is now established, without a King of House of Lords'. In October 1649, the requirement was extended to MPs, clergymen, and government officeholders; and in January 1650, to all men in England eighteen years old and upward. The Engagement thus provided the discursive context in which a theory of political obligation to the new government 'capable of … justifying the duty to obey a merely de facto and usurping political power' was forged in dialogue with vigorous royalist and Presbyterian opposition (Skinner 1972, 79–80). Though we do not know whether Marvell subscribed the oath, the Ode seems to me clear in accepting engagement with the Commonwealth as the condition of 'forwardness' within its twin spheres of concern, politics and poetry. Wallace (1968) thus found the Ode revealing of Marvell's 'loyalism', by which he meant a form of political conscience which granted the transference of allegiance after the death of a former sovereign; 'he may be loyal "to the existing form of government" provided the old government is extinct' (5). But this was in some ways merely a rebranding of 'de facto' theories of obligation worked out in the Engagement Controversy, which bear some brief rehearsal here in light of what I would claim is the Horatian Ode's key word: *forward*.

As Glenn Burgess (1986) has shown, defenders of the Engagement typically deployed what were held to be mutually supporting arguments from providence and from ideas of 'political society'. Providentialist arguments rested on the famous passage from St Paul: 'Let every soul be subject unto the higher powers. For there is no power but of God: the powers that be are ordained of God' (Romans 13:1). Nedham, like nearly all de factoist writers, gives vent to this doctrine in *The Case of the Commonwealth of England, Stated* (1650), the first pamphlet we have from his pen after gaining his release from Newgate prison. But he also reasons, in a Hobbesian vein, 'That non-submission to government justly deprives men of the benefit of its protection', for which purpose states and kingdoms were first set up. In particular, he exhorts the need for preserving 'civil communion', whose two main ends are 'public safety' and 'public equity'. By this latter term he means, 'the administration of justice, encouragement of virtue, and punishment of vice, without which it's impossible to enjoy peace or happiness' (17–18). Any government satisfying these criteria, according to Nedham, may be lawfully obeyed, and indeed, where such conditions obtain, to refuse obedience is to transgress against the law of God and nature 'and open a gap to confusion' (18). 'It must needs be as much madness', he says, echoing Marvell, 'to strive against the stream for the upholding of a power cast down by the Almighty, as it were for the old sons of Earth to heap up mountains against heaven' (5). (On Marvell and Nedham's de factoism, see Worden 2007, esp. 67–9).

Even if it's true of the Ode that 'phrase after phrase bears ironic or hostile implications' (Creaser 2002, 47), there can be little doubt of Cromwell's being backed by the arguments of providence and the sword. Indeed, in a remarkable passage in a poem full of remarkable passages, Marvell explicitly yokes usurpatory violence to a state of civic 'happiness'. 'This was that memorable hour', Marvell says of the moment when the executioner's axe separated the king's head from his body, 'Which first assured the forcèd power' (ll. 65–6). The simile which follows draws a comparison between Charles's bloody head and the 'bleeding head' discovered at the foundations of Jupiter's Temple in Rome, a prospect which frightened its architects, 'And yet', the poet avers, 'in that the State / Foresaw its happy fate' (ll. 71–2). Critics have tended to focus on 'happy fate' at the expense of 'forcèd power' in a rush to affirm Marvell's forecasting of a glorious republican future. Cromwell and his party have indeed seized the moment, the Machiavellian *occasione*, in overthrowing the monarchical government, and have even succeeded in putting the new state on a footing that can be termed 'happy'. But Marvell's rather chilling identification of the republic's happy hour with 'forcèd power' sets providence and fate within a deeply contingent 'de factoist' frame. 'Now that you may understand what fate is', Nedham writes in the opening pages of *The Case*, 'Minucius Felix calls it, *Quod de unoquoque nostrum fatus est Deus*, that which God hath spoken or determined concerning every man. *It is* (saith Seneca) *that Providence which pulls down one kingdom or government, and sets up another; nor is this done leisurely and by degrees, but it hurls the powers of the world on a sudden, from the highest pinnacle of glory, to nothing*' (2). At the conclusion of the Ode, Marvell advises Cromwell, 'the War's and Fortune's son', to 'keep thy sword erect', coolly observing, 'The same arts that did gain / A pow'r must it maintain' (ll. 113, 116, 119–20).

Within a year (1649–1650) Cromwell has subdued the Irish; he now goes to tame the 'Caledonian deer'; 'A Caesar he ere long to Gaul, / To Italy an Hannibal, / And to all states not free / Shall climacteric be' (ll. 101–4). 'Free' has most often been understood in a republican sense, but if we take the measure of Marvell's subsequent allegiances, such freedom evidently has more to do with an ideal of moderate Christian liberty than it does with particular constitutional frameworks. Cromwell's victories in the Ode are over the Catholic Irish and the Presbyterian Scots (Marvell, we recall from the poem to Lovelace, was no friend of 'severe Presbytery'), while France and Italy are persecutingly Romish states. Much has been made of Marvell's double-edged praise for Cromwell as not 'yet grown stiffer with command, / But still in the Republic's hand' (ll. 81–2). But when, in 1653, it is the *falcon* who has the *falconer* sure, when the Rump and the Nominated Assembly have alike been dissolved and Cromwell installed as Lord Protector, Marvell's support, judging from 'The First Anniversary', is hardly thereby diminished. There he praises Cromwell's defence of 'sober liberty' (l. 289) against the rage of the sects, 'The shame and plague both of the land and age' (l. 294). Like Amphion, Cromwell plays upon the rude heap of the English polity, raising the martial tower and palace sweet, but above all the graver temple, its Doric columns rising high. As a Restoration MP and clandestine satirist, Marvell repeatedly scourged Stuart foreign policy, but he also played an active role in encouraging the king's indulgence of tender conscience in the face of Anglican retrenchment and an intolerant Parliament (see *Chameleon*, esp. 217–18). This helps us understand why attempts to bracket Marvell's politics under convenient labels have so often foundered: Marvell's allegiances—as the Ode teaches us— pivot around the twinned questions of where 'forwardness' appears (a question of ideological 'sides') and of getting or appearing forward in the sense urged on the forward youth.

Can something also be said of those stanzas in which Marvell so affectingly replays Charles's gracious comportment upon the scaffold? Caught in a web of fear and hope woven, it is intimated, by Cromwell himself, the king fled to Carisbrooke Castle:

> That thence the royal actor born
> The tragic scaffold might adorn,
> While round the armèd bands
> Did clap their bloody hands.
> He nothing common did, or mean,
> Upon that memorable scene;
> But with his keener eye
> The axe's edge did try.
> Nor called the Gods with vulgar spite
> To vindicate his helpless right;
> But bowed his comely head
> Down, as upon a bed.
> (ll. 53–64)

Here Marvell entombs what I earlier called the poem's 'emotional royalism', in a still frieze flanked on either side by Cromwell's restless activity. Norbrook (1990) comments superbly on this passage: 'If Cromwell is the republican sublime', he writes, 'Charles is the courtly beautiful; Marvell is establishing a similar relationship between his forebears the cavalier poets and the new and more innovative genre of poetry he is now founding [in the HO] ... monarchical culture is weighed at its own highest self-evaluation, as the source of grace, decorum, elegance, exclusiveness, and found beautiful but limited' (156). This is penetrating criticism, even if it seems too irrevocable and unruffled in its conclusions. If we scratch the polished surface of Marvell's 'courtly beautiful', we discover traffic once again with the newsbooks, which reported how the aftermath of king's execution became nothing less than a street circus, a raree show, or indeed a marketplace organised by parliamentary soldiers (see *Mercurius Elencticus* 1, 31 January–7 February 1649, sig. A2ᵛ). Moreover, with respect to the 'new and more innovative genre of poetry' Marvell is said to be founding, we must ask, 'founding for how long?' Marvell's next dateable poem is the bitter satire on May, a 'son of Ben' turned historian of Parliament, which is not only written in a Cavalier mode but in Jonson's voice, or at least in that of his ghost. The lyrics composed at Nun Appleton frequently return to the well of classical and continental verse cherished and nurtured by the Stanley circle. While in 'The Last Instructions', Marvell brilliantly re-inhabits the courtly beautiful, his Ovidian paean to Archibald Douglas shines the brighter beside his curdled portraits of court corruption. Marvell is indeed a forward and innovative, even a 'restless' poet, but his art does not move in a straight line.

A Staggering Reversal?: 'Tom May's Death'

Still, there is something about 'Tom May's Death' that does not compute. Though current understandings of seventeenth-century politics and political culture hedge against assumptions of ideological consistency, it is nonetheless jarring to turn from the scrupulous appraisal of Cromwell in the Ode to what looks like royalist satire in 'Tom May's Death' a few months hence. Moreover, the satire's vehement tone is hard to square with the apparent lack of biographical circumstance connecting the poem's target and its author. The translator and historian May was a generation older than Marvell, and it has proven difficult to place them at less than one or two removes from each other. May contributed some commendatory verses to James Shirley's *Poems* of 1646, though this volume predates Shirley's and, later, Marvell's association with the Stanley circle; May can be linked to Nedham who can be linked to Marvell; and so on. This is also to be reminded that May was a London figure, and it is hard to think 'Tom May's Death' was not written with some of Marvell's London friends in mind. However, May died on 13 November 1650, and most think Marvell likely entered Fairfax's service in London and accompanied him to his Yorkshire estate sometime after the latter resigned his post at the end of June. 'Tom May's Death' has not seemed 'the sort of poem Marvell would have written under Fairfax's roof' (*P&L*, 1:277).

May first came to attention in the 1620s and 1630s as the author of plays, poems, and translations composed in Jonson's milieu; on more than one occasion, he sought preferment in dedicating works 'To the Most High and Mighty Monarch Charles'. Passed over in favour of William Davenant for the honour of succeeding Jonson as unofficial poet laureate, however, by 1642 May had switched his allegiances to Parliament and turned to writing parliamentary propaganda, for which he was rewarded with a secretaryship in January 1646. May's *The History of the Parliament of England which Began November the Third, 1640* was published in May 1647. A *Breviary* of the same history, condensing May's earlier account and bringing the narrative of events from September 1643 up to the verge of the regicide, appeared in June 1650, coincident with Marvell's presumed writing of the Horatian Ode. In an oft-cited article, Blair Worden (1984) pondered how 'Horace, the republican soldier of Philippi, came to terms with the rule of Augustus Caesar', and looked to the political odes to explain this 'painful transition' (526). 'The ode of 1650' accordingly 'tells us about *Marvell's* Horatian transition. It may even', says Worden, 'have assisted it' (my emphasis). So too may have 'Tom May's Death', if in a counter-intuitive way: that is, I suggest we try reading the poem as displacing the pain of Marvell's Horatian transition into a mould which allowed Marvell once more to invoke the Cavalier muse set aside in the Ode and to mete out poetic justice to one who—for the poet's purposes anyway—made the same transition all too easily.

'Tom May's Death' reflects Marvell's reading of May's Lucan and of his history of Parliament, fashioning a playful metaphorics out of the principles of just translation (literally 'to carry across'). The poem thus begins with May waking up to a frightening hangover on the wrong side of the River Styx (according to Aubrey, May choked by tying his bonnet too tight after a night of heavy drinking). He stumbles through the Elysian dusk with 'eye uncertain' until he comes upon a figure whom he first takes to be a tapster but who turns out to be Ben Jonson, singing of ancient heroes. 'But seeing May, he varied straight his song, / Gently to signify that he was wrong':

'Cups more than civil of Emathian wine,
I sing' (said he) 'and the Pharsalian Sign,
Where the historian of the Commonwealth
In his own bowels sheathed the conquering health.'
By this May to himself and them was come,
He found he was translated, and by whom.
(ll. 21–6)

Jonson's speech pointedly rewrites the opening lines of May's Lucan:

Wars more than civil on Emathian plains
We sing; rage licensed; where Rome distains
In her own bowels her victorious swords …
(1.1–3)

Emathia was the Thessalian province where the Battle of Pharsalia was fought between Pompey and Caesar. In Jonson's rendering, the Pharsalian field becomes a pub, the rage and pathos of 'wars more than civil', of the victorious sword sheathed in its bearer's own bowels, transferred bathetically to

May's Pyrrhic turn as parliamentary flack, his death by drink a parody of noble Roman suicide.

But readers of May's Lucan also would have recalled Jonson's commendatory verses 'To My Chosen Friend', which prefaced every edition of the *Pharsalia*. There Jonson praises the 'due proportion' given by Lucan to 'Pompey's popularity, / Caesar's ambition, Cato's liberty, / Calm Brutus' tenor' (ll. 9–11) and wonders what god of harmony 'Taught Lucan these true moods!' (ll. 14–15). 'Arts, and eloquence', 'Phoebus, and Hermes', he answers himself, thus denominating the tutelary gods of both Lucan and of May's Lucan 'Englished' (ll. 15–16). When Marvell's Jonson, on seeing May, varies 'straight his song / Gently to signify that he was wrong', it is thus 'he', Jonson, who corrects himself as much as he corrects May. The partisan history of Parliament casts the *Pharsalia* in a new light, its proportions now found wanting or imperfect, as Hobbes would find them in introducing his translations of Homer: of Lucan, Hobbes says he 'shows himself openly in the Pompeyan faction, inveighing against Caesar throughout … And a great part of the delight of his readers proceedeth from the pleasure which too many men take to hear great persons censured' (Hobbes 1677, sig. A9^r). The affinity with Lucan displayed by May, formerly hymned by Jonson 'in terms that reveal an awareness of both poets' participation in the sublime, which in turn inspir[ed] Jonson with sublimity' (Day 2013, 234), is here recast as a conspiracy between the two poets, Lucan and May, inspiring parody and invective: as May's hangover lifts, 'He found he was translated, and by whom'.

May's shade nonetheless persists in pressing for his place 'among the learned throng' (l. 28) headed by Jonson, who, like St Peter in Milton's 'Lycidas', responds by shaking his locks and brandishing his staff of office, not St Peter's apocalyptic 'two-handed engine' but his laurel wand, whipping May 'o'er the pate' (l. 37). 'Far from these blessèd shades tread back again', Jonson commands,

> Most servile wit and mercenary pen.
> Polydore, Lucan, Alan, Vandal, Goth,
> Malignant poet and historian both.
> Go seek the novice statesmen, and obtrude
> On them some Roman-cast similitude,
> Tell them of liberty, the stories fine,
> Until you all grow consuls in your wine.
> ....
> Foul architect that hadst not eye to see
> How ill the measures of these states agree;

And who by Rome's example England lay,
Those but to Lucan do continue May.
(ll. 39–54)

The charges put to May are clear cut: he's betrayed an allegiance to arts and eloquence—and to Jonson's 'tribe', their cult of worship—so that he might flatter his parliamentary paymasters with 'Roman-cast similitudes', thus 'manufacturing' (Smith's word) an English classical republicanism. But it is somewhat more difficult to specify the offending acts (see Reedy 1980, 141–8). In the epistle dedicatory to the *Pharsalia*, May insists that Lucan's is 'the greatest of histories, the affairs of Rome, whose transcendent greatness will admit no comparison with other states either before, or after it' (sig. A3ᵛ). Its *Continuation* (1631) was dedicated to Charles I. May's *Breviary* likewise notably eschews Roman parallels. This leaves the 1647 *History*, and given Jonson's earlier swipe, in 'Tom May's Death', at Brutus and Cassius as 'the people's cheats' (l. 18), Marvell may have in mind May's rehearsal there of praise for Brutus and Cassius as defenders of Roman liberty against the tyranny of Caesar and Antony (3:30–1). More suggestively, however, the charge falls anticipatively on dressing up the Rump and Council of State in Roman garb; surely these are Marvell's 'novice statesmen', and we recall that May had only taken his history of Parliament up to the end of the second civil war.

There is something slightly trumped up about this harangue, suggesting perhaps that Marvell's real concerns lie elsewhere, and indeed, the poem's most oratorical passage firmly sets politics within the frame of poetry and the poet's calling:

When the sword glitters o'er the judge's head,
And fear has coward churchmen silencèd,
Then is the poet's time, 'tis then he draws,
And single fights forsaken Virtue's cause.
He, when the wheel of empire whirleth back,
And though the world's disjointed axle crack,
Sings still of ancient rights and better times,
Seeks wretched good, arraigns successful crimes.
But thou, base man, first prostituted hast
Our spotless knowledge and the studies chaste,
Apostatizing from our arts and us,
To turn the chronicler to Spartacus.
(ll. 63–74)

Jonson's commendatory poem on the *Pharsalia* began by invoking the figure of a climbing stair, a metaphor for Pompey's and Caesar's mighty ambitions, but also for the epic sublimity of Lucan and his inspired translator. As much as going over to the side of Parliament, May is rebuked for apostatizing from poesy, becoming a writer of gazettes and chronicles unworthy of Phoebus and Hermes. This replays yet once more the fear of cultural degeneracy aired in the poem to Lovelace while at the same time supplying an antidote in the passage's tough Horatian-Jonsonian eloquence.

But is Thomas May really here at all? Or is he a screen against which Marvell could play out the discomfort of his own de facto loyalty to the new regime, which he had seemed to declare in the Horatian Ode? Was his praise of Cromwell 'due'? Was his posture upright (as opposed to 'base')? In his earlier poem, Marvell sang of course of 'ancient rights', but as their elegist not their champion; he had looked on successful crimes, but judged them by their results: was this the poet's task? And what of the Ode's own Roman-cast similitudes? Reading backward from 'Tom May's Death', the ill fit of such analogies in that poem becomes more intelligible: they brace against the apprehension of cheaply manufactured virtue, of a 'servile pen', perhaps not least in and by the poet himself. The painful compromises and calculations of the Horatian Ode are paid for by the uncompromising satire of 'Tom May's Death': having vaporised his double—May vanishes 'in a cloud of pitch' following Jonson's anathematising sentence—Marvell marches indefatigably on towards his poetic destiny, first as Fairfax's, then as Cromwell's poet.

Paradise's Only Map: Reading 'Upon Appleton House'

In his *Short Memorials of Himself*, composed after the restoration of the monarchy in 1660, the Lord Fairfax (1699) looked back upon 'the sad calamities of the war' so as to clear himself of 'those actions which seemed to the world most questionable' (93–4). There he ruefully recounts the divisions that grew up between Parliament and the army which led to Pride's Purge and the trial and execution of the king, which he regarded with 'dislike and abhorrence' (121). 'All the power being got into the army', he writes in summary,

> … they cut up the root of kingly government; after this were Engagements made to abolish that title. Then was war declared against Scotland for assisting the king, and several leagues made with foreign princes, to confederate with their new government, which was now a commonwealth, against the kingly power.

All this I saw with grief and sorrow, and though I had as much the love of the army as ever, and was with great importunity solicited by that remaining Parliament and soldiers, to continue my command; and though I might, so long as I acted their designs, have attained what height of power, and other advantages I pleased; yet by the mercies and goodness of God, I did, so long as I continued in the army, oppose all their ways and councils, and when I could do no more, I then declined their actions (126–7).

Thus did Fairfax recall the circumstances of laying down his commission in June 1650, refusing to make war on the Scots, 'to whom', the Presbyterian general reminded the Council of State, 'we are engaged in a solemn league and covenant' (Whitelocke 1853, 3:209). Preparations were made to remove to Yorkshire with his family, wife Anne, and only child Mary, who would be twelve that summer. For her tutor, Fairfax chose Andrew Marvell, a fellow northerner whose father may have been known to the Fairfaxes, and moreover a man 'of an approved conversation', as Milton put it in his letter to President Bradshaw (see Hopper 2007, 202). Marvell's poem 'To His Worthy Friend Doctor Witty upon His Translation of the Popular Errors', written no later than November, contains what is surely an allusion to Mary Fairfax's progress in the acquisition of foreign languages, progress evidently well begun.

'Tom May's Death', which dates to late autumn or winter 1650, would thus seem to belong with the nymphs and mowers, the fauns and fairies of Marvell's Nun Appleton period, the most fruitful years of this fitful poetic career. This untidy chronology has the salutary effect of reminding us that neither poet nor patron was hermetically sealed from the outside world at Nun Appleton. However much pastoral retreat may have constituted for Marvell both the condition and the abiding theme of the verse we associate with his time in Fairfax's employ, above all his meditations on the dilemmas of engagement and withdrawal in 'Upon Appleton House', the illusion of a timeless pastoral world is just that, a projection which shelters Marvell's complex negotiation of contingent events and material circumstances. We began with the notion of embodied reading as one of the keys to understanding this literary life: nowhere is Marvell drawn more ineluctably into relations of reading and writing than at Nun Appleton, as language tutor to young Maria, as sharer in Lord Fairfax's literary and intellectual enthusiasms, as historian and poet of the Fairfax estate and of Fairfacian dynasty, as transcriber of the dialectic between self and world, as surveyor 'of the mind contemplating its own creations' (Friedman 1970, 136).

Criticism has taken a long time in overcoming T. S. Eliot's deprecation of 'Appleton House' as 'misshapen', though of late it has come to be recognised as perhaps the supreme text of Marvell's poetic achievement. Accordingly, 'Appleton House' will occupy our attention for the rest of this chapter, and so serve, in its abundant variety, as a kind of proxy for Marvell's brilliant experiments in lyric, which have long been identified with this period. By learning to read 'Appleton House' well, we stand to gain an appreciation for the tropes and tactics which animate this extraordinary body of verse. Eliot of course is notorious for making offhand aesthetic judgments which nevertheless prove surprisingly productive or revealing: his estimation of Milton's 'bad influence' and lack of direct sensuous apprehension were clearly motivated by the Anglo-Catholic and royalist Eliot's repugnance for Milton's politics, but out of Eliot's vandalism there sprang a sweeping reassessment of Milton's poetry, culminating in Christopher Ricks's *Milton's Grand Style* (1963). And indeed, there is something indecorous and disproportionate about 'Appleton House', though rather than judging these faults in the poem we might regard them instead as formal signatures.

To that end, I want to explore the potential of what critical theorists call 'queer form'. In so doing, I want also to trouble the false binary between historicism and 'theory'. Marvell's playfully critical revisionist approach to genre has been a touchstone of Marvell studies since Rosalie Colie's *'My Echoing Song'* (1970). More recently, scholars have begun to ponder the mysteries of the poet's sexuality. Fresh consideration has been given to the obviously slanderous but nonetheless persistent and repeated accusations of sexual deviance and difference bruited by Marvell's Restoration enemies; as later chapters will explore more fully, he was jeered as a eunuch, a castrato, a 'rosemary'. Criticism has also thoroughly reconceived the erotic intensities of a body of verse that treats, as we have seen, with coy mistresses and cruel lovers but sings as well of fragrant mowers, immolated soldiers, and young girls. To ask after the meanings and possibilities of 'queer form' is no more than to bring these two strands of inquiry together.

In David J. Getsy's words (2017), 'A life is thrown into relief as queer through its commitment to unauthorized or unorthodox relations and the transformative potential they represent', the 'organizing synecdoche' for this commitment being 'a set of sexual relations that refuse "natural" rites of procreation and, by extension, propose new modes of desire, pleasure, family, and kinship' (254). Getsy's elegant formulation carries with it a sense of social and artistic activism—he is a scholar of modern and contemporary art and theory—but we need not import this into the seventeenth century. For there can be little doubting the friction between the contours of the life Marvell led and imagined—and indeed which was imagined for him—and the social and sexual ideals of his culture. In the last chapter, we began to draw a 'figural map of Marvellian sexuality', which included representations of the self-seeking gaze as well as the recurrent eroticising of liminal figures who fall outside the bounds of heteronormativity. Such sexual imagining may be subsumed under Marvell's broader ambivalence towards patriarchy, a subject steadily excavated by Derek Hirst and Steven Zwicker since the 1990s (see esp. Hirst and Zwicker 1999). Landless, childless, and isolate, Marvell sought advancement by means of the patronage of great men, a dependent relation that seems to have mingled and conditioned gratitude, even love, with resentment and resistance. That Marvell's celebration of patriarchal authority and familial destiny in 'Appleton House' should have brought such ambivalence to the surface we can well believe. It is but another step to regard such complex valencing of ideology as the work of 'queer form', of 'queering form', the enactment of 'unauthorized or unorthodox relations' within the sphere of aesthetic kinds, that is, 'in the associations, frictions, and bonds between and among forms' (Getsy 2017, 254).

'Upon Appleton House' is a country house poem, but its promiscuous tonalities stretch far beyond that of Jonson's urbane praise for the Sidneys as benevolent patrons of organic community in 'To Penshurst'. It is a landscape poem or chorography, and clearly takes some inspiration from John Denham's much-admired 'Cooper's Hill' (1642/1655), but the perspectives it adopts are hardly limited to the naturalistic, as Marvell 'forces his reader to an awareness of the perplexities of vision in a fallen world' (Roth 1972, 271). As 'mini-epic', 'Appleton House' contains multitudes: history, satire, panegyric, ode, the poem's various modes and episodes querying and subverting one another and often disquieting its centrally sanctioned praise. The poem holds the mirror up to nature, though this mirror proves capable of being inverted or reversed, and the poem's self-reflexive mirrorings more challenging and vertiginous still. As with other Marvellian lyrics only more so, every time we read 'Appleton House', it seems, something that we took for granted now appears baffling or strange, while something which had escaped our attention leaps into new significance.

The first ten stanzas of 'Upon Appleton House' seek to fashion master and manor within a set of emblematic terms flattering to both, preparing the ground for the poem's meditations on greatness and humility. 'Within this sober frame expect / Work of no foreign architect', Marvell begins, 'That unto caves the quarries drew, / And forests did to pastures hew' (ll. 1–4). This is a poem about place, and Marvell insists at once on the house's native design and on its builders' respect for local resources and ecology, in that its raising spared the over-exploitation of surrounding quarries and forests. (The house described by Marvell seems to be the modest structure built out of the ruined nunnery at Nun Appleton, not the 'new and noble house' designed by John Webb and completed by c. 1657; see Erickson 1979). In these opening lines, Marvell also opens a critical dialogue with Davenant's heroic poem *Gondibert* (1651), which exults in the 'delightful conveyances of probable fictions' over 'austere' truth, and whose form Davenant compares to a richly accoutred building, 'In which I did not only observe the symmetry [of English drama] (proportioning five books to five acts, and cantos to scenes) … but all the shadowings, happy strokes, secret graces, and even the drapery (which together make the second beauty) I have (I hope) exactly followed' (16–17).

The arguments of modesty and sobriety are extended through Aesopian moralising, deflating the pretensions of 'man', who builds so far in excess of his physical needs, unlike beasts, who are content with dwellings measured out by the proportions of their own bodies. '[A]ll things are composèd here', the poet emphasises, 'Like Nature, orderly and near:'

> In which we the dimensions find
> Of that more sober age and mind,
> When larger-sizèd men did stoop
> To enter at a narrow loop;
> As practising, in doors so strait,
> To strain themselves through heaven's gate.
> (ll. 25–32)

The allusive frame shifts in this stanza from fable and emblem book to the lofty Virgil, recalling the rustic hospitality of Evander's house in an interlude to the war with the Latins in Book VIII of the *Aeneid*. Cattle low about the house, and when Evander and Aeneas reach the doorstep, the Arcadian asks of Aeneas: '"Have the courage, my guest, to scorn riches; make yourself, too, worthy of deity, and come not disdainful of our poverty." He spoke, and beneath the roof of his lowly dwelling led towering Aeneas …' (8.359–65). In Virgil, this episode is a digression from the main, heroic action; Marvell's tactic is to make digression central to his poem, and to invert Virgil's heroic script, rendering Fairfax's retirement from action, his conscientious lowering or stooping of himself, the nobler heroism. The low architecture of 'Appleton House' thus also finds its argument, again counterpointing Davenant's high-ceilinged *Gondibert*. We observe here as well Marvell's habit of repurposing the same tropes and allusions in different generic contexts and to opposite effect: in 'Flecknoe', the titular figure's narrow cell and malnourished body occasioned jokes about the ease of passing through the eye of a needle; here, Fairfax's Aeneas-like stooping stands as a genuine type of Christian grace.

It is a commonplace that great works of art teach us how to read them, but nonetheless instructive for being so. The opening of 'Appleton House' habituates us to the way metaphors in the poem propagate unexpectedly, and so stretch and challenge the ways of seeing figures of speech invite. As he continues to play on the topic of Fairfax's moral greatness relative to the modest dimensions of his dwelling, Marvell ventures the ('ridiculous' according to T. S. Eliot) image of the house 'sweating' and 'swelling' to accommodate its master (ll. 49–53); of course there is no material basis for the metaphor; Marvell is hardly looking at humid walls and poetically taking the moisture for 'sweat'. But once it has been insinuated into the poem, this organic idea of the house soon develops into something more warrantable, in the way Marvell depicts the social community of Nun Appleton as part and parcel of its architecture:

> A stately frontispiece of poor
> Adorns without the open door:
> Nor less the rooms within commends
> Daily new furniture of friends.
> (ll. 65–9)

Lord Fairfax's other estates, at Bishop's Hill, or Denton, or Bilbrough, may hold him better than Appleton House, but the sweet disorder of the latter's 'fragrant gardens, shady woods, / Deep meadows, and transparent floods' (ll. 79–80), would only be 'defaced' by art. At Nun Appleton, nature prevails, a claim which extends of course to the poem, which shadows in its form the house and its surrounds; but the poem also gently confounds that which is reflected in its mirror and that which its mirror produces.

Such confounding persists as the poem shifts from emblematic framework to recounting the history of the house. For this chronicle of the family's founding and its reconstitution of the Cistercian priory at Nun Appleton in its own Protestant image is at once much embellished and too long with respect to the proportions of the poem, occupying twenty-five of its ninety-seven stanzas. The nunnery scene's extended scale makes room for anti-Catholic satire and for illustrating the designs of providence in the Fairfaxes' possession of Nun Appleton, where oak and bud of English virtue were cultivated. Equally and oppositely, however, this also means elaborating on the sensuous economies of the former priory, the attractions of which are extensively ventriloquized by a nun in what Jonathan Crewe (1994) calls 'a deliciously subversive closet poem embedded in the obligatory recital of Fairfax succession' (283). In other words, inscribed within the poem's work of service and patronage is a potent counternarrative, brilliantly and ironically justified as a necessary adjunct to Marvell's dynastic 'founder's myth'.

Sir William Fairfax of Steeton had married the heiress Isabel Thwaites in 1518. According to a grant of livery of that year, Thwaites was at the time of her marriage an underage ward of the king (Erickson 1979, 160); the prioress of Nun Appleton, Lady Anna Langton, was her guardian. At the dissolution of the monasteries, more than twenty years after the Fairfax-Thwaites marriage, the building and estate came into the family's possession. Marvell turns these rather unremarkable facts into a pseudo-romance narrative according to which Fairfax had to forcibly rescue his bride from the 'gloomy cloister' (l. 89) where she had been shut up by her guardian and inveigled with promises of a specious religious life amongst 'virgin Amazons' (l. 106). In the nun's speech, it becomes clear how far the convent's devotional practices are conditioned by a physics of likeness, which provides an alternative both to biological reproduction and to the implicit violence of heterosexual congress. When they have done praying their rosary, says the prioress, one of the sisters reads from the lives of the saints while 'all the rest with needles paint' (l. 123), embroidering holy legends with which to decorate the altar. '"But much it to our work would add"', the nun entreats Thwaites, 'If here your hand, your face we had"':

'By it we would Our Lady touch;
Yet thus She you resembles much.
Some of your features, as we sewed,
Through every shrine would be bestowed.
And in one beauty we would take
Enough a thousand saints to make.'
(ll. 129–36)

In Catholic doctrine, the Virgin Mary is venerated as a figure who specially mediates redemption through Christ; here, the nun imagines virgin Thwaites as a conduit to the Holy Mother, and her features as a pattern for Our Lady's image, which, according to the nun, the busy collective of the priory will scatter through the land. Needlework pattern books were a staple of continental print culture and were widely imported into England; scenes from Biblical narratives were one of the predominant categories of design. Thwaites is thus figured both as textual exemplar and embroidered icon, and so offered a futurity quite apart from the sexual destiny of marriage, one all the holier for being a product of the cloister.

This equation between sexual likeness and the prospect of eternity reaches its climax, as it were, in a scene which parodies the traditional *droit du seigneur* (Jankowski 2011, 76):

> 'Each night among us to your side
> Appoint a fresh and virgin bride;
> Whom if Our Lord at midnight find,
> Yet neither should be left behind.
> Where you may lie as chaste in bed,
> As pearls together billeted.
> All night embracing arm in arm,
> Like crystal pure and with cotton warm.'
> (ll. 185–93)

The conjunction of Thwaites and her 'virgin bride', as here envisioned by the prioress, is far more perfect than that between bride and bridegroom or feudal lord: the 'chaste' nuns are billeted so close one could not be translated to heaven without the other, their mirrored genders an emblem of unimpaired spiritual union, whereas sexual difference aligns with other forms of incommensurability and with the threat of coercion. The overt ironies impugn the perverse practices of 'chaste' nuns and argue for the providential intervention of William Fairfax within this scene of Catholic sensual error. But other energies and echoes cross-hatch its Protestant rectitude: for one, there is a frisson of voyeurism in the revelation of two women so enwrapt, an act of looking which includes the narrator, his audience, and indeed God, should he visit this midnight bower. But later Marvellian readers might also identify thematic links to 'The Nymph Complaining', with its metamorphic tableaux of 'undifference', or to 'CoyMistress', in which the speaker exhorts his lady, 'Let us roll all our strength, and all / Our sweetness, up into one ball' (ll. 41–2), an image often glossed by reference to the hermaphroditic spheres of Plato's *Symposium*. The cloistered nuns are the satiric negative of a lyric imagination afforded wide liberty elsewhere in Marvell's poetry, including elsewhere in this poem. In activating the axiomatic connections between writing and 'spinning, weaving, sewing, and other forms of textile labour' (Lees-Jeffries 2017, 165), Marvell also draws together the aesthetic economy of the convent and his own activities as a poet who stands outside of the patriarchal order. 'And do not believe that you are sterile, albeit … an exile from women', Marvell writes in the Latin epigram 'Upon an Eunuch: a Poet', 'By you will Fame be forever pregnant, and you will lay hold of the nine sisters from the mountain, while Echo, repeatedly struck, will give birth to music as your offspring' (*Poems*, 188).

As Graham Hammill (2012, 188–9) has observed, it is notable that Thwaites's own voice is wholly elided: at the conclusion of the nun's speech, the narrator turns, as if in a play, to address William Fairfax and direct his heroic recovery of the virgin: 'Now Fairfax, seek her promised faith: / Religion that dispensèd hath, / Which she hence forward does begin; / The nun's smooth tongue has sucked her in' (ll. 197–200). Fairfax's ensuing meditation of his right is bolstered by the narrator's preview of this couple's 'offspring fierce' fighting 'through all the universe' (ll. 241–2), a reverse-engineering of providential mandate which justifies the martial act of storming the nunnery. Waving aside the prioress and her sharp-tongued sisters 'like flies' (l. 257), Fairfax apprehends Thwaites waiting and weeping at the altar and bears her away without a word, leaving the nuns to bemoan their loss. In view of the narrator's description of Thwaites as the one true jewel of the convent, a smack at the decorative relics of unreformed worship, her shining tears offer themselves as signs of her true faith, to Fairfax and to right religion. But this requires us to forget that sexually loaded line wherein Thwaites was said to be 'sucked in' by the subtle tongue of the nun, which seems to suggest that she had in fact been well persuaded by the prioress. Fairfax's dynastic prerogative conquers at the cost of Thwaites's silence. Withdrawal into self-enclosed, self-pleasing languor, punctured by importunate time, by history and its climacterics, is a motif which plays across Marvell's verse and indeed over his whole career. Here he ventriloquizes destiny itself, identifying with progenitive male authority: from the union of William Fairfax and Isabel Thwaites will come not just a line of Protestant heroes but the triumph of Parliament and religion in the late civil war. But Marvell also appears to sympathise with Isabel Thwaites, whose ambiguous tears silently register the loss of a subjectivity and of a potentiality unfathomed and indeed unfathomable by the patriarchal order into which she is here carried.

With the marriage of William Fairfax and Isabel Thwaites and the transfer of Nun Appleton to their posterity, the poem returns to its survey of the estate, moving from house to gardens. It accomplishes this transition by way of an awkward telescoping of William and Isabel's heirs. 'From that blest bed the hero came', says the poet, still playing genealogist, 'Whom France and Poland yet does fame:'

> Who when retirèd here to peace,
> His warlike studies could not cease;
> But laid these gardens out in sport

In the just figure of a fort;
And with five bastions it did fence,
As aiming one for every sense.
(ll. 281–8)

The 'hero' alluded to in this passage would seem to be Sir Thomas Fairfax, great-grandfather of Marvell's patron, son of William and Isabel. In the stanzas which immediately follow, however, Marvell describes the bees and flowers of these gardens performing a reveille at the rising of the sun, followed by a salute at the entrance of the present Sir Thomas, his lady, and their nymph-like daughter. This odd elision glosses over entirely Fairfax's own military career, tumbling him into a retirement that pantomimes his ancestor's and indeed into a like pantomime of 'warlike studies' amidst the garden fortress. That couplet, with its pointed rhyme, deliberately reverses the scenario of the Horatian Ode, which sees Cromwell climbing from his private gardens by industrious valour to ruin the great work of time: 'So restless Cromwell could not cease / In the inglorious arts of peace' (ll. 9–10). The rehearsal of military drills and ceremonies within the hortulian enclosure of Fairfax's mock fort produces some of the most brilliant instances of metaphysical wit in Marvell's verse. Particularly striking is the precision with which pastoral imagery is yoked to the idiom of the officer's manual and the heraldry catalogue. There are bee-soldiers in Virgil's *Georgics*, and more than one Renaissance poet stumbled upon the metaphor of a 'troop' of flowers, but only in Marvell does each flower dry 'its pan yet dank with dew' and fill 'its flask with odours new' (ll. 295–6), discharging 'fragrant volleys' with a 'shrill report' (ll. 298, 307), then re-pressing its 'charge' of gunpowder (l. 300). By virtue of the same analytic method, as Elaine Grummitt (2000) remarks, 'Marvell's description of the three "regiments" (l. 311) of the "tulip, pink, and rose" (l. 312) evokes the Fairfax shield, with its red bars …, while the image of the stars walking "about the Pole" particularly compliments Lady Fairfax, daughter of Sir Horace Vere', whose armorial bearings incorporated a burst of 'five points argent' (207–8).

But Marvell's wit is not merely diverting; the heraldic iconography is surely meant to honour the Fairfaxes' benevolent command over the natural community at Nun Appleton. This well-governed world of sight, sound, and smell also recalls the allegorical Castle of Alma in Spenser's *Faerie Queene*, reason's fortress, and a bulwark against those 'strong affections' which vie 'to bring the soul into captivity' (*FQ*, 2.11.1–10). Nor was such moral casuistry as Marvell here performs under cover of mock-heroics merely a tendentious exercise, a caressing of his patron's conscience; for at the time Marvell was assembling 'Upon Appleton House', there was a real possibility of Fairfax's retirement being put to the test by external events. As its most searching chronologists have pointed out, 'Appleton House' is 'very much a summer's poem', and Marvell's tutelage of Mary Fairfax could hardly have begun much before August 1650; Fairfax was still in London as late as 17 July (see Hirst and Zwicker 1993, 249 and *passim*). The summer of 1652, Marvell's last at Nun Appleton, was memorably scorched by drought, which ill comports with the poem's colourful parade of flowers, its 'grassy deeps', or its flooded meadows. This leaves 1651, a summer troubled by rumour of war and civil unrest and not too far from Fairfax's Yorkshire doorstep. The Scottish campaign over which Fairfax had resigned had yielded Cromwell's miraculous victory at Dunbar in September 1650 and the occupation of Edinburgh. A decisive conclusion to the war was delayed, however, by relentlessly atrocious weather, which disrupted English supply lines and plagued Cromwell's troops with ague and dysentery, and by the Lord General's own poor health that winter and spring, thus allowing the Scots to regroup. The *Memorials* of the MP Bulstrode Whitelocke refer to intelligence of 23 May 1651 of the Scots' 'design to slip by the English army into England, and to draw the seat of war out of their own country into England, where they expected many to befriend them' (3:303). Though the expectations of the Scots and their king were to be disappointed in this respect, Whitelocke's intelligence was sound: by early August the Scottish army had pushed south of the border, and the Commonwealth was looking for assurances from Fairfax. During those same fraught weeks in August, there were Leveller-led enclosure riots in south Yorkshire, commotions glanced at in the mowing sequence of Marvell's poem.

This is to begin to make sense of those more reflective and surely more challenging stanzas of the garden survey, in which the poet takes stock of the cost of England's civil wars and the possibility for national regeneration, questions which touch delicately on the grounds of Fairfax's actions. Comparing 'that dear and happy isle' (l. 321) of pre-war England to lost paradise, Marvell asks, with sensible pathos, 'What luckless apple did we taste, / To make us mortal, and thee waste?' (ll. 327–8). Smith cites several parallels for the view of England as Eden, the most suggestive of which is John of Gaunt's speech in act two scene one of *Richard II*, an extended paean to England's unspoiled glory which is hedged by a prophecy of moral blot and national decay. Duly noted are Gaunt's epithets 'This other Eden, demi-paradise' (2.1.41–2), but the more striking lines, with regard to this precise moment in 'Upon Appleton House', come as we read on in Gaunt's speech: England is 'This fortress built by Nature for herself / Against infection and the hand of war' (2.1.43–4), once 'bound in with the triumphant sea' (2.1.61), but 'now bound in with shame' (2.1.63), 'a shameful conquest of itself' (2.1.66). Lord Fairfax's garden fortress doubles the Shakespearean image of unfallen England, an island within that once 'dear and happy isle'. But such immunity and self-enclosure as the garden offers is obviously highly tenuous, shadowed as it is by Gaunt's prophetic doom, and indeed by mustering troops at Ripon, some thirty miles northwest of Nun Appleton, and by rioters at Hatfield Chase to the south and east. Where before Marvell portrayed the Fairfaxes' garden exertions as a parody of military organisation, he here inverts his figures, taking the garden and the gardener as the originals of such discipline, afterward copied and perverted by the soldier. Lord Fairfax's retirement to the garden thus seeks to repair this original relation, 'But war all this'—all 'gentler forts', all gardens, nurseries, greenhouses—'doth overgrow: / We ordnance plant and powder sow' (ll. 343–4).

In one of the small miracles of 'Upon Appleton House', Marvell exquisitely poses and unfolds this dialectic of reparation versus epidemic blight before his patron:

>   XLIV
> And yet there walks one on the sod
> Who, had it pleased him and God,
> Might once have made our gardens spring
> Fresh as his own and flourishing.
> But he preferred to the Cinque Ports
> These five imaginary forts:
> And in those half-dry trenches spanned
> Power which the ocean might command.
>   XLV
> For he did, with his utmost skill,
> Ambition weed, but conscience till.
> Conscience, that heaven-nursèd plant,
> Which most our earthly gardens want.
> A prickling leaf it bears, and such
> As that which shrinks at every touch;
> But flowers eternal, and divine,
> That in the crowns of saints do shine.
> (ll. 345–60)

The first of these two stanzas treads the brink of decorum, setting the disappointment with which it presents Fairfax's premature retirement, and the potential he represented for healing England's wounds and making it green again, against the near-bathos of 'had it pleased him and God', of Fairfax's preference for his garden fortress to command of the Cinque Ports. The succeeding stanza translates these apprehensions into the elevated language of tender conscience and heavenly reward, and so abates their force, recalling Fairfax's speech upon laying down his commission: 'What my conscience yields unto as just and lawful I shall follow; and what seems to me to be otherwise I will not do. My conscience is not satisfied, and therefore I must desire to be excused' (Markham 1870, 360). To assert, and to honour, the demands of private conscience within the public sphere is of course the very mark of Christian liberty, under which sign Marvell at once compasses and neutralises perceptions of Fairfax's retirement as a shameful self-conquering (recall John of Gaunt) and as a betrayal of hopes for national redemption. Allowing the 'prick' of Fairfax's decision was a most delicate piece of honesty on all sides.

Having faced directly the thorny circumstance of Lord Fairfax's retirement in stanzas 44–5, the speaker abruptly diverts his gaze, throwing a 'quarrelsome' beam of sight towards Cawood Castle, former seat of the Archbishop of York, a gesture immediately deflated as the eye falls innocently onto the meadow below: 'And now to the abyss I pass' (l. 369). The extravagance of Marvell's wit in these scenes is surely performative, in that we find the poet rapidly shuffling a set of figures that reflect on the metamorphic powers of nature and art and dramatize the contingency of perspective, toggling between above and below, within and without, near and far. Men appear grasshoppers, grasshoppers, giants; rural labourers are divers within a green sea, then Israelites crossing the parted deep, then rustics kissing within the hay like Ametas and Thestylis; the mown field resembles one of Lely's canvasses, a Spanish bullring, or the society the Levellers would create; the cattle look like freckles on a face, or like a flea refracted through a multiplying glass, or like slowly moving constellations (see stanzas 47–58).

Foregrounding aesthetic device in this way allows the poet to gain some distance on the topical by heightening the element of mediation, even as he continues to worry the topical within his pastoral vision. The comparison of mowers to Israelites evokes the idea of England as elect nation, a type of new Israel, but also the competing visions of providence and national destiny over which the civil war had been fought. James I and Charles I had both rested their claims to *jure divino* authority on Davidic precedent, and in the *Eikon Basilike*, Charles deliberately fashioned himself after David in his afflictions, borrowing liberally from the psalms in the meditations which closed each section of the book. For this he was much mocked by Milton, who, in *Eikonoklastes*, blasted the king for 'the vain ostentation of imitating David's language, not his life' (*CPW*, 3:555), and indeed fitted him with quite another Biblical parallel—that of Pharaoh. Easy as it is to lose ourselves in Marvell's shifting tableaux of mower-soldiers, we do well to bear in mind the edge of scriptural politics in the summer of 1651, which saw the son of Pharaoh mustering an army over the northern border, and the erstwhile captain of the Israelites withdrawn into his solitude.

'What should he do?' This is the question asked of William Fairfax in the context of his own crisis of conscience, the sequestering of his future helpmeet and dynastic partner by Prioress Langton, and it resounds through the poem. There has been some debate about Marvell's standing with Fairfax and within the Fairfax household, specifically as to whether young Mary's language tutor was in a position to counsel, much less criticise, his employer, and to be sure the lessons of 'Upon Appleton House' are of a most extraordinary kind. But we can hardly doubt the poem's intimacy with its patron, or at least its assumption of, ventriloquism of Fairfax's interests and preoccupations, or of family history and memory. And though not resolved within the poem, which ends in a prospect of displacements and ambiguities, the drama of conscience it plays out in its mirror was in fact resolved in the world without. In the last week of August, readers of Nedham's *Politicus* would hear of 'Letters from my Lord General, which advertise us that the headquarter was at Ferry Briggs, Aug. 19 and would be at Doncaster or Rotheram Aug. 20. That my Lord Fairfax met my Lord General, and went three miles with him in his coach, and expressed his willingness to raise forces, if there were occasion' (*Mercurius Politicus* 64, 21–28 August 1651, 1016). Fairfax's determination to act ('if there were occasion') lends a certain formal perfection to the nunnery episode, recapitulating his ancestor's heroic purpose. That he went out riding in Cromwell's coach—away from the domestic scene—and there gave his promise to defend the Commonwealth may not be a wholly incidental detail. Fairfax was widely reputed to be overmastered by his wife, whose convictions were Presbyterian-royalist, 'and so had unhappily concurred in her husband's entering into rebellion, never imagining what misery it would bring upon the kingdom; and [afterward] abhorred the work in hand as much as anybody could do, and did all she could to hinder her husband from acting any part in it' (Hyde 1888, 4:486–7). The symmetries of the nunnery scene touched close to home in more ways than one.

'Upon Appleton House' is clearly an obliging performance, but not all its projects and purposes can be ascribed to Fairfax. Its peculiar 'mock' or 'anti-' pastoral mode, most evident in the meadows and woods sequences, links it with other Marvellian pastorals traditionally dated to this period, not all of which can have been written in the same season, nor are they so encumbered with the business of clientage. Sukanta Chaudhuri (1989) has suggestively termed this mode 'a paradoxical pastoral of disharmony and alienation' (432).

One of the key substitutions in this inverted pastoral is that of the mower for the shepherd; for while the mower enjoys a certain empathy with nature—'The sun himself licks off my sweat', boasts Damon the Mower—his archetypal reaping more often places him at odds with his heavily symbolic environment. Marvell's anthropomorphising of nature also blurs the moral order of conventional pastoral, in which pristine nature promises to restore man's lost innocence; whereas nature anthropomorphised mirrors and rivals human acts and arts to unsettling effect.

To return, then, to those curious meadows, in which nature and art compete to dazzle the eye and to assert their respective claims to authority. 'No scene that turns with engines strange / Does oft'ner than these meadows change', avows the narrator, 'For when the sun the grass hath vexed, / The tawny mowers enter next' (ll. 385–8). The theatre, with its changeable scenery, is said to be outgone by nature, which 'vexes' the grass by blanching and withering it, turning the lush green meadows brown and dry; in turn, the mowers seem both to collaborate in and to outgo nature's 'masque', transforming the green sea of the meadows into a battlefield, a rustic masquing hall, a levelled plain. The lines seem deliberately to confuse temporal logic—the sun withers the grass before the mowers enter, yet the mowers 'seem like Israelites to be, / Walking on foot through a green sea' (ll. 389–90), which they then reduce to yellow 'hay' (l. 421). Indeed, it is scarcely an exaggeration to say that Marvell's is a pastoral of cognitive dissonance as we encounter the mowers at work:

> L
> With whistling scythe, and elbow strong,
> These massacre the grass along:
> While one, unknowing, carves the rail,
> Whose yet unfeathered quills her fail.
> The edge all bloody from its breast
> He draws, and does his stroke detest;
> Fearing the flesh untimely mowed
> To him a fate as black forbode.
> LI
> But bloody Thestylis, that waits
> To bring the mowing camp their cates,
> Greedy as kites, has trussed it up,
> And forthwith means on it to sup:
> When on another quick she lights,
> And cries, 'He called us Iraelites;
> But now, to make his saying true,

Rails rain for quails, for manna, dew.'
(ll. 393–408)

Death is of course a classic topos of pastoral, so fully as to constitute a genre unto itself, that of pastoral elegy. But pastoral loss almost always finds compensation; we might even say that this is the work which pastoral performs. The shepherd Daphnis in Virgil's fifth eclogue, mourned by his friends Mopsus and Menalcas, is both immortalised in their epitaphs of remembrance and becomes himself a kind of pastoral spirit, inspiring tributes of wine and song. Milton's 'Lycidas', for all its famed digressiveness, closely follows Virgil's pattern, staging the poet's triumph in the act of writing a pastoral elegy and proclaiming Lycidas, 'Sunk though he be beneath the watery floor' (l. 167), risen through Christ, and henceforth 'the genius of the shore' (l. 183). The spectre of death in the Marvellian scene is shorn of such comfort—violent, bloody, metaphysically hollow. An emblem of death, the mower simultaneously fears death, and what might be a vision of cyclical renewal becomes instead a scene of alienated dread: the grass is 'massacred', and the mower's accidental murder of the rail, he fears, 'To him a fate as black forbode[s]'. Marvell replays this incident with even greater thematic point in 'Damon the Mower', in which Damon's scythe also 'whistles' as he 'depopulates the ground' (ll. 74–5), but this time bites into his own flesh, 'And there among the grass fell down, / By his own scythe, the mower mown' (ll. 79–80).

Then there is bloody Thestylis, who overhears the narrator and who truculently speaks back to him, a moment of estrangement that rivals anything in Marvell's poetry or for that matter in early modern literature for ontological disruptiveness, that is, for the way it momentarily shatters the generic conventions which hold together a poetic world, and indeed, more radically suggests how the 'real world' is likewise held together by nothing firmer than the stitches of language. Her interjection coarsely deflates the comparison of the mowers to Israelites, in effect charging the speaker with imposing self-serving fictions on her and her fellows, scoffing that the helpless rails felled by the mowers' whistling scythes must be manna from heaven. This upbraiding of Biblical typology surely colours our reading of those lines in which the stubbled meadows are said to resemble 'A camp of battle newly fought' (l. 420), the stacks of hay standing in for piles of slain bodies. For the 'anti-pastoral' of death acted out in the meadows of Nun Appleton, the desacralisation of violence, the accusation of the camp follower who knows death intimately and finds in it little sign of special providence, here provide the discursive context for recollecting the battlefields of the English civil war. In one of the text's signal inversions, Thestylis's crying out of the poem introduces a demotic, bottom-up perspective on scenes of 'massacre' which stubbornly defies providentialist gloss. To royalist and roundhead command, all battles were either deliverances or judgments, but this was a distinction which ultimately mattered little to the piles of dead on either side.

It is perhaps no wonder then that the meadow episode culminates in a flood—a flood of images in which the violent flux of nature and the poet's restive eye blend and clash, the seasonal flooding of the River Wharfe, which further transforms the meadows into a space of paradox, as 'boats ... over bridges sail / And fishes do the stables scale' (ll. 478–9), but one which also washes away that which came before it, as the poet takes sanctuary in the 'green, yet growing ark' of the wood (l. 484). Underneath these arching boughs the poet is offered a fresh chance at pastoral communion and renewal; but here are also fresh dangers, insofar as the retreat to the woods mirrors Isabel Thwaites's seclusion in the nunnery and as well Lord Fairfax's retirement to his 'more gentle fort'. These stanzas also play out an imaginative sequence which mirrors that of 'The Garden', a poem Marvell also translated into Latin verse ('Hortus'). In previous chapters, I suggested some of the reasons why we might be reluctant to accept a Restoration date for 'The Garden', not the least of which is its strong thematic and stylistic resonance with 'Appleton House': both poems use the same octosyllabic couplets, the same eight-line stanzas, to ruminate on like dilemmas, the quarrel between *otium* and *negotium*, philosophical leisure and worldly pursuit. More than this, the conjunction of these not two but three poems, two in English, one in Latin, allows us to see Marvell approaching the same set of questions at slightly different angles and in poetry of different depths and tones, that is, to see a poet engaging in self-reflective experiment of a kind which is quite explicitly the concern, above all, of 'The Garden'. To site these verses c. 1668 does not altogether alter this picture, giving the impression of looping recursivity as opposed to a concentrated programme of linked composition, and perhaps one day the archive shall produce definitive evidence one way or another of the poem's date. Until then, Occam's principle to me suggests that poems which go together most likely grew together.

'The Garden' begins in unmistakably Horatian fashion, coolly exposing the vanity of human endeavour and the delight of meditative seclusion: 'How vainly men themselves amaze / To win the palm, the oak, or bays' (ll. 1–2). Its argument advances wittily and assuredly by means of unmetaphor, taking these emblems of military, civic, and poetic achievement at face value and asking whether it were not better to be surrounded by plants and bathed in shade than to strive for bare sprigs. Marvell's speaker then gives this line of thinking another turn, pretending that the gods gave chase to beautiful women only so the gods could possess them as plants, retelling the stories of Apollo and Daphne, Pan and Syrinx (ll. 25–32). As if overhearing him, the plants of the garden of a sudden begin to draw the speaker into their embrace, reaching their fruits into his hands, crushing their wine upon his mouth, as he falls innocently on grass (ll. 33–40). Thus are we brought to that unforgettable stanza:

> Meanwhile the mind, from pleasures less,
> Withdraws into its happiness:
> The mind, that ocean where each kind
> Does straight its own resemblance find;
> Yet it creates, transcending these,
> Far other worlds, and other seas,
> Annihilating all that's made
> To a green thought in a green shade.
> (ll. 41–8)

William Empson (1935) thought there was 'something very Far-Eastern about this'. He arrived at this notion by pondering the Oxford editor's annotation of 'annihilating': 'Either "reducing the whole material world to nothing material, *i.e.* to a green thought", or "considering the material world as of no value compared to a green thought"'. 'Evidently', Empson concluded, 'the object of such a fundamental contradiction (seen in the etymology: turn all *ad nihil*, *to* nothing, and *to* a thought) is to deny its reality; the point is not that these two are essentially different so far as either is to be known. So far as he has achieved his state of ecstasy he combines them, he is "neither conscious nor not conscious", like the seventh Buddhist stage of enlightenment' (119–20). Of course, this is make-believe; but Empson's comment nonetheless has about it an undeniable suggestiveness. And indeed, he was not wrong to surmise the presence of a mystical element that is scarcely Horatian, deriving not from the teachings of Buddha but rather, as scholarship has since discovered, from Plotinus and from Hermes Trismegistus (see e.g. Klonsky 1950; Røstvig 1959).

In the Renaissance, Hermes was held to be an Egyptian high priest of Biblical antiquity to whom was revealed more of God and nature than was to all the prophets (in reality, the hermetic texts were a Hellenistic congeries of early Christian doctrine and neo-Platonism). Understood aright, the *Corpus Hermeticum* promised the sage or virtuoso knowledge to rival Adam before the fall. These 'books of secrets' were long mined by alchemists and occultists, but they found readers as well among upright Protestants like Thomas Lord

Fairfax, who at one time seems to have begun work on a learned edition of John Everard's English translation of *The Divine Pymander of Hermes Trismegistus* (1650/1657). According to Everard, Hermes is called 'thrice-greatest' for having 'perfect and exact knowledge of all things contained in the world; which things he divided in three kingdoms (as he calls them), viz: mineral, vegetable, animal; which three, he did excel in right understanding of; also, because he attained to … the knowledge of the quintessence of the whole universe' (Everard 1650, sig. A3^v–A4^r). The speaker of 'The Garden' is clearly a hermetic figure, one whose being is anatomised into three parts—the body, the mind, and the soul—and who, in stanza six, epitomises quintessential knowledge in his radiant green thought, comprehending all of creation (the mind holds within itself images of all that is in the world) but moreover comprehending *creativity*, rearranging those images into novel relations, 'Far other worlds, and other seas' (see Teskey 2019, 366). No less is the woods sequence of 'Appleton House' a hermetic progress: at first dark and uncertain, the true nature of things is gradually revealed within the wood, as the speaker's ears are opened to the tongues of birds and beasts, and in the leaves shadowy truths show forth to the mind's eye:

> Out of these scattered sibyl's leaves
> Strange prophecies my fancy weaves:
> And in one history consumes,
> Like Mexique paintings, all the plumes.
> What Rome, Greece, Palestine, ere said
> I in this light mosaic read.
> Thrice happy he who, not mistook,
> Hath read in Nature's mystic book.
> (ll. 577–84)

In another kind of annihilation, the books of scripture, the book of nature, and the hermetic text dissolve into a single truth.

But it is the differences as much as the resemblances between these parallel passages that invite our consideration. In 'The Garden', Platonic hierarchies are duly observed: the body is not despised but the satiation of bodily desire permits the mind to withdraw into its proper sphere and to experience the higher pleasures of intellectual happiness; 'Casting the body's vest aside' (l. 51), the soul glides up to the bough of a tree like a bird, anticipating its ultimate freedom from the body and ascent to heaven. Marvell may be thinking here of Plato's *Phaedrus*, which philosophises deeply on the wings of the soul: 'when it is perfect and fully winged', Plato's Socrates instructs Phaedrus, 'it mounts upward, and governs the whole world' (Plato 1914, 473). Moreover, the speaker is soon carried from his state of ecstasy back to the world, and in contemplating the 'fragrant zodiac' of the last stanza—a sundial whose twelve segments are planted with different herbs and flowers—the speaker gestures towards a new perspective on time reckoned according to a consciousness far wider than the vain self-regard of individual humans. (In the *Phaedrus*, Socrates says it takes ten thousand years for the incarnate soul to regrow its wings and return to where it came).

The adventures of the hermetic seeker in 'Appleton House' are far more wayward than those described in 'The Garden'. By stanza 73, as we have seen, Marvell's speaker has already advanced to the verge of Adamic wisdom, speaking the 'learned original' of birds and beasts and reading in the sibyl's leaves the secrets of philosophers and prophets. There is the perception of retrograde motion, then—especially when read against 'The Garden'—as sympathetic nature *now* begins to clasp and curl itself around the speaker, as he transforms into 'some great prelate of the grove' (l. 592). In the next stanza, cool zephyrs winnow the chaff of his thoughts, language which recalls the gospels, but this sense of spiritual and intellectual purification is surely compromised by the speaker's apparent arousal under the ministrations of sensual nature, 'languishing with ease … / On pallets swoll'n of velvet moss' while the wind cools his 'panting brows' (ll. 593–4, 596). Indeed, his next thought is of beauty, albeit to glory in his insusceptibility to love's arrows while safely encamped behind these hermetic woods, but the ground of this indifference to human beauty and what Marvell elsewhere calls love 'sorted by pairs' turns out to be a vegetal eroticism acted out in the postures of an ecstatic crucifixion:

> Bind me ye woodbines in your twines,
> Curl me about ye gadding vines,
> And oh so close your circles lace,
> That I may never leave this place:
> But, lest your fetters prove too weak,
> Ere I your silken bondage break,
> Do you, O brambles, chain me too,
> And courteous briars nail me through.
> (ll. 609–16)

What was the starting point in 'The Garden' for spiritual ascent—the satiety of the body in the 'luxuriant nirvana of vegetable Nature' (Berger 1988, 269)—is here the climax of the speaker's hermetic pursuits, a blatant disordering of Christian-Platonic prerogatives, and a reorganising of eros under the sign—to combine a Freudian term with a Marvellian—of polymorphously perverse vegetable love. The speaker of 'The Garden' muses that 'Apollo hunted Daphne so, / Only that she might laurel grow; / And Pan did after Syrinx speed, / Not as a nymph, but for a reed' (ll. 29–32). In 'Upon Appleton House', Marvell's speaker reads in nature's mystic book, goes out to nature and tosses himself on 'pallets swoll'n of velvet moss' (l. 594), so that he might become plant-like and be ravished by gadding vines and courteous brambles.

The stage is thus set for nearly (but not quite) the last of the poem's inversions, as, three stanzas later, the young Maria enters the picture, and the recumbent and discomposed poet is recalled to himself by the chastening presence of his tutee: 'But now away my hooks, my quills, / And angles, idle utensils. / ... / 'Twere shame that such judicious eyes / Should with such toys a man surprise; / She that already is the law / Of all her sex, her age's awe' (ll. 649–56). 'Loose Nature' follows suit (l. 657), precipitating an ode to evening in which the four elements of earth, air, water, and fire majestically slow, still, quiet, and compact until 'Nature is wholly vitrified' (l. 687). There are hints here of Milton's great Nativity Ode, of that modesty which Nature shows to the 'heaven-born-child' (l. 30), covering her 'guilty' front with innocent snow (ll. 32, 39). Audacious as this parallel is, it is under the influence of Mary Fairfax's 'judicious eyes' that fallen nature and with it the poem's fallen vision stand to be reformed. So too is she the providential emblem of futurity and moral regeneration:

> Hence she with graces more divine
> Supplies beyond her sex the line;
> And, like a sprig of mistletoe,
> On the Fairfacian oak does grow;
> When, for some universal good,
> The priest shall cut the sacred bud;
> While her glad parents most rejoice,
> And make their destiny their choice.
> (ll. 736–44)

The wisdom is that of Ecclesiastes: 'To every thing there is a season, and a time to every purpose under the heaven: A Time to be born, and a time to die; a time to plant, and a time to pluck up that which is planted' (3:1–2). In the Horatian Ode, we saw Oliver Cromwell seizing the moment to climb from his private gardens and cast the kingdom into another mould; 'Upon Appleton House' in turn sees Lord Fairfax retiring from warlike study to his private garden (ll. 283–4), thereby inciting the philosophising and extenuating of the poem; these perturbations find their end, appropriately enough, in the reverse-mirroring of the earlier lines, as Mary Fairfax is here imagined as a plant grown to perfection under the care of Lord and Lady Fairfax, one destined to be 'grafted' onto the public good through dynastic marriage. High summer 1651 was the season of Mary Fairfax's thirteenth birthday, and the symbolic commencement of her adulthood.

The poem ends in that image of the salmon fishers hoisting their canoes above their heads 'like Antipodes in shoes' (l. 771), and so puts to bed the topsy-turvy imaginary which has proliferated across its survey of house, gardens, meadows, and woods:

> How tortoise-like, but not so slow,
> These rational amphibii go!
> Let's in: for the dark hemisphere
> Does now like one of them appear.
> (ll. 773–6)

Recalled by the entrance of Maria from the untamed fringes of poetic play and self-imagining in the wood, the poet, and with him his audience (if he had one), are turned back to the 'sober frame' of the house and its 'discipline severe' (l. 723). With this somewhat abrupt and somewhat languid close, we are left to ask after the meaning of those strange scenes which seemed to grow so far in excess of the poem's apparent illocutionary aims, those scenes which tangle and inveigle the reader in their queer sympathies. It has been suggested that the hermetic passages warn against the dangers of spiritual solipsism and enthusiasm by investing those qualities in the figure of the poet, who submits himself to the embarrassment of being caught out *in flagrante delicto* in his mystic antics as 'easy philosopher' (l. 561). Or we might plausibly read the retreat to the grove as enacting and abandoning the 'instantly recognizable' pattern of royalist seclusion—a là Thomas Stanley at Cumberlow Green—and the sublimation of Cavalier verse into the meditative poetics of the garden (see Werlin 2019). The garden is a fine and private place, but its embraces prove little less threatening or perverse than those we observed in the nunnery, and little less hostile to heroic futurity (cf. Picciotto 2010, 362–3).

As it ever is with Marvell, topical explanation takes us far with this poem, but only so far. *Topos*, as Marvell well knew, is Greek for 'place', and as Gordon Teskey (2019) valuably reminds us, in the humanist culture of the Renaissance, with its reverence for the best that has been thought and said:

literary *invention* (L. *inventio*, from *invenio* 'to come upon a thing') is a matter of finding one's way to an often-visited 'place': age is wiser than youth; it is better to be flexible than strong; to die for your country is good; destiny cannot be eschewed; meditative detachment is better than unreflecting engagement; all human efforts are vain. Our colloquial expression, 'don't go there', that is, 'don't talk about that', retains a trace of this spatialised conception of rhetorical possibilities as *topoi*. The poet goes to one of these mental places, whatever it may be, and expands on it rhetorically, by 'amplification'. On the topic of the superiority of leisure to labour, what better place to go than a garden? (359)

The overt work of 'Appleton House' may thus be described as a wide survey of topics related to conscientious retirement, which are in turn mapped onto the architectural and topographical survey of the country house poem. The text's insistent digressiveness and its no less insistent estrangement of 'place'—topographical as well as rhetorical—track, however, with a more singular vision, one which seeks to eschew the hegemonic authority of the 'commonplace'. Digression and defamiliarisation are the signs both of Marvell's literary modernity in 'Upon Appleton House' and of a certain transgressiveness ('don't go there'). In its shadows and at its margins, the once-promising Cambridge scholar and would-be cleric, reduced by circumstance to household service, fantasises himself 'some great prelate of the grove', a peer not to corrupt bishops or grim presbyters but to Adam in his innocence. The erotic overtones of this transformation go somewhere else, somewhere beyond solipsism or misogyny ('Two Paradises 'twere in one / To live in Paradise alone'), refusing 'natural' rites of procreation and proposing new modes of desire and pleasure in the sentient embrace of self-moving nature. Marvellian eroticism is a radically open tuning, Echo presides over it, and their offspring, Marvell's echoing song.

References

Berger, Harry, Jr. 1988. *Second World and Green World: Studies in Renaissance Fiction-Making*. Berkeley and Los Angeles: University of California Press.

Booth, Stephen. 1974. On the Value of *Hamlet*. In *Literary Criticism: Idea and Act*, ed. W.K. Wimsatt, 284–310. Berkeley and Los Angeles: University of California Press.

Burgess, Glenn. 1986. Usurpation, Obligation, and Obedience in the Thought of the Engagement Controversy. *HJ* 29 (3): 515–536.

Chaudhuri, Sukanta. 1989. *Renaissance Pastoral and Its Development*. Oxford: Oxford University Press.

Creaser, John. 2002. Prosody and Liberty in Milton and Marvell. In *Milton and the Terms of Liberty*, ed. Graham Parry and Joad Raymond, 37–56. Woodbridge: D. S. Brewer.

Crewe, Jonathan. 1994. The Garden State: Marvell's Poetics of Enclosure. In *Enclosure Acts: Sexuality, Property, and Culture in Early Modern England*, ed. Richard Burt and John Michael Archer, 270–289. Ithaca: Cornell University Press.

Davenant, William. 1651. *Gondibert: An Heroic Poem*. London.

Day, Henry J.M. 2013. *Lucan and the Sublime: Power, Representation and Aesthetic Experience*. Cambridge: Cambridge University Press.

Dzelzainis, Martin. 2019. "A Greater Errour in Chronology": Issues of Dating in Marvell. In *The Oxford Handbook of Andrew Marvell*, ed. Martin Dzelzainis and Edward Holberton, 317–336. Oxford: Oxford University Press.

Empson, William. 1935. *Some Versions of Pastoral*. London: Chatto & Windus.

Erickson, Lee. 1979. Marvell's *Upon Appleton House* and the Fairfax Family. *ELR* 1: 158–168.

Everard, John. 1650. *The Divine Pymander of Hermes Trismegistus*. London.

Fairfax, Sir Thomas. 1699. *Short Memorials of Thomas Lord Fairfax, Written by Himself*. London.

Friedman, Donald. 1970. *Marvell's Pastoral Art*. London: Routledge.

Gardiner, S.R., ed. 1906. *The Constitutional Documents of the Puritan Revolution*. 3rd ed. Oxford: Clarendon Press.

Getsy, David J. 2017. Queer Relations. *ASAP/Journal* 2 (2): 254–257.

Grummitt, Elaine J. 2000. Heraldic Imagery in Seventeenth-Century English Poetry. Ph.D. diss., Durham University.

Hammill, Graham. 2012. *The Mosaic Constitution: Political Theology and Imagination from Machiavelli to Milton*. Chicago: University of Chicago Press.

Hirst, Derek, and Steven N. Zwicker. 1993. High Summer at Nun Appleton, 1651: Andrew Marvell and Lord Fairfax's Occasions. *HJ* 36 (2): 247–269.

———. 1999. Andrew Marvell and the Toils of Patriarchy: Fatherhood, Longing, and the Body Politic. *ELH* 66 (3): 629–654.

Hobbes, Thomas. 1677. *The Iliads and Odysseys of Homer*. 2nd ed. London.

Hopper, Andrew. 2007. *'Black Tom': Sir Thomas Fairfax and the English Revolution*. Manchester: Manchester University Press.

Horace. 2004. *Odes and Epodes*. Ed. and trans. Niall Rudd. Loeb Classical Library 33. Cambridge, MA: Harvard University Press.

Hyde, Edward, Earl of Clarendon. 1888. *The History of the Rebellion and Civil Wars in England by Edward, Earl of Clarendon*. Ed. W. Dunn Macray. 6 vols. Oxford: Clarendon Press.

Jankowski, Theodora. 2011. "Virgins" and "Not-Women": Dissident Gender Positions. In *The Lesbian Premodern*, ed. Noreen Giffney, Michelle M. Sauer, and Diane Watt, 75–89. New York: Palgrave Macmillan.

Kelliher, Hilton. 1978. *Andrew Marvell: Poet & Politician*. London: British Library.

Klonsky, Milton. 1950. A Guide Through the Garden. *Sewanee Review* 58 (1): 16–35.

Lees-Jeffries, Hester. 2017. "My Mother's Maids, When They Did Sew and Spin": Staging Sewing, Telling Tales. *Shakespeare Survey* 70: 165–173.

[Lilburne, John]. 1649. *The Hunting of the Foxes from Newmarket and Triploe Heath to Whitehall*. London.

Markham, Clements. 1870. *A Life of the Great Lord Fairfax*. London: Macmillan.

Marvell, Andrew. 2007. *Poems of Andrew Marvell*. Ed. Nigel Smith. Rev. ed. London: Longman.

May, Thomas. 1650. *Lucan's Pharsalia, Or, The Civil Wars of Rome, Between Pompey the Great and Julius Caesar*. 4th ed. London.

McDowell, Nicholas. 2012. Marvell Among the Cromwellians. In *The Oxford Handbook of Literature and the English Revolution*, ed. Laura L. Knoppers, 481–497. Oxford: Oxford University Press.

Milton, John. 1953–82. *Complete Prose Works of John Milton*. Ed. Don M. Wolfe et al. New Haven: Yale University Press.

———. 2008. *The Major Works*. Ed. Stephen Orgel and Jonathan Goldberg. Oxford World's Classics. Oxford: Oxford University Press.

Norbrook, David. 1990. Marvell's "Horatian Ode" and the Politics of Genre. In *Literature and the English Civil War*, ed. Thomas Healy and Jonathan Sawday, 147–169. Cambridge: Cambridge University Press.

Picciotto, Joanna. 2010. *Labors of Innocence in Early Modern England*. Cambridge, MA: Harvard University Press.

Plato. 1914. *Euthyphro. Apology. Crito. Phaedo. Phaedrus*. Trans. Harold North Fowler. Loeb Classical Library 36. Cambridge, MA: Harvard University Press.

Raymond, Joad. 2018. "Small Portals": Marvell's *Horatian Ode*, Print Culture, and Literary History. In *Texts and Readers in the Age of Marvell*, ed. Christopher D'Addario and Matthew C. Augustine, 33–55. Manchester: Manchester University Press.

Reedy, Gerard. 1980. "An Horatian Ode" and "Tom May's Death". *SEL* 20 (1): 137–151.

Røstvig, Sofen-Marie. 1959. Andrew Marvell's "The Garden": A Hermetic Poem. *English Studies* 40: 65–76.

Roth, Frederic H., Jr. 1972. Marvell's "Upon Appleton House": A Study in Perspective. *Texas Studies in Language and Literature* 14 (2): 269–281.

Skinner, Quentin. 1972. Conquest and Consent: Thomas Hobbes and the Engagement Controversy. In *The Interregnum: The Quest for Settlement, 1646–1660*, ed. G.E. Aylmer, 79–98. London: Macmillan.

Teskey, Gordon. 2019. Greenland: Marvell's "The Garden". In *The Oxford Handbook of Andrew Marvell*, ed. Martin Dzelzainis and Edward Holberton, 357–370. Oxford: Oxford University Press.

Virgil. 1918. *Aeneid: Books 7–12: Appendix Vergiliana*. Trans. H. Rushton Fairclough. Revised by G. P. Goold. Loeb Classical Library 64. Cambridge, MA: Harvard University Press.

Wallace, John M. 1968. *Destiny His Choice: The Loyalism of Andrew Marvell*. Chicago: University of Chicago Press.

Werlin, Julianne. 2019. Upon Appleton House. In *The Oxford Handbook of Andrew Marvell*, ed. Martin Dzelzainis and Edward Holberton, 481–498. Oxford: Oxford University Press.

Whitelocke, Bulstrode. 1853. *Memorials of English Affairs*. 4 vols. New ed. Oxford: Oxford University Press.

Woolrych, Austin. 2002. *Britain in Revolution 1625–1660*. Oxford: Oxford University Press.

Worden, Blair. 1984. The Politics of Marvell's Horatian Ode. *HJ* 27 (3): 525–547.

———. 2007. *Literature and Politics in Cromwellian England: John Milton, Andrew Marvell, Marchamont Nedham*. Oxford: Oxford University Press.

6

'With my most humble service': England and the Continent, 1652–1659

What was life like for Marvell at Nun Appleton? We would very much like to know, though the evidence for Marvell's experience in the Fairfax household comes mostly from the poems he appears to have written at this time and is thus filtered by the constraints of patronage and by a concern to write poetry and not history or autobiography (or, as we have seen, by Marvell's habit of sheltering history and autobiography within poetic convention). Still, 'Appleton House' must reflect something of the shared reality of poet, patron, and pupil. The poem's length, complexity, and densely allusive texture argue ample time for study: in the library at Nun Appleton, Marvell could have perused the manuscripts of Fairfax family records as well as the Lord General's numerous volumes of poems and translations, church history, and hermetic philosophy. Evidently, Fairfax liked to walk the grounds of the estate. Marvell's poem shows him strolling in the garden with Lady Fairfax and young Maria, but we have a sense of wider perambulations with the poet, and in Marvell's text are caught Lord Fairfax's small talk, his anecdotes, his literary conversation, and his tenderness of conscience. Marvell of course also read and conversed with Mary Fairfax, and he seems to have taken particular delight in her elocution of foreign languages. For all the pleasures of country life, however, Marvell kept half an eye, and perhaps more than half an eye, on the London literary and political scene, presumably using the post to disseminate his verse ('Tom May's Death', the poem to Witty), send and receive news, and canvass for job openings. His appointment as Mary's language tutor was obviously a temporary arrangement, providing the finish to her education and polishing her graces for the dynastic marriage which was her destiny. In turn, Marvell received from his association with the Fairfaxes a useful polishing of his own

© The Author(s), under exclusive license to Springer Nature Switzerland AG 2021
M. C. Augustine, *Andrew Marvell*, Literary Lives,
https://doi.org/10.1007/978-3-030-59287-5_6

credentials, an overwriting of his erstwhile royalist connections. When Marvell left Nun Appleton for London in autumn 1652, he could be commended as a man 'fit for the State to make use of', as Milton would put it in his letter to Bradshaw.

In the exceptionally hot summer of that year, in his final weeks or months at the estate, Marvell likely wrote that beguiling sequence of pastorals we know as the Mower poems: 'The Mower against Gardens', 'Damon the Mower', 'The Mower to the Glow-worms', and 'The Mower's Song', printed in that order in *1681* (on the date of 'The Mower against Gardens', see Hammond 2006). Before our narrative re-joins what will be a swiftly flowing current of history and events with Marvell's entrance into Cromwell's service and affairs of state, the lyrics merit our attention as important developments of Marvell's pastoral mode, the contours of which we began to explore in 'Appleton House'. Then there is Damon himself, at once a bricolage of pastoral types and a screen for sexual and psychological alienation that surely goes beyond convention, inviting our speculation as to what Damon may reveal, consciously or unconsciously, of his maker's own sexuality and self-imagining. Ultimately, we can never be sure when we have got hold of Marvell's subjectivity and when we are, as it were, merely grasping at intertextual straws, but recent criticism has been disposed to see in Damon's looking and longing a submerged script of the self.

The Mower Poems

'The Mower against Gardens' reads like a kind of pastoral manifesto, a sustained harangue directed at 'Luxurious man' by a figure who identifies with uncorrupted Nature. As is characteristic of the Mower poems, a complex irony is generated through the uncertain distance between the poet and his pastoral persona. Here, the Mower deplores grafting and other sophisticated horticultural techniques as perversions of the creative impulse in Nature. Yet the poem tangles any number of pastoral antecedents into its language, producing as it were a new species of pastoral from these intertextual cuttings. The form of 'The Mower against Gardens' is that of an Horatian epode, with alternating lines of iambic pentameter and tetrameter forming closed couplets, and it owes a general debt to Horace's second epode, 'The Praises of a Country Life'. More particularly, Marvell's lyric has been seen to echo and overturn contemporary poems by Thomas Randolph and Henry Vaughan, thus drawing together the contrapuntal uses of pastoral in Cavalier poetry and in devotional verse.

Though little remembered now, Randolph won early renown as a poet and dramatist at Cambridge and was adopted as a 'Son of Ben' before his untimely death in 1635 at the age of twenty-nine. His *Poems* were printed four times between 1638 and 1652, including the longish lyric 'Upon Love fondly refus'd for Conscience sake', which uses the same metre as 'The Mower against Gardens' and features grafting as a central conceit. In this poem, Randolph fashions a myth of pastoral innocence on behalf of libertine pleasure, recalling a time when women were accounted free to dispense their charms as the violet her odour, before 'envious avarice / Made women first impropriate' (ll. 12-13). The capacity of trees and plants to support a variety of stock (through grafting) at once and paradoxically figure the naturalness of promiscuity and the perfectibility of Nature by dealing promiscuously, as Marvell will put it, 'between the bark and tree' (l. 21).

The accusatory force of this phrase in Marvell's poem suggests his undoing of Randolph's Cavalier blandishments in 'The Mower against Gardens': pointedly, the Mower's only consorts in the 'sweet fields' (l. 32) and unfallen meadows are 'fauns and fairies' (l. 35); human sexual passion is described as always already tainted and indeed furnishes the metaphorics for censuring gardens and gardening. As the Mower relates, 'Luxurious man, to bring his vice in use, / Did after him the world seduce: / And from the fields the flowers and plants allure, / Where Nature was most plain and pure' (ll. 1-4). First, he imperiously enclosed the free-breathing earth into stagnant parcels, encompassing 'A dead and standing pool of air' (l. 6); then he nutrified the soil to change the nature of that which grows in it, cultivating ostentatious pinks with double flowers, wantonly perfumed roses, and painted tulips. Seducing the world after him in this way, fallen man is said by the Mower to undergo a second fall as he learns to value things not in themselves but at the rate of exchange, that is, as commodities: the tulip's 'onion root they then so high did hold / That one was for a meadow sold' (ll. 15-16). (The Mower's commentary on global commodities markets—referring here to the 'tulip mania' of the 1630s and in the lines following to the '*Marvel of Peru*', which also puns on the poet's name—is obviously too specific and too knowing for this rustic figure). The poem's cataloguing of the 'debasement of natural ends to perverse human uses' (McKeon 1983, 60) climaxes with the practice of grafting, which the Mower abhors in language that evokes Biblical proscriptions against 'Forbidden mixtures' (l. 22) but which he moreover likens to the sexual dealings of the Turk, placing the gardener in his 'green *seraglio*' (l. 27) where he 'does Nature vex / To procreate without a sex' (ll. 29-30).

If, however, 'The Mower against Gardens' thus explodes Randolph's myth of innocent libertinage in a golden age before the invention of property rights—in the land as well as in women's bodies—neither does it hark back to Eden. This is the animating motif of Vaughan's 'Corruption', a poem less certainly connected to Marvell's but one which indexes the widespread hope in seventeenth-century England of recreating Paradise, bringing about a second golden age. 'Corruption' refers of course to original sin but more precisely to the 'doctrine of progressive decay', the idea that man and nature fall farther away from God and from original perfection over time (see Wilson 1970, 121). Though Adam in his exile 'sighed for Eden, and would often say / "Ah! what bright days were those!"' (ll. 19-20), the countryside nonetheless continued to shine with the memory of Edenic splendour, angels lay in 'each bush, and cell, / Each oak, and highway knew them; / Walk but the fields, or sit down at some well, / And he [Adam] was sure to view them' (ll. 25-8). Vaughan's poem derives pathos from the way these manifestations of God's love fade from view in the course of human history, down to the dark hour of the poem's utterance, only to find its end in the prospect of Paradise restored: 'But hark! what trumpet's that? what angel cries / "Arise! thrust in Thy sickle?"' (ll. 39-40). For all that Marvell has been linked to seventeenth-century apocalyptic, it is notable how deliberately 'The Mower against Gardens' turns its back on Christian revelation, eschewing the corrupt gardens of civilisation not for the new Edens of prophecy but for the meadows 'Where willing Nature does to all dispense / A wild and fragrant innocence' (ll. 33-4). If some of the poem's attitudes align with those of reformers who resisted the enclosure of common lands as 'the coming in of bondage [which] … doth dam up the spirit of Peace and Liberty' (Everard et al. 1649, 7), and who sought to establish utopian communities based on 'the free use of the earth' (Winstanley 1652, 18), the Mower remains an isolated figure, and his world is not ours. Like that other Marvellian isolate, the Unfortunate Lover, he prevails in story only, dwelling with the fauns and fairies, with the fictions of pastoral.

Judith Haber (1994) has argued that the other Mower poems 'merely unpack what is already there in "The Mower against Gardens"' (123). And indeed, given the arc Marvell describes at the start of the sequence, from eros to alienation from nature, it should hardly surprise us that the entrance onto the scene of Juliana in 'Damon the Mower' heralds the Mower's self-division as well as his division from the 'enchanted landscape which once nurtured him' (Prawdzik 2015). As we shall see, however, this relatively simple idea is complicated by the jostling of intertexts which threaten to burst in and displace the ostensible content of Marvell's poem and so to reveal or suggest alternative imaginative scripts to the conventional one the Mower sequence offers. That script is announced in the opening lines of 'Damon the Mower': 'Hark how the mower Damon sung, / With love of Juliana stung!' (ll. 1-2). It is recapitulated in the refrain of 'The Mower's Song': 'For Juliana came [comes], and she / What I do to the grass, does to my thoughts and me'. The American poet and musician David Berman once described two of his records as saying the same thing, only in the latter 'I'm trying to say it again, to someone else, after having accepted it' (Berman 2008). So we might conceive the different psychological vantages of 'Damon the Mower' and 'The Mower's Song'. Damon's complaint in 'Damon the Mower' is framed by an initial stanza spoken by a poetic narrator who uses the past tense; however, the following eight stanzas are spoken by Damon in the present, as he relates the effects of Juliana's scorching beams on 'the fields and mower both' (l. 20), allowing the pathos of Damon's bewilderment and self-alienation to come to the fore. Only in the final two stanzas is the narrative frame reasserted. 'The Mower's Song' compresses the story of Damon and Juliana into five stanzas, the first three of these providing an emotional digest of events that have already happened ('Juliana *came*, and she / What I do to the grass, does to my thoughts and me'). Damon's resort to the future tense in stanza four signals Juliana's imminent return and the revenge the mower seeks to exact on her returning, such that the 'flow'rs, and grass, and I and all, / Will in common ruin fall' (ll. 21-2).

The flames of love and the icy chill of a mistress's disdain are of course elemental to Petrarchan tradition, as are the effects of alienation and angst. Despite their rural setting, the Mower poems also seem to reflect the social dynamics of Petrarch's courtly *canzones* through Juliana's aloof indifference towards Damon's humble gifts ('Damon the Mower', ll. 33-40). But in that charged moment where Damon looks at himself in the mirror of his scythe, other worlds of feeling, and other permutations of story, are opened to the reader. '"Nor am I so deformed to sight"', he insists defensively, '"If in my scythe I looked right; / In which I see my picture done, / As in a crescent moon the sun"' (ll. 57-60). Damon's protestation unmistakably echoes Virgil's second eclogue: 'Nor am I so unsightly [nec sum adeo informis]; on the shore the other day I looked at myself, when, by grace of the winds, the sea was at peace and still. With you for judge, I should fear not Daphnis, if the mirror never lies!' (ll. 25-7). The Virgilian speaker is Corydon; but the one to whom he addresses himself, the one he burns for, is no haughty mistress but his fellow shepherd, Alexis. As Damon boasts of his demesne and of his bucolic wealth—'"I am the mower Damon known / Through all the meadows I have mown"' (ll. 41-2)—so Corydon to the hills and woods; from Corydon, too, Marvell translates the pain of being neither seen nor known by his beloved. But Virgil, in his second eclogue, 'as in those infinitely receding perspectives of Chinese boxes' (Kalstone 1974, 177), is also remembering a precursor text, the eleventh idyll of Theocritus, in which the cyclops Polyphemus complains for love of Galatea. Polyphemus, of course, really is 'informis', a 'shaggy brow' stretching over his whole forehead and 'beneath it … a single eye' (see ll. 30-3). Polyphemus's unseemliness makes him a figure of earthy comedy, but his reflection is also a source of pain ('I know why you avoid me, lovely girl'), all the more so when we recall that his unsightly eye (a grim pun) is the site of his wounding by Odysseus.

Despite the unceasing efforts to uncover the historical reality behind, for instance, the Dark Lady or the Young Man in Shakespeare's sonnets, we know that not all love poetry necessarily reflects the experience of being in love and that lyric verse may serve any number of purposes within the social contexts in which poetry is written. Marvell's 'To His Coy Mistress' is a good case in point, insofar as it seems to be more interested in exploring, perhaps exploding the tropes and conventions of love poetry than it is in any actual coy young lady—'An hundred years should go to praise / Thine eyes, and on thy forehead gaze. / Two hundred to adore each breast: / But thirty thousand to the rest' (ll. 13-16). It may have been written for the amusement of a homosocial coterie, with in-jokes and allusions tailored to the coterie's shared tastes (see McDowell 2008, 31-52). The Mower poems offer vexingly little in the way of either a biographical or a social point of reference. 'Appleton House' gives no report of rural feasts or entertainments such as we find in 'To Penshurst', and a hired man like Andrew Marvell would not have had entrée to young gentlewomen visiting the great house. The idea that 'Damon's relationship to the unreachable Juliana translates, in some way, the relationship between Marvell and his tutee' (Prawdzik 2015) is made plausible by Marvell's imaginative capacity, in poems like 'The Picture of Little T. C. in a Prospect of Flowers' and 'Young Love', for placing prepubescent girls within the compass of eros; but the Juliana of the Mower poems seems threateningly mature. Yet neither has it been satisfying to think that Marvell is simply playing language games, combining the Petrarchan and the pastoral into new forms to pass the time, as if shuffling cards.

So affecting are the Mower poems, in other words, we want their apparent emotional disclosures to have some referent in the world equal to the poems' force, but if not the love of a woman, what is the poet 'really' telling us about? William Empson (1984) offered one answer: 'I think he fell in love with the Mower'. 'Damon keeps saying he is in despair for love of a woman', Empson explains, 'and this allows love to be talked about, but he would not have accepted the situation so passively. It is the poet who is in love with Damon; Freud calls the device "displacement", when interpreting dreams. They are exquisite poems, and much better when this obvious point is admitted'

(14-15). We have already noted several instances of homoeroticism in Marvell's verse: the Ovidian beauty of young Francis Villiers, the eroticised death of Archibald Douglas, the delightful pungency of the mowers in 'Appleton House', a detail recalled in Damon's boast, 'And, if at noon my toil me heat, / The sun *himself* licks off my sweat' ('Damon the Mower', ll. 46-7). Indeed, there is often more sensual directness in Marvell's representation of male figures than in his lyric portraits of female lovers. In 'Coy Mistress', he wholly ironises the conventional blazon, and when he approaches the topic of consummation, his thoughts turn first to worms and corpses, then to 'amorous birds of prey', tearing their 'pleasures with rough strife / Thorough the iron gates of life' (ll. 43-4). The rough strife endured by the Unfortunate Lover, as we saw in Chap. 4, is something altogether apart from the destiny of those 'Sorted by pairs' with whom 'the infant Love yet plays' (ll. 2-3), while within the semantic and geometrical abstractions of 'The Definition of Love' is a union 'begotten by Despair / Upon Impossibility' (ll. 3-4).

Empson's reading of the Mower poems as enacting the displacement of same-sex desire has much to recommend it and makes legible the homoerotic energy that surfaces elsewhere in Marvell's poetry, as Paul Hammond has elaborated (1996, 87-123). It also sharpens the accusations of sodomy which attached to Marvell in the pamphlet warfare of the 1670s. To read these polemics is of course to be reminded of 'the revulsion and violent hostility which homosexuality aroused' in Renaissance England (Bray 1995, 58). But it is also to confront the truth of Alan Bray's observation that homosexuality was part of 'the symbolic universe of Elizabethan and Stuart England', in which it functioned as a sign of heresy and treason (20-1). It is far from clear what if anything the accusations about Marvell's sexuality may reveal of his actual habits or preferences once we account for their conventional force. And we cannot forget that Marvell's takedown of Samuel Parker in *The Rehearsal Transpros'd* includes several riffs on the archdeacon's sexual profligacy, a page Marvell took from Milton's attack on Alexander More in *Pro Se Defensio* (see Augustine 2018, 138-41). When one of Parker's cronies produces some doggerel verse alleging Marvell to have been Milton's catamite, the shuttle is simply being returned over the polemical net (see Butler 1673, 135).

More peculiar, however, are the persistent innuendoes, in the half-dozen responses to *RT*, not merely of 'impotence', as Empson says, but of Marvell's castration or sexual disfigurement. In the most explicit of these, the answerer adopts the mode of Marvell's painter satires, instructing Marvell's portraitist:

> [I]f ever he draws him below the waist, to follow the example of that artist, who, having completed the picture of a woman, could at any time, with two strokes

of his pencil upon her face, two upon her breast, and two between her thighs; change her in an instant into man: but after our author's female figure is completed, the change of sex is far easier; for nature or *sinister accident* has rendered some of the alteration strokes useless and unnecessary. (Butler 1673, 134)

Here too there is a symbolic logic at work apart from or in addition to mere personal slander: Marvell's allegedly ambiguous gender reflects the threatening indeterminacy of his stance as one who proclaimed loyalty to the crown and to the Established Church even as he defended the liberty of nonconformists and was known to associate with rebels and republicans like his 'dear friend Mr Milton' (Butler 1673, 110). But the cruel glee with which these innuendoes are fashioned by Marvell's enemies is not without resonance in the alternately anguished and defiant representations of trauma and incapacity which play across Marvell's verse: the eunuch of 'Upon an Eunuch: a Poet', 'unable to thrust a sickle at the virgin corn' (l. 2), the Unfortunate Lover, singular, isolate, 'dressed / In his own blood' (ll. 55-6). Damon too is wounded, seemingly excluded from sexual reproduction, and recognises in Death an image of himself ('Damon the Mower', ll. 87-8; see Hirst and Zwicker 2012, 113). Then there is Marvell's rueful self-characterisation in his letter to John Trott, where he writes, 'But I myself, who live to so little purpose, can have little authority or ability to advise you … who are a person that are and may be much more so generally useful', the letter's occasion being the death of Trott's son (*1681*, 69). In the end, these are all representations, and perhaps one lesson we can take from this juxtaposition of Marvell's private verse and the public controversies in which he was embroiled is how far political and religious identity and how far even eros and inwardness are mediated by and negotiated through a culture's available symbolic figures, its resources of myth and literature. But it is telling nonetheless that the figures Marvell reached for in giving voice to Damon's pain were Corydon and Polyphemus.

Cromwellian Service

If Juliana's scorching beams do indeed tally with the heat and droughts observed in the summer of 1652, then Marvell was likely still in residence at Nun Appleton through July, when the fields were mown. We do not know exactly when he left Fairfax's service and returned to London, but records attest his presence there later in the year (see *Chronology*, 37). By February 1653, as we have seen, Milton was recommending him to John Bradshaw as a replacement for the late George Weckherlin in the office of the Secretary of

State. It seems likely that there was sustained contact between the two men before Milton was prepared to advocate as he did on behalf of 'Mr Marvile'. I have speculated that Marvell made use of news networks to keep abreast of activities in the capital from his seclusion in Yorkshire. The nearly seventy-year-old Weckherlin (b. 1584), Milton's predecessor as Latin secretary, had been recalled from retirement in March 1652 to assist with foreign affairs as the sight in Milton's right eye failed. But Weckherlin was in poor health, so not only might Marvell have thought himself well-qualified for a secretarial role, he may also have had reason to believe there would be an opening in Milton's office sooner rather than later. In any case, it is evident from Milton's letter that the younger poet's approach was both cannily timed and judiciously calibrated.

Around this time Marvell composed his satire on 'The Character of Holland', and as Nicholas von Maltzahn has observed, 'The Miltonic allusions in the poem coincide conspicuously with [his] approach to Milton for employment' (*Chronology*, 38). These verses marked the English victory over the Dutch in the Battle of Portland and fought for control of the English Channel over three days in February (18-20), though the first two-thirds of the poem comprises anti-Dutch satire of a more general kind. Privately circulated in 1653, a truncated version with an eight-line epilogue bringing naval matters up to date was printed in 1665 and again in 1672, moments of renewed hostility with the Dutch. The poem was thus transformed from a piece of Commonwealth propaganda into a work flattering to royalist and Yorkist interests. The apparent incongruity of the politics at play in these versions, as well as that between the 1665 'Character' and Marvell's Painter satires, which are so scabrously critical of the court, has until recently led most commentators to conclude that some other, opportunistic hand must have been responsible for the 1665 alteration and for seeing the poem into print. But it has never been explained who might have had access to Marvell's copy, apart of course from Marvell himself, and indeed, Martin Dzelzainis (2015) has now made the case for Marvell as the responsible agent. We are reminded that Marvell had been part of an embassy to Muscovy and Sweden from July 1663 to January 1665, service undertaken with 'his Majesty's good liking', and that Marvell, on his return, may have been eager to signal his further utility to the crown. This sequence of Anglo-Dutch poems thus provides further evidence of Marvell's plasticity—perhaps opportunism—as a writer and political creature, of his capacity to modulate praise and blame as the coordinates of his self-interest and of the national interest shifted over time.

Despite Milton's backing, Marvell did not obtain the secretarial post he had sought in early 1653. He did, however, succeed in coming to the attention of the good and great. He soon became tutor to Cromwell's ward and prospective son-in-law William Dutton, and by July 1653 had set up with Dutton in the household of John Oxenbridge at Eton. In a letter dated 28 July, Marvell writes his new employer to assure him the boy is well looked after: 'The care which your Excellence is pleased to take of him', Marvell affirms, 'is no small encouragement and shall be so represented to him. But above all I shall labour to make him sensible of his duty to God. For then we begin to serve faithfully when we consider that he is our Master. And in this both he and I owe infinitely to your Lordship, for having placed us in so godly a family as that of Mr Oxenbridge whose doctrine and example are like a book and a map, not only instructing the ear but demonstrating to the eye which way we ought to travel' (*P&L*, 2:304-5). But overseeing Dutton's learning and spiritual formation was also a kind of soft state appointment which placed Marvell at the disposal of the Council. By the winter of 1653–1654, Marvell was being called on remotely to aid in a diplomatic mission to Sweden. He contributed a Latin epigram accompanying a miniature portrait of Cromwell meant for Queen Christina ('In Effigiem Oliveri Cromwell'), and moreover, a verse epistle, also in Latin, which played an important role in the embassy's happy outcome ('Angelo suo Marvellius'). Marvell's poem was received by the English ambassador, Bulstrode Whitelocke, on 23 March 1654, after some weeks of mostly fruitless negotiations. It had come via Whitelocke's chaplain, Nathaniel Ingelo, fellow of Eton College, and Marvell's recent acquaintance there. One evening, when conversation with the Queen turned to matters of poetry, Whitelocke was happy 'to show her a copy of Latin verses made by an English gentleman, a friend of [his], and sent over to him hither, and which he had now about him, and knew that such diversions were pleasing to the Queen'. Whitelocke recorded that 'the Queen was much delighted with these and other verses which [he] showed her; read them over several times, and desired copies of them, which [he] sent her; and in this good humour she wished Whitelocke to leave with her a copy of his articles as he had now revised them, and to come to her again the next day, when she would give him a further answer, and, she hoped, to his contentment' (Whitelocke 1855, 2:71-2). (On Whitelocke's embassy to Sweden, see Holberton 2008, 6-36.)

If young William Dutton did not much engage Marvell's energies of attention (see *Chameleon*, 112-13), their hosts, John Oxenbridge and his wife Jane, most certainly did. Oxenbridge was a nonconformist divine, educated at Cambridge and Oxford, who had been deprived of his post as tutor of Magdalen Hall by Archbishop Laud in 1634. He subsequently met and married Jane Butler, herself said to be 'a scholar beyond what is usual in her sex, and of a masculine judgment in the profound points of religion', so much so that Oxenbridge did not like to preach on a passage of Scripture without first consulting her opinion on it (qtd. in Winship 2004). In 1635 they left England for Bermuda, beginning a six-year sojourn in that island, in the course of which John Oxenbridge fell afoul of Bermuda's governing council for his Congregationalist preaching (see Donoghue 2013, 49). An itinerant minister after returning to England in 1641, Oxenbridge found favour under the Commonwealth, gaining his appointment as fellow of Eton College in October 1652. The following summer—around the time William Dutton and his tutor were being taken into the Oxenbridges' care—Cromwell made John Oxenbridge a commissioner to the Somers Island Company, which had responsibility for the administration of Bermuda.

This may have been the occasion for Marvell's poem 'Bermudas', the most obviously, indeed perhaps the only obviously 'Puritan' poem Marvell wrote, notwithstanding his reputation as a 'great Puritan poet' (so termed in the *Encyclopedia Britannica* [1911] at the height of its cultural authority). Framed by a pair of four-line stanzas in the voice of a poetic speaker, 'Bermudas' presents a song of praise which rings out from a small boat of Puritan settlers as they row off the Bermudian coast, sounding His name 'Till it arrive at heaven's vault: / Which thence (perhaps) rebounding, may / Echo beyond the Mexique Bay' (ll. 34-6). Their song is modelled on the Psalms, evoking in particular George Sandys's much-admired verse paraphrases of the Psalms, which were published in 1636, 1638, and 1648. Sandys's psalms were popular at court and were set to music and published in libretti by the court musician Henry Lawes in 1638 and 1648. As Smith remarks, 'To transfer this kind of verse into an obviously Puritanical context was to perform the kind of generic relocation characteristic of Marvell's political poems', as, for instance, in Marvell's refitting of royalist Horatianism for praise of Cromwell in the Horatian Ode (*Chameleon*, 114). The mention of Lawes might also remind us of the parallel to Milton's *Comus*, perhaps a refashioning of court masque for more austerely Protestant purposes. Lawes composed the music for *Comus*, acted the part of the Attendant Spirit in its original performance, and served in effect as the first publisher of Milton's text. We have reason to question Marvell's alleged closeness to Milton in the early 1670s, when such closeness was touted by Marvell's enemies as a way of discrediting his moderate defence of nonconformity. But we have perhaps underestimated the assiduity with which Marvell cultivated Milton as a professional sponsor, 'honoured friend', and literary touchstone in the 1650s. The 'Character of Holland' seems to imagine Milton among its close circle of initial readers and strategically echoes Milton's poetry and prose. 'Bermudas', too, though it may have been written for the Oxenbridge household, scans as a kind of Miltonic imitation and may well have found its way back to Milton at Westminster. In June 1654, Marvell would write Milton at his house in Petty France street to relate his (Marvell's) presentation of a copy of *Defensio Secunda* to John Bradshaw at Eton, professing at the same time his intention to 'study it even to the getting of it by heart' (*P&L*, 306). He may even have had a hand in polishing Milton's Latin tract for the press earlier that winter. At Saumur with William Dutton in 1655–1656, Marvell would circulate copies of Milton's *Pro Se Defensio* amongst the Protestant pilgrims there. If Marvell had a 'Miltonic moment', it was in the mid-1650s (see Connell 2011).

The Bermudians thank God for delivering them from the dangers of their sea voyage; for the paradisal bounty of their new home—'He makes the figs our mouths to meet, / And throws the melons at our feet' (ll. 21-2), Marvell's rowers aver, recalling those memorable lines from 'The Garden', 'The nectarene, and curious peach, / Into my hands themselves do reach; / Stumbling on melons as I pass, / Insnared with flow'rs, I fall on grass' (ll. 37-40); and for framing a natural temple in the island the better to exalt his praises. As we might by now expect, however, problems emerge once we begin to scratch the poem's surface. Though early seventeenth-century reports did indeed make Bermuda out to be an isle of plenty, its fame was owing to its notorious shipwrecks, and it was moreover a tobacco colony which relied on indentured servitude and slavery. While there 'is nothing in Bermuda's early history to compare with the horrors of … the mainland colony' (Bernhard 1985, 58), a place of leisured otium it was not. Neither was it especially Puritan: when news of the regicide reached Bermuda, the settlers proclaimed Charles II king, forced a change of Governor, and persecuted Independent ministers and church members (see Pestana 2004, 91-2). How much of Bermuda's natural, economic, and religious history Marvell was aware of is of course difficult to say, but it would be unwise to assume Marvell's naiveté in matters about which he wrote. To be sure, Marvell's poem conjures Bermuda as a godly paradise in a way that might be pleasing to John Oxenbridge, stamping classical gardens of sensual delight with a firmly Protestant poetic. But like so many of Marvell's poems, it seems spring-loaded with ironies and ambiguities, qualities which are activated as the poem circulates beyond its immediate illocutionary context. These qualities are exacerbated by the eerie frame which introduces the rowers' 'holy and cheerful note': 'Where the remote Bermudas ride / In th'ocean's bosom unespied, / From a small boat, that rowed along, / The list'ning winds received this song' (ll. 1-4). Are the islands 'unespied', or the settlers rowing in the ocean's bosom? From what vantage does the speaker thus espy a prospect he declares unperceived? Between the water and the air, where does he tread to listen? And where are these pilgrims going, since their praise for the island's bounty makes clear they have already arrived? Thus the superb Rosalie Colie (1970): 'We know a great deal about the poem and its content, perhaps even its occasion'; 'What we do not know, though, is what is going on in this poem' (141).

'The First Anniversary'

On or about 17 January 1655 (the day the bibliophile George Thomason collected his copy), Marvell's 'The First Anniversary of the Government under His Highness the Lord Protector' appeared in London bookshops, though the anniversary of its title fell on 16 December. In it, Marvell reflected on the first year of Protectoral rule, celebrating Cromwell's achievements while also deflating the resistance to Cromwell's government which had found outlet in political pamphlets, in popular preaching, and in conspiracies real and imagined against the Protector's life. Indeed, Marvell's poem is remarkable for the way it filters newsbook reportage and hostile propaganda into its deliberative rhetoric of praise: 'The First Anniversary' is composed at the unruly interface of classical decorum and demotic print (see Raymond 1999). Though published anonymously, the poem was belatedly entered into the Stationer's Register under Marvell's name, so its authorship cannot have been altogether a secret. It was registered by the bookseller Thomas Newcomb, the government's printer and publisher of Milton's *Defensio Secunda*, and so has a quasi-official status, though the extent to which Cromwell or the Council of State may have been involved in its commissioning remains unclear. But Marvell was certainly at a stretch when he claimed never to have had any, 'not the remotest relation to public matters, nor correspondence with the persons then predominant, until the year 1657', when he finally entered the secretarial service (*PW*, 1:288).

How did we get here? The regicide, the dissolution of monarchy, and the dismantling of the English Church had effectively alienated both traditional elites and popular feeling. The Rump government's blanket imposition of oaths of allegiance to the Commonwealth reflects the depth of its insecurity after a year of ruling without a king or House of Lords. Still, a certain segment of radicals and reformers were optimistic about the nation's future at the inception of the republic. Shortly after the regicide, the Puritan divine John Owen (whose side Marvell would later take against Samuel Parker) looked hopefully on England as God's elect nation, 'given to the people of the Most High', whence God would 'sooner or later shake all the monarchies of the Earth' (Owen 1862, 8:261). Following Cromwell's decisive victory over

Charles II's Scottish army in September 1651, Owen preached the thanksgiving sermon before the Right Honourable Commons assembled in Parliament, declaring: 'Of all the times which the Holy One of Israel hath caused to pass over the nations of the world, there hath not any from the days of old been so filled with eminent discoveries of his presence, power, and providence ... as the season wherein he hath made you a spectacle unto men and angels, being the instrument in his hand to perform all his pleasure' (Owen 1862, 8:313). Yet less than two years later, in April 1653, Cromwell vehemently addressed this same Parliament, telling the remaining Rumpers, '"Come, come, I will put an end to your prating"; then walking up and down the House like a madman, and kicking the ground with his feet, he cried out, "You are no Parliament, I say you are no Parliament; I will put an end to your sitting": whereupon the serjeant attending the Parliament opened the doors, and Lieutenant-Colonel Worsley with two files of musketeers entered the House' (Ludlow 1894, 353).

Cromwell's expulsion of the Rump has prompted considerable debate amongst historians, but it can probably best be explained as a judgement on the Rump's inertia, its failure to legislate the election of a new representative and to settle the religious question—whether there was to be a national church and how far liberty of conscience should be extended. Following its initial flurry of activity, the Rump was paralysed by tension with the army and internally by divisions between its radical and conservative elements. The Rump's successor, the Nominated Assembly, also known as Barebone's Parliament, fared little better. These 138 'persons of approved fidelity' (one from each county in England, plus six apiece for Ireland and Wales and five for Scotland) were hand-picked by Cromwell and his Council of Officers and charged with providing for the 'peace, safety, and good government of this Commonwealth' (*ConstDoc*, 405), taking up where the Rump had left off before its ignominious dismissal. An auspicious start to the Assembly's sitting, however, soon gave way to the same ideological gridlock which had plagued the Rump. As moderates increasingly stayed away from the fractious proceedings, the well-organised millenarian wing of MPs was able to sustain razor majorities in voting measures which 'deeply antagonized the political nation' (Woolrych 2002, 555). In response to Parliament's wayward drift, the disaffected Major-General John Lambert set about drawing up a new constitutional document which provided for a limited monarchy; he presented it first to a small number of fellow officers and then, in late November 1653, to Cromwell. Sensitive to charges of vainglory, ambition, and self-dealing, Cromwell would not forcibly dismiss the assembly he had invested with supreme authority just a few months before, nor would he accept the title of king. Lambert and the Council of Officers settled on another tack, contriving with the Speaker, Francis Rous, to bring a motion for Parliament's self-dissolution. Within a few days, nearly eighty members had subscribed to Parliament's abdication of authority. Lambert's new constitution, the Instrument of Government, duly revised to provide for an elected, non-monarchical executive, was adopted by the Council of Officers on 15 December. Cromwell was installed as Lord Protector the following day.

The first year of Protectoral rule saw a number of important achievements, especially on the diplomatic front. The Dutch War, to which Marvell's 'Character of Holland' bears witness, was concluded on terms favourable to England in April 1654 with the signing of the Treaty of Westminster. The successful negotiation of a peace between England and Holland had the effect of easing England's relations with other Baltic nations, specifically Denmark (a Dutch ally) and Sweden (under the commercial treaty advanced by Whitelocke's embassy). In July the Protectorate concluded a peace with the crown of Portugal. So Marvell declares of Cromwell, at the opening of 'The First Anniversary':

> 'Tis he the force of scattered Time contracts,
> And in one year the work of ages acts:
> While heavy monarchs make a wide return,
> Longer, and more malignant than Saturn:
> And though they all Platonic years should reign,
> In the same posture would be found again.
> Their earthy projects under ground they lay,
> More slow and brittle than the China clay:
> Well may they strive to leave them to their son,
> For one thing never was by one king done.
> (ll. 13-22)

Marvell redeploys the trope of Cromwell's 'industrious valour' from the Horatian Ode (l. 34), drawing a contrast between the singularly energetic figure of the Protector and slothful European monarchs. Marvell's comparisons are astrological: Saturn was the most distant known planet with the widest and slowest orbit, while Cromwell, contracting the scattered force of time, is implicitly imagined as a mercurial inner planet, racing round the sun. The stress laid on Cromwell's extraordinary individuality is balanced by a republican rhetoric of disdain for the ponderousness of monarchy as an institution, a duality recapitulated towards the poem's close, where foreign princes wonderingly inveigh of Cromwell: 'He seems a king by long succession born, /

And yet the same to be a king does scorn. / Abroad a king he seems, and something more, / At home a subject on the equal floor' (ll. 387-90). The astrological metaphors also place Cromwell within a providential scheme as heaven's flame and climacteric to all who oppose him (cf. Ode, ll. 26, 104), and indeed, Cromwell insisted to his first Protectoral Parliament 'I called not myself to this place!', but rather received his commission from God (Cromwell 1850, 373).

The deliberations of this Parliament, which was summoned to meet on 3 September, however, produced a set of quandaries for the Lord Protector, quandaries which are taken up by his most humble and faithful servant in 'The First Anniversary'. What Cromwell wanted from the people's representative was 'healing and settling', namely, the formal recognition of the Instrument's constitutional authority and of the ordinances he had issued over the last nine months. But it soon became clear that members saw the constitution as an open question, and some, including Cromwell's erstwhile comrade-in-arms, the radicalised millenarian Thomas Harrison, spoke openly against the Protectorate's legitimacy and called on Parliament 'to extirpate the new tyranny'. When Cromwell demanded members take an oath recognising the indentures by which they were summoned, and so promise not to 'propose, or give my consent, to alter the government, as it is settled in one person and a Parliament', a hundred of the newly elected representatives to this 'free Parliament' were thereby excluded (Cromwell 1850, 3:401). Even so, there was debate in the House about curtailing the Protector's executive and military powers as well as the religious liberty afforded under the Instrument. The religious clauses of the Protectoral settlement had struck a compromise solution to the thorny question of religion, maintaining a state church and a public ministry while extending toleration to all those 'such as profess faith in God by Jesus Christ (though differing in judgment from the doctrine, worship, or discipline publicly held forth)', 'provided this liberty be not extended to Popery or Prelacy, nor to such as, under the profession of Christ, hold forth and practice licentiousness' (*ConstDoc*, 416). This made it the most liberal English regime of the seventeenth century in point of religion, but it nevertheless awkwardly straddled conservative and radical opinion—a feature of Cromwellian rule more generally.

To millenarians like the Fifth Monarchists, a small but highly vocal sect in the 1650s, the fall of the Stuarts was a sign on the road to the second coming, and they hoped to see the establishment of a government of visible saints who would usher in Christ's reign, as prophesied in the Book of Daniel. In their view, the dissolution of the Nominated Assembly (in which a number of their Fifth Monarchist brethren had sat), the institution of Cromwellian rule, and the maintenance of a system of church patronage were works of anti-Christ. Cromwell was 'the dissemblingest perjured villain in the world' (Rymer 1737–1745, 9:251). Less hysterical Independents like Secretary Milton were little more approving of the civil authority's role in church government. In his unpublished sonnet to 'Cromwell, our chief of men' (1652), Milton had implored Cromwell to help 'save free conscience from the paw / Of hireling wolves whose gospel is their maw' (ll. 13-14). *Defensio Secunda* puts it more baldly, asking Cromwell not to 'permit two powers, utterly diverse, the civil and the ecclesiastical, to make harlots of each other', and to 'leave the church to the church' (*CPW*, 4:678). But to a considerable number of MPs, the pro-liferation of sects and of unregulated worship and belief was a direct threat to civil society, and a parliamentary committee was convened to investigate and suppress 'damnable heresies', a programme which had all the appearance of a 'persecutor's charter' (Woolrych 2002, 612). Cromwell dissolved the first Protectoral Parliament five days after 'The First Anniversary' was published.

Marvell could not have anticipated this eventuality, but this is all to explain the poetic and thematic significance of *discordia concors* or harmonious dis-cord within Marvell's poem. In its most well-known passage, Marvell com-pares Cromwell's statecraft to the magical skill of Amphion, who built the walls of Thebes by the music of his lyre:

> So when Amphion did the lute command,
> Which the god gave him; with his gentle hand,
> The rougher stones, unto his measures hewed,
> Danced up in order from the quarries rude;
> This took a lower, that an higher place,
> As he the treble altered, or the bass:
> No note he struck, but a new story layed,
> And the great work ascended while he played.
> The list'ning structures he with wonder eyed,
> And still new stops to various time applied:
> Now through the strings a martial rage he throws,
> And joining straight the Theban tow'r arose;
> Then as he strokes them with a touch more sweet,
> The flocking marbles in a palace meet;
> But, for he most the graver notes did try,
> Therefore the temples reared their columns high:
> Thus, here he ceased, his sacred lute creates
> Th'harmonious city of the seven gates.
> Such was that wondrous order and consent,
> When Cromwell tuned the ruling Instrument.
> (ll. 49-68)

Where the sources are bare in their details of Amphion's feat, Marvell emphasises the roughness and rudeness of Cromwell's building materials and the attendant difficulty of hewing them into 'wondrous order' (Apollonius Rhodius says only that the rocks Amphion moved by his lute were 'large', Horace nothing at all). Marvell's conceit admits into the poem the dissentious condition of the body politic while admiring Cromwell for fitting such disagreeable parts into a working whole. But this is also what Marvell's poem is doing in absorbing dissenting print into its praise. The Fifth Monarchist Anna Trapnel had gained notoriety in January 1654 for falling into an eleven-day trance, during which the Spirit moved her to pray, sing, and prophecy, with a scribe by her bed and frequent visits from notable sectaries. The fruits of this episode were published in a pamphlet called *The Cry of a Stone*. Marvell seems at several points in 'The First Anniversary' to answer this prophetess of Protectoral ruin, and he directly blasts the Fifth Monarchists and their leaders Christopher Feake and John Simpson at l. 293ff (Trapnel was a member of Simpson's congregation, and Marvell's abuse of Feake and Simpson as foaming Mahometans is also a sidelong glance at Trapnel's epileptic-like trance). In one of many articulations of chiliastic expectation, the *Cry* records Trapnel insisting, 'Let him not say as they said of old, who put the day [of Christ's return] far from them, that the vision was for many days, for a time yet far off; but let them accept of the day and time that thou has put into their hand: the Lord is building his temple, it is no time for them to build tabernacles; now thou art upon thy temple-work, shall they be building great palaces for themselves' (Trapnell 1654, 29). Cromwell's Protectorate, Trapnel suggests, is more intent on building up its temporal authority than in making ready for God's rule on earth, and we may recall Milton's warnings about church hirelings and civil power making a harlot of religion. The Amphion passage answers Trapnel by making an architectural emblem out of Cromwell's just priorities: while he plays notes of 'martial rage' and alabaster sweetness, thus raising the tower and the palace, he chiefly 'the graver notes did try / Therefore the temples reared their columns high'. Cromwell may be another Amphion, but his poet is no less a magician.

But what are we to make of Marvell's extended recollection of Cromwell's near-fatal brush with disaster in September 1654 when the coach he was driving in Hyde Park overturned and he was dragged behind at peril of his life? More curious still is the mock-eulogising of Cromwell which follows the report of the accident, the premise of which is that true praise may be more easily spoken of the dead (see ll. 187-8). Marvell turns the incident to his advantage by regarding it as the providential wages of political sin against the Protector: 'Thou, who so oft through storms of thund'ring lead / Hast born securely thine undaunted head', he writes, 'Thy breast through poniarding conspiracies, / Drawn from the sheath of lying prophecies; / Thee proof beyond all other force or skill, / Our sins endanger, and shall one day kill' (ll. 169-74). 'Panic groans' accompany rumour of Cromwell's death; but the apocalyptic tenor of these noises disconcertingly underscores the fragility of the body politic, held together as it is by this singular figure who will one day die. Moreover, the pretence of Cromwell's death as a means to speaking true praise, while it insists on the ultimate *falseness* of misapprehensions about Cromwell—that he would make himself king, that he desired to be rid of Parliament—it does not stipulate their *groundlessness.* Such fears and uncertainties would only be made void, Marvell seems to argue, by the finality of death, thereby allowing for the genuine difficulty of assessing this sui generis figure or of guessing 'which way the protector was about to jump' (Hirst 1985, 25). Marvell's poem steers not away from but into those 'thick clouds' which lie about the morning and 'intercept the beam of mortal eyes' (ll. 141-2)—a figure for millennial uncertainty but also for practical politics in the first year of Protectoral government. Marvell thus unknowingly echoes another shrewd English observer, who in September 1654 wrote to the French first minister of Cromwell: 'His enterprises are only known to himself ... Certainly we are led into the clouds; we know no longer what to believe' (qtd. in Hirst).

A different question is what 'The First Anniversary' tells us about *Marvell's* politics c. 1654. Here too we are liable to being led into the clouds. I am not persuaded by accounts which suggest the poem has a shadow agenda which runs against its overt support for the Protector's 'quasi-republican', 'quasi-imperial' stance—either urging him to accept the crown or subtly warning against the erosion of liberty under the Instrument. We can go pretty far down the road with Derek Hirst, who sees the poem's languages and figures as a kind of symbolic paraphrase of Cromwell's complex self-presentation. But then, this is how Marvellian panegyric works, on a principle akin to what Hugh Kenner identified as the 'Uncle Charles principle' in Joyce (see Kenner 1978, 16-17, here and as follows). Kenner was responding to the critic Wyndham Lewis, who had faulted Joyce's style for lapsing into middlebrow cliché. The sentence Lewis picked out to illustrate his point was this one: 'Every morning, therefore, Uncle Charles repaired to his outhouse but not before he had greased and brushed scrupulously his back hair and brushed and put on his tall hat'. 'People', Lewis sniffed, '*repair* to places in works of fiction of the humblest order'. What Kenner saw was that *repaired* 'wears invisible quotation marks. It would be Uncle Charles's own word, should he chance to say what he was doing. [...] Not that he does so speak, in our hearing. Rather, a speck of his characterizing vocabulary attends our sense of him. A word he need not even utter is there like a gnat in the air beside him, for us to perceive in the same field of attention in which we note how scrupulously he brushes his hat'. Marvell has fastened onto a similar technique in fashioning his praise for great men like Fairfax and Cromwell. Marvell ventriloquises their conversation, their writing and speeches, the books with which they surround themselves, the speech and writing of those they endorse or with whom they associate, he intuits and rhetoricises the whole manifold of his patrons' self-presentation and self-imagining at a given historical moment and layers this virtual penumbra into his remarkable panegyrics.

The dilemma for the biographical critic, of course, is that the quality of *listening* which governs Marvell's panegyrics is relatively impersonal; it works to service his patrons, not his private convictions, whatever they may have been. We may say that Marvell was willing to be heard speaking as he does in 'The First Anniversary', for his name was attached to the poem in the Stationer's Register. From this we can conclude that Marvell's conscience could accommodate itself to the phenomenon of Cromwellian rule as it stood in January 1655. But if he was a closet republican, as some have argued, he remained closeted: the die-hard republicans who felt betrayed by the dissolution of the Rump and the investment of authority in a Lord Protector would not have recognised the author of 'The First Anniversary' as a fellow traveller (and why would they when the poem came from the government's printer, as was clear from its title page). And it would have been an exceptionally flexible republican conscience which could also accommodate itself to restored Stuart rule and indeed to the royal prerogative as an instrument of liberty. To speak of 'the curve of Marvell's political development' (to borrow a phrase of Cleanth Brooks's) too much assumes that his politics were *going* somewhere, developing towards some end, or into some more or less permanent shape. The parallel career of John Milton is especially unhelpful in this regard, insofar as Milton *does* develop from a conformist of some sort—recall, for instance, the young Milton's Latin elegy on the ceremonialist bishop Lancelot Andrewes—into a religious and political Independent who became disillusioned with Cromwell and complied with the Stuart regime as far as was necessary to stay alive and no further and only after the Restoration was a fait accompli (witness the two editions of *The Ready and Easy Way to Form a Commonwealth* in February and April 1660). Marvell's devotion to the ideal of 'sober liberty', as he phrases it in 'The First Anniversary', was real and lasting, and in the Restoration, he became a forceful satirist and polemicist where such liberty was threatened. But he was as ready to ally with a strong-armed Protector or a prerogative monarch in liberty's defence as he was with Parliaments, and he defended nonconformists while remaining suspicious of men of a zealous spiritual itch. Marvell's dual reputation as a Platonic idealist and uncompromising Whig patriot belies the fundamental worldliness of his engagement with relations of power as a writer in public life.

'A Notable English Italo-Machavillian'

In the autumn of 1655, Marvell and his tutee William Dutton embarked on what would be roughly a year's stay in the French town of Saumur, home to the famous Huguenot academy, at the behest of Dutton's uncle and benefactor John Dutton. Founded by Phillippe du Mornay in 1593, the Académie de Saumur was a centre of French Protestant theology during the time when reformed religion was protected under the Edict of Nantes. Saumur itself, as noted briefly in Chap. 4, 'offered a safe place to stay to reformed students from abroad and to young aristocrats who stopped there on the way to Geneva', though this description somewhat understates the religiously mixed and cosmopolitan commerce of the town as a 'resort and as a touring center' in the Loire valley (Pittion 2018, 3, 4). While much more limited than the Grand Tour Marvell oversaw in the 1640s, Dutton's visit to Saumur served much the same purpose, to acquire the refinements of a young gentleman and a taste of the wider world. But Marvell was also working, and not merely as a tutor Hartlib Papers (2013). He was noticed right away: in October, a correspondent of the English intelligencer Samuel Hartlib reported, 'There is [here] one Marvel of 40 y[ears] of age who ... is skilled in several languages', one who has made his living as a tutor but 'who is fitter to be a Secretary of State' (*Hartlib Papers* 2013). And indeed, it has emerged that Marvell was in regular communication with John Thurloe, secretary to the Council of State, director of Cromwell's intelligence service, and Marvell's future superior (see *Chronology*, 43). Marvell was also in contact with Milton and endeavoured to serve Milton's purposes while in Saumur. Confirmation of this is second-hand but well corroborated by circumstance. In the summer of 1657, Milton sent copies of the second *Defence* and perhaps also of his *Defence of Himself against Alexander More* to Henry Oldenburg, then in Saumur. On receiving this packet, Oldenburg wrote to Milton, somewhat awkwardly demurring to publicise Milton's works there for fear of making himself unwelcome. In his reply, Milton explained, through what we might imagine to be clenched teeth: 'A certain learned friend of mine spent last summer at Saumur. He wrote me that the book was in demand in that region. I sent him just one copy. He wrote back that some of the learned men with whom he had shared it had been more than pleased. Had I not thought I should please them, I would certainly have spared you the trouble and me the expense' (*CPW*, 7:502-3). Marvell was without doubt Milton's 'certain learned friend'.

Oldenburg's letter to Milton had included mention of the fact that More had recently been appointed minister in the French town of Charenton on the outskirts of Paris. Oldenburg's reticence to show about Milton's writings against More in Saumur speaks to the support More then enjoyed there. Moses Amyraut, the leading theologian at Saumur, was a noted critic of English religious Independency and saw its influence amongst the French Reforme community as destabilising (see Pittion 2018, 11-12). That Marvell was willing to do what Oldenburg declined to perform a year later suggests Marvell's determination to retain Milton's patronage as well as his aptitude for underground work. This is also to make sense of that most famous description of Marvell from another observer in Saumur. In August 1656, James Scudamore wrote the Stuart councillor Sir Richard Browne in Paris, observing that there were many English at Saumur but few of note, one exception being William Dutton, 'called by the French Le Genre du Protecteur [*gendre*, son-in-law] whose governor is one Mervill, a notable English-Italo Machavillian' (qtd. in Kelliher 2008). Historians and critics have tended to strain the import of this remark in construing it as revealing of Marvell's political philosophy. Though Marvell had clearly read his Machiavelli, the label serves here as a common epithet. If Scudamore knew who Marvell was, he may also have known of his erstwhile royalist connections and thus of his side-changing as a man now in service to Cromwell. In any case, Scudamore's report identifies Marvell as a political operator, and there is a whiff as well of suspected clandestine activity. In other words, it is the comment of a spy on another spy, and then as now, 'Machiavellian' was shorthand for cunning, shrewdness, and political expediency.

Secretary Marvell

Marvell and Dutton's time in Saumur was cut short by the failing health of John Dutton. In September 1656 he successfully petitioned Cromwell for William to be recalled from France so that the elder Dutton might impart to his nephew 'all the business of his estate and have his assistance' (*Chronology*, 44). Marvell spent the next several months as a go-between for John Dutton and was entrusted to press the matter of William's marriage to Frances Cromwell with the Protector. But greater opportunities lay before Cromwell's poet. Philip Meadows, who had been preferred to Marvell as assistant Latin secretary in 1653, was in February 1657 chosen as special envoy to Denmark. Meadows sailed for Copenhagen in August and Marvell was selected to fill his place, reporting to Secretary Thurloe's office on 2 September. Having followed a contingent and circuitous career for some fifteen years, since the death of his father and the loss of his place at Cambridge, Marvell, now thirty-six, had finally found work equal to his talents and was clearly a man on the rise.

Remarkably, Marvell's colleagues in the Office of Foreign Tongues included not only his senior secretary John Milton but also John Dryden, the future Stuart laureate with whom Marvell would spar after the Restoration. Students of literary modernism have often remarked on the proximity of several of its key figures to the workings of bureaucracy—Kafka at the Worker's Accident Insurance Institute, Wallace Stevens at the Hartford, T. S. Eliot at Faber & Faber—but in the Cromwellian secretariat we find together no less than the three greatest poets of the later seventeenth century. It is a matter of speculation as to whether they exchanged verse with one another during the brief period of their shared employment. Milton was now beginning *Paradise Lost*; Marvell had already written most of the poems for which he would later gain fame; Dryden virtually nothing which has survived, though he distinguished himself as a student at Cambridge, and was said to have 'read over and very well understood all the Greek and Latin poets' (qtd. in Hammond 2009). Critics have found in both Milton and Dryden allusions to the Horatian Ode, though these are disputed. Possibly Marvell had sight of Milton's epic in its earliest stages (see *Poems*, 302; *Chameleon*, 151). But surely theirs was a complicated camaraderie if such they had. Milton was by this point completely blind. Marvell already had a relationship with Milton, but he was plainly the 'junior partner' and Milton's direct subordinate, to say nothing of Marvell's instinctive guardedness. Dryden was only a few years out of university, and of a diffident nature himself, though we may imagine he was more at home in the Latin office than he would be at the debauched court of Charles II.

There were political and religious differences as well. Milton was more of a republican than Marvell, and we have noted their divergence on the matter of religion in *Defensio Secunda* and 'The First Anniversary', the latter of which Philip Connell (2011) has read 'as an oblique but urgent attempt to disarm the older poet's objections to the Protector's role as at once godly magistrate and supreme arbiter of "sober liberty"' (565). Dryden came from a Puritan gentry family but seems not to have been disposed towards Puritanism himself, though he would later show, like Milton and Marvell, a strong disdain of clerical power. The political climacteric of the Restoration would obviously set these three men on very different courses, but their literary association would endure, if somewhat vexingly for Dryden. As Stuart laureate, he would make a rhyming opera out of *Paradise Lost*, for which he sought Milton's permission. Marvell's commendatory poem to the second edition of *Paradise Lost* suggests Milton told him about the meeting and contains several barbs at Dryden's expense. While in *The Rehearsal Transpros'd*, Marvell will recast Samuel Parker in the Dryden role of Buckingham's farce.

Latin was the lingua franca of diplomatic correspondence in early modern Europe, and the Office of Foreign Tongues was where such correspondence was translated into English for the use of the Council of State or (usually) into Latin for dispatch to foreign commissioners and potentates. Such work required speed and diligence as well as a finely tuned sense of audience and decorum, moulding the diktats of harried officials—including His Highness the Lord Protector—into the language of diplomacy. It was work for which a superb ventriloquist like Marvell was preternaturally suited. He was soon asked to write a petition to the King of Portugal over the loss of a Scottish merchant ship, which had been seized by the Portuguese and its crew murdered before the civil wars. Over the next twelve months, he would be kept busy with the Anglo-Spanish War, in which England was allied with the French, and with Dutch and Baltic affairs. Marvell also acted as something like a diplomatic liaison, both receiving and visiting foreign ambassadors. Ever prudent, Marvell kept close account of his coach rides while on public business ('to the French ambassador's thirteen times', 'to the Portugal ambassador's seven times', 'three days fetching the Dutch ambassador from Gravesend', etc.), for which he was duly reimbursed by the state (see *Chronology*, 53).

Marvell's enjoyment of the dignity and security of his position as a civil servant to the Commonwealth was to be short-lived: almost a year to the day after his appointment, on 3 September 1658, Oliver Cromwell died of a fever, perhaps brought on by the stress of his daughter Elizabeth's own suffering and death from an unknown illness in the months previous. The Instrument of Government had been superseded in May 1657 by the parliamentary Humble Petition and Advice as the recognised constitution of England, Scotland, and Ireland. Unlike the Instrument, which had provided for the election of a new Protector by the Council of State, the Humble Petition allowed the Protector to designate his successor. At Cromwell's death, however, no written designation could be found. It was reported that Cromwell had appointed his eldest son Richard to succeed him, and he was sworn in as Lord Protector the same day. To the providentially minded, Oliver Cromwell's posthumous fortunes did not bode well for his son. The embalming of the late Lord Protector's body was botched, leading to the corpse's rapid putrefaction. A wax mask of his face was made, and the body secretly interred in Westminster Abbey a few days later. Cromwell's elaborate lying in state at Somerset House was thus accomplished by way of props, a wooden effigy being apparelled in a 'robe of purple velvet, laced with a rich gold lace, and furred with ermines; upon the kirtle was the royal large robes of the like purple velvet, laced and furred with ermines, with rich strings and tassels of gold, the kirtle being girt with a rich embroidered belt, wherein was a fair sword, richly gilt and hatched with gold … In the right hand was the golden sceptre, representing government; in the left hand the globe, denoting principality; upon the head a purple velvet cap furred with ermines, signifying regality' (Carrington 1659, 233-4). The royal trappings Cromwell had eschewed in life were lavished upon him in death. A state funeral was observed on 23 November and the 'body' carried in a progress from Somerset to Westminster attended by a train of dignitaries and government functionaries. Among them were Cromwell's Latin secretaries, John Milton, Andrew Marvell, and John Dryden.

Marvell's 'A Poem upon the Death of His Late Highness the Lord Protector' was meant to appear in a quarto volume registered by Henry Herringman on 20 January 1659 as *Three poems to the happy memory of the most renowned Oliver, late Lord Protector of this Commonwealth, by Mr Marvell, Mr Driden, Mr Sprat*. When *Three Poems* did appear that spring, however, it was under the imprimatur of William Wilson, and Marvell's poem had been withdrawn and replaced by one by Edmund Waller. This is interesting enough and bears further comment, but the circumstances of the elegy's disappearance from the volume are perhaps less strange than the actual poem. Pierre Legouis (1965), among the elegy's most ardent appreciators amidst a generally taciturn reception, traced an arc from the 'approving admiration' for Cromwell in 'The First Anniversary' to the poem on the death, where, he professed, 'love adds its intimate note' (114). This remark has a double valence, identifying Marvell's counter-intuitive emphasis on Cromwell as private man of feeling as opposed to soldier and statesman, but as well the poem's own affective investments and disclosures. Thus Marvell's aetiology of Cromwell's demise:

> To Love and Grief the fatal writ was signed;
> (Those nobler weaknesses of human kind
> From which those powers that issued the decree,
> Although immortal, found they were not free),
> That they, to whom his breast still open lies,
> In gentle passions should his death disguise:
> And leave succeeding ages cause to mourn,
> As long as Grief shall weep, or Love shall burn.

Straight does a slow and languishing disease
Eliza, Nature's and his darling, seize.
Her when an infant, taken with her charms,
He oft would flourish in his mighty arms;
And, lest their force the tender burden wrong,
Slacken the vigour of his muscles strong;
Then to the mother's breast her softly move,
Which while she drained of milk, she filled with love.
....
With her each day the pleasing hours he shares,
And at her aspect calms his growing cares;
Or with a grandsire's joy her children sees
Hanging about her neck or at his knees.
Hold fast, dear infants, hold them both or none!
This will not stay when once the other's gone.
(ll. 21-52)

In assigning to Love and Grief the cause of Cromwell's death, Marvell glances back, as he does frequently in this poem, to 'The First Anniversary' and to the figure of Amphion. For not only was Amphion renowned as a musician and builder, he also died of grief over the death of his children (his wife, the unfortunate Niobe, herself appears parenthetically in 'The Nymph Complaining' as mythic counterpart to the nymph's grief). But this nursery scene also finds the self-imagined orphan Andrew Marvell at once imagining and imagining himself into the Cromwells' tender domesticity. Eliza was but a few years younger than Marvell, and his affecting recollection of how her father dandled her in his arms as an infant is pure fantasy. By occupying such a position in the poem, within the Cromwells' domestic space, Marvell seems to view Cromwell as a surrogate father and so also to re-enact his own orphaning. And well may he have wondered, without the Lord Protector's patronage, what would become of him?

The poem's most famous passage is a moment of gothic intensity that recalls Hamlet in the graveyard, one that begins with startling directness and ends in purple apostrophe:

I saw him dead. A leaden slumber lies
And mortal sleep over those wakeful eyes:
Those gentle rays under the lids were fled,
Which through his looks that piercing sweetness shed;
That port which so majestic was and strong,
Loose and deprived of vigour, stretched along:

All withered, all discoloured, pale and wan,
How much another thing, no more that man?
Oh human glory vain, Oh death, Oh wings,
Oh worthless world, Oh transitory things!
(ll. 247-56)

Marvell's resort to the grammar of the first person cuts through the elaborate decorum of panegyric. The four monosyllables 'I saw him dead' land like a blow. There is some debate as to whether Marvell means he saw the Protector's body before its interment or whether he is meditating on the wax effigy. The passage seems to me almost wholly enervated if we are not meant to imagine the poet caught in the intimate grip of death besides the corpse. The effect Marvell is working up is one of horror as he observes the signs of disanimation. But this does not rule out its being a poetic fiction, and we might ask when and how Marvell may have gained such a private audience with the Lord Protector's body. At his death, Cromwell was attended by family, physicians, and councillors of state. An autopsy and the embalming were performed the night he died, shortly after which the body's purulence became evident. This is slightly to temper our sense of the elegy's personal nature, of its offering, as Alex Garganigo (2018) puts it, Marvell's 'unvarnished, heartfelt response to Cromwell's death' (206). The emotive couplet which concludes this verse paragraph notably abandons the grammar of the first person, shifting from embodied witnessing of 'the man' to the ejaculations of a stage character; the lines also dimly reprise Aeneas's apprehension of Hector's ghost in Book II of the *Aeneid*. If the poem transcends politics through love, it here slips free of what Paul Hammond (2003) calls 'the grammar of commitment' (232).

'A Poem upon the Death' ends by voicing support for Richard Cromwell's succession, though this has struck most readers as perfunctory at best, and indeed, the terms of Marvell's praise seem to glance at expectations of Richard's impotence next to his father. And discerningly enough: hamstrung with severe financial problems and without the native respect of the army, over which he assumed supreme command as Lord Protector, Richard soon found himself in political limbo between the army and Parliament. By 22 April 1659 he would be effectively deposed by the army, and on 25 May he signed a formal letter of resignation, promising to demean himself 'with all peaceableness' under the new regime 'and to procure to the uttermost of my power, that all in whom I have any interest do the same' (qtd. in Gaunt 2008). For the next year, Parliament and the army would alternately bid to establish a working government and constitutional framework; their failure to do so would result in the restoration of Charles Stuart as king of England, Scotland, and Ireland on 29 May 1660.

Sometime after January 1659, Henry Herringman decided to get out of the business of publishing praise for Cromwells, presumably selling his copyright to *Three Poems* to William Wilson. Herringman would soon become Dryden's publisher, and one of the Restoration's leading producers of *belles-lettres*. Dryden may have wished Herringman had better counselled him about going ahead with publication of his 'Heroic Stanzas on the Death of Oliver Cromwell', which he would have to live down for the rest of his long career. Characteristically, Dryden's ambition to be noticed and preferred mitigated his caution. No less characteristically did Marvell prevent his poem from being cast into turbulent political waters, despite his far greater investment in the figure of Oliver Cromwell. 'A Poem upon the Death of His Late Highness the Lord Protector' may justly be called Marvell's 'personal elegy', but its withdrawal at the eleventh hour from *Three poems to the happy memory of the most renowned Oliver* was the act of a politician, and sure enough, politician was to be the next act in Marvell's career.

References

Augustine, Matthew C. 2018. *Aesthetics of Contingency: Writing, Politics, and Culture in England, 1639-89*. Manchester: Manchester University Press.

Berman, David. 2008. '*Post' Rock Podcast* with Chris Richards and David Malitz. 27 June 2008. Retrieved from http://voices.washingtonpost.com/postrock/2008/06/.

Bernhard, Virginia. 1985. Bermuda and Virginia in the Seventeenth Century: A Comparative View. *Journal of Social History* 19 (1): 57–70.

Bray, Alan. 1995. *Homosexuality in Renaissance England*. 2nd ed. New York: Columbia University Press.

Butler, Samuel. 1673. *The Transproser Rehears'd*. London.

Carrington, Samuel. 1659. *The History of the Life and Death of His Most Serene Highness, Oliver, Late Lord Protector*. London.

Connell, Philip. 2011. Marvell, Milton, and the Protectoral Church Settlement. *RES* 62 (256): 562–593.

Cromwell, Oliver. 1850. *Oliver Cromwell's Letters and Speeches: With Elucidations*. Ed. Thomas Carlyle. 4 vols. London: Chapman & Hall.

Donoghue, John. 2013. *Fire under the Ashes: An Atlantic History of the English Revolution*. Chicago: University of Chicago Press.

Dzelzainis, Martin. 2015. Marvell and the Dutch in 1665. In *A Concise Companion to the Study of Manuscripts, Printed Books, and the Production of Early Modern Texts*, ed. Edward Jones, 249–265. Oxford: Wiley-Blackwell.

Empson, William. 1984. *Using Biography*. London: Chatto & Windus.

Everard, William, et al. 1649. *The True Levellers Standard Advanced.* London.

Gardiner, S.R., ed. 1906. *The Constitutional Documents of the Puritan Revolution, 1625–1660.* 3rd ed. Oxford: Clarendon Press.

Garganigo, Alex. 2018. Marvell's Personal Elegy? Rewriting Shakespeare in *A Poem upon the Death of O. C.* In *Texts and Readers in the Age of Marvell*, ed. Christopher D'Addario and Matthew C. Augustine, 206–223. Manchester: Manchester University Press.

Gaunt, Peter. 2008. Cromwell, Richard (1626-1712), lord protector of England, Scotland, and Ireland. *ODNB.*

Haber, Judith. 1994. *Pastoral and the Poetics of Self-Contradiction: Theocritus to Marvell.* Cambridge: Cambridge University Press.

Hammond, Paul. 2009. Dryden, John (1631–1700), poet, playwright, and critic. *ODNB.*

———. 1996. Marvell's Sexuality. *SC* 11 (1): 87–123.

———. 2003. Marvell's Pronouns. *Essays in Criticism* 53 (3): 219–234.

———. 2006. The Date of Marvell's "The Mower against Gardens". *N&Q* 53 (2): 178–181.

The Hartlib Papers. 2013. Edited by Mark Greengrass, Michael Leslie, and Michael Hannon. Published by The Digital Humanities Institute, University of Sheffield. https://www.dhi.ac.uk/hartlib.

Hirst, Derek. 1985. "That Sober Liberty": Marvell's Cromwell in 1654. In *The Golden and the Brazen World: Papers in Literature and History, 1650–1800*, ed. John M. Wallace, 17–53. Berkeley and Los Angeles: University of California Press.

Hirst, Derek, and Steven N. Zwicker. 2012. *Andrew Marvell, Orphan of the Hurricane.* Oxford: Oxford University Press.

Holberton, Edward. 2008. *Poetry and the Cromwellian Protectorate: Culture, Politics, and Institutions.* Oxford: Oxford University Press.

Kalstone, David. 1974. Marvell and the Fictions of Pastoral. *ELR* 4 (1): 174–188.

Kelliher, W. H. 2008. Marvell, Andrew (1621-1678), poet and politician. *ODNB.*

Kenner, Hugh. 1978. *Joyce's Voices.* Berkeley and Los Angeles: University of California Press.

Legouis, Pierre. 1965. *Andrew Marvell: Poet, Puritan, Patriot.* Oxford: Clarendon Press.

Ludlow, Edmund. 1894. *The Memoirs of Edmund Ludlow, Lieutenant-General of the Horse in the Army of the Commonwealth of England, 1625–1672.* Ed. C.H. Firth. 2 vols. Oxford: Clarendon Press.

Marvell, Andrew. 1971. *The Poems and Letters of Andrew Marvell.* Ed. H. M. Margoliouth, rev. Pierre Legouis with E. E. Duncan-Jones. 3rd ed. 2 vols. Oxford: Clarendon Press.

———. 2003. *Prose Works of Andrew Marvell.* Ed. Annabel Patterson, Martin Dzelzainis, Nicholas von Maltzahn, and N.H. Keeble. 2 vols. New Haven: Yale University Press.

———. 2007. *Poems of Andrew Marvell.* Ed. Nigel Smith. Rev. ed. London: Longman.

McDowell, Nicholas. 2008. *Poetry and Allegiance in the English Civil Wars: Marvell and the Cause of Wit*. Oxford: Oxford University Press.

McKeon, Michael. 1983. Pastoralism, Puritanism, Imperialism, Scientism: Andrew Marvell and the Problem of Mediation. *Yearbook of English Studies* 13: 46–65.

Milton, John. 1953–1982. *Complete Prose Works of John Milton*. Ed. Don M. Wolfe et al. 8 vols. New Haven: Yale University Press.

———. 2008. *The Major Works*. Ed. Stephen Orgel and Jonathan Goldberg. Oxford World's Classics. Oxford: Oxford University Press.

Owen, John. 1862. *The Works of John Owen*. Ed. William H. Goold. 16 vols. Edinburgh: T & T Clark.

Pestana, Carla Gardina. 2004. *The English Atlantic in an Age of Revolution, 1640-1661*. Cambridge, MA: Harvard University Press.

Pittion, Jean-Paul. 2018. Marvell and Protestant Saumur in the 1650s. *Marvell Studies* 3 (1): 5.

Prawdzik, Brendan. 2015. Damon the Mower. *The Literary Encyclopedia*. www.litencyc.com. Accessed 23 Aug 2019.

Randolph, Thomas. 1652. *Poems*. 4th ed. London.

Raymond, Joad. 1999. Framing Liberty: Marvell's "First Anniversary" and the Instrument of Government. *HLQ* 62 (3/4): 313–350.

Rymer, Thomas. 1737–1745. *Rymer's Foedera*. 10 vols. The Hague.

Smith, Nigel. 2010. *Andrew Marvell: The Chameleon*. New Haven: Yale University Press.

Theocritus. 2015. *Theocritus. Moschus. Bion*. Ed and trans. Neil Hopkinson. Loeb Classical Library 28. Cambridge, MA: Harvard University Press.

Trapnell, Anna. 1654. *The Cry of a Stone, Or a Relation of Something Spoken in Whitehall by Anna Trapnell, Being in Visions of God*. London.

Virgil. 1916. *Eclogues. Georgics. Aeneid: Books 1-6*. Trans. H. Rushton Fairclough. Revised by G. P. Goold. Loeb Classical Library 63. Cambridge, MA: Harvard University Press.

von Maltzahn, Nicholas. 2005. *An Andrew Marvell Chronology*. New York: Palgrave Macmillan.

Whitelocke, Bulstrode. 1855. *A Journal of the Swedish Embassy in the Years 1653 and 1654*. 2 vols. London: Longman.

Wilson, G.E. 1970. A Characteristic of Vaughan's Style and Two Meditative Poems: "Corruption" and "Day of Judgement". *Style* 4 (2): 119–131.

Winship, Michael P. 2004. Oxenbridge, John. *ODNB*.

Winstanley, Gerrard. 1652. *The Law of Freedom in a Platform, or, True Magistracy Restored*. London.

Woolrych, Austin. 2002. *Britain in Revolution: 1625–1660*. Oxford: Oxford University Press.

7

'His anger reached that rage which passed his art': England, the Netherlands, and the Baltic, 1659–1667

> This day, his Majesty, Charles II came to London, after a sad and long exile and calamitous suffering both of the King and Church, being seventeen years. This was also his birthday, and with a triumph of above 20,000 horse and foot, brandishing their swords, and shouting with inexpressible joy; the ways strewn with flowers, the bells ringing, the streets hung with tapestry, fountains running with wine; the Mayor, Aldermen, and all the companies, in their liveries, chains of gold, and banners; Lords and Nobles, clad in cloth of silver, gold, and velvet; the windows and balconies, all set with ladies; trumpets, music, and myriads of people flocking, even so far as from Rochester, so as they were seven hours in passing the city, even from two in the afternoon till nine at night. (Evelyn 1901, 1:322)

Thus did the diarist John Evelyn record the return of the king on 29 May 1660, as well as the holiday mood which accompanied the end of the Commonwealth and the restoration of Stuart monarchy. A few weeks before, on the first of May, the king's Declaration from Breda had been read in Parliament and supply voted for bringing him in, occasioning 'Great joy ... at London: and at night more bonfires than ever, and ringing of bells and drinking of the King's health upon their knees in the streets', according to Evelyn's more famous counterpart Samuel Pepys. To which Pepys added that 'everybody seems to be very joyful in the business—insomuch that our sea-commanders now begin to say so too, which a week ago they would not do' (*Pepys*, 2 May 1660). Just two months earlier, on 6 March, Pepys had heard from his patron Sir Edward Montagu 'that there was great endeavours to bring in the Protector again; but he [Montagu] told me, too, that he did believe it would not last long if he were brought in; no, nor the King neither (though he seems to think that he will come in), unless he carry himself very soberly and well.… Everybody now drinks the King's health without any fear', Pepys remarked, 'whereas before it was very private that a man dare do it'. The question with which this chapter begins, then, is how to explain the apparent political sea change in the spring of 1660, how the raising of toasts to Charles Stuart spread from the private houses of closet royalists to the streets of London and indeed across the three kingdoms of England, Scotland, and Ireland. This is also, of course, to ask how Marvell, late a member of Cromwell's government, navigated the shifts and eddies in political life to become a dedicated MP for his hometown of Hull and a leading writer of oppositional satire in the decade after the Restoration.

The Collapse of the Commonwealth and the Restoration of Monarchy

Upon succeeding his father as Lord Protector, Richard Cromwell summoned a new Parliament, which was seated on 27 January 1659. It was to this Third Protectorate Parliament that Andrew Marvell was first elected MP for Hull, having been made a free burgess of the Hull Corporation at the behest of his brother-in-law Edmund Popple the previous December (*P&L*, 2:372). The Hull Corporation was the unitary authority for the borough. Its recognition of Marvell as a freeman or free burgess—one enjoying the rights and privileges of citizens of the borough, despite Marvell's not being resident there— was preliminary to his election. This Parliament was short-lived: army grandees forced Richard to dissolve it in April when it appeared that republicans in Parliament were moving to retake control of the militia and restore the Commonwealth. But the army proved divided against itself and the expectations of its more radical faction deeply unrealistic. So it fell out that the grandees were pressured by the rank-and-file to recall the Rump Parliament, which on 7 May declared 'that the nation should be governed in the way of a Commonwealth, without a King, single person, or House of Lords' (Ludlow 1894, 2:83). When the Rump failed to heed the army's petitions, it was prevented from sitting and ultimately expelled in an army coup d'état of 13 October.

The political floundering of Parliament and the army in London was closely followed by General George Monck, the commander-in-chief of English forces in Scotland (he would later have a prominent role in Marvell's satires on the second Anglo-Dutch War). With the benefit of hindsight, it is perhaps too easy to see Monck's choices, which would ultimately lead to the restoration of monarchy, as more purposive than they likely were. And indeed, it was ostensibly in support of the distressed Rump that Monck crossed the Tweed on 2 January 1660 at the head of 5000 foot troops and 2000 horse. Shortly after the expulsion of the Rump, Monck had written the military junta in London, condemning his fellow officers for their 'late violent proceedings upon the Parliament of England' and entreating that they 'would speedily invite the members of Parliament to return to the discharge of their duties in that freedom and liberty in which the supreme authority of these nations ought to sit' (Monck 1714, 12-13). Instead, the ruling council of officers mobilised regiments to neutralise Monck's threatened intervention. A bloody internecine clash was only avoided through Monck's alliance with Lord Fairfax, Marvell's patron, who raised the northern countryside and took the garrison at York without a blow in the wake of widespread defection and desertion in the opposing army.

The way south was opened to Monck and his troops, and they arrived at Westminster on 2 February, by which time the beleaguered military government had been forced to recall the Rump once more. But the ground was now cracking beneath the Commonwealth: the press was rife with petitions from the provinces calling for a free Parliament. On 10 February, Lord Fairfax joined the good and great of Yorkshire in subscribing a petition for the recalling of the Long Parliament or the election of a new without qualifying tests and threatening to refuse to pay taxes in the interim. Desperately clinging to its vanishing authority, the Rump ordered Monck to bring the City of London to heel and issued writs for the arrest of petitioners. But by 21 February, Monck had seen enough to know which way the wind was blowing, forcibly restoring the 73 surviving MPs purged in 1648. With adherents of the Good Old Cause now outflanked by moderates, Parliament voted on 16 March to dissolve itself and for the calling and holding of a new Parliament on 25 April, all but assuring the return of the king.

To the question of political sea change, then, we might well give a Hobbesian answer. 'The sovereignty is the soul of the Commonwealth', Hobbes wrote in *Leviathan* (1651), 'which once departed from the body, the members do no more receive their motion from it' (114). The political chaos of the months following Cromwell's death effectively absolved subjects of their obedience to the government established—indeed, sovereign power was transferred no fewer than six times between September 1658 and April 1660—leaving the restoration of monarchy the only viable option for securing public safety. But the fact remains that the Commonwealth never enjoyed more than minority support. The 'marvellous providences' of Cromwellian rule convinced many who had called Oliver 'no better than a traitorous hypocrite', as the Presbyterian divine Richard Baxter put it, that they owed Richard their subjection (Baxter 1696, Bk. 1, Pt. 1, 100). The Rump was another story, a self-interested oligarchy 'masquerading' as the people's representatives. Having been returned to power in May 1659 'by exploiting the radical enthusiasms of soldiers and sectaries', the Rump became 'doubly obnoxious to the Parliamentarian gentry … who had never aimed further than a limited or "mixed" monarchy, and hated swordsmen, regicides, fanatics and all other disrupters of social and political order' (Woolrych 1958, 608). Choking deficits, army arrears, rising prices, tax strikes, these only deepened the political dislocation of 1659-60 and hastened the collapse of the Commonwealth.

The king's Declaration from Breda also did much to ease fears of retribution and religious persecution in the event that Charles Stuart returned. To 'all our subjects, of what degree or quality soever', the king promised 'a free and general pardon … excepting only such persons as shall hereafter be excepted by Parliament'. 'And because the passion and uncharitableness of the times have produced several opinions in religion', the declaration went on state, 'we do declare a liberty to tender consciences, and that no man shall be disquieted or called in question for differences of opinion in matters of religion, which do not disturb the peace of the kingdom; and that we shall be ready to consent to such an Act of Parliament, as, upon mature deliberation, shall be offered to us, for the full granting of indulgence' (*ConstDoc*, 465-6). The caveats in the tail of these promises of grace would prove more significant than perhaps even Charles anticipated. But such assurances were enough to move the Convention Parliament, which was duly called after the Long Parliament dissolved itself on 16 March, to vouchsafe its readiness 'immediately [to] apply ourselves to the preparing of these things' and to appoint an embassy to bring the king home (*HPHC*, 1:8).

MP, Committee-Man, and Diplomat

Having been unseated by the dissolution of Richard's Parliament and the recalling of the Rump, Marvell was returned as MP for Hull in the Convention Parliament with 141 votes, polling second to John Ramsden's 227. In this sense and capacity, he was party to the king's restoration, though it was not just royalists who now put their hopes in Charles Stuart—while die-hard republicans could only expect to be left out in the cold (or worse), a wide and varied spectrum of political and religious interests in 1660 perforce looked to the king for healing and settling. Expressions of loyalism at the Restoration were tactical and often necessary for those who had accommodated with the

Interregnum and its various regimes. In his constituency letters to the Hull Corporation, Marvell typically adopts the politic language of the House in giving reports of 'his Majesty', which can make gleaning his personal attitude towards the monarch difficult to gauge. In the *Rehearsal Transpros'd*, however, Marvell several times refers to the king's restoration as 'happy' and 'miraculous' (*PW*, 1:90, 192, 261). Proponents of a Whig Marvell are of course right to observe in these pamphlets Marvell's strategic support for the king's Declaration of Indulgence in the teeth of an intolerant Parliament and persecuting bishops, and that the whole gambit of fashioning religious polemic as dramatic burlesque seems meant to attract the support of courtiers and coffeehouse wits (see Keeble 1999). But in some of Marvell's earliest and—by his standards—most candid constituency letters, there appear signs of Marvell's readiness to accept the Restoration and moreover of his faith in Charles's beneficence, a faith greater, it would seem, than that which he lodged in Parliament.

In his first surviving letter as MP, dated 17 November 1660, Marvell wrote to 'the right wor[shipful] Christopher Richardson, Mayor, and the Aldermen his Brethren, of Kingston upon Hull', advising them of Parliament's fresh slate of business following a long recess. Towards its close, he foresees that Parliament will soon make effective its earlier vote to raise the king's revenue to £1,200,000 per annum. 'I do not love to write so much of this money news', he confesses, 'But I think you have observed that Parliaments have been always made use of to that purpose, and though we may buy gold too dear yet we must at any rate be glad of peace, freedom, and good conscience' (*P&L*, 2:3). On the 29th, the day after the king's mooted religious settlement was scuttled in Parliament, Marvell writes with yet greater expectation of the king, 'We must henceforth rely only upon his Majesty's goodness who I must needs say hath hitherto been more ready to give than we to receive' (2:6). Marvell's commentators have sometimes given the impression that he entered the Restoration as some kind of Machiavel, hiding his commonwealth stripes in order to oppose the new regime from within. But to imagine Marvell's politics c. 1660 in this way seems not entirely in keeping with the evidence or indeed with political reality. In the Horatian Ode, Marvell had wrestled from what we might think of as his grief over the regicide a way of making accommodation with Cromwell and the republic. 'The First Anniversary' shows him a willing mouthpiece and mythologist of Cromwellian rule. In 1658, he lamented the death of Oliver Cromwell and welcomed, but surely with half a heart, Richard's succession, only to withdraw the publication of that piece as the political calculus rapidly shifted. The republican experiment having crashed and burned, there were no real alternatives to recalling the exiled king, and what was the lesson of the Ode if not the madness of blaming or resisting the force of providence.

Notwithstanding Marvell's energy and diligence in representing the interests of his hometown—his 294 letters to the Hull Corporation are the fullest record we have of constituency work in this period (see Keeble 1990; Seaward 2019)—the holiday mood is not likely to have lasted long for Marvell. While there was honour in being an MP, he had risen quickly in John Thurloe's service and might reasonably have hoped to become a senior secretary or diplomat had the Protectorate endured; he had little traction with the restored court. Certainly, the pay was worse. The £200 per annum he had earned as a secretary for foreign tongues was seven or eight times the average wages of a skilled tradesman; for his services as MP, the Hull Corporation paid him 6s. 8d. (6 shillings and 8 pence) per day of parliamentary attendance, or about £23 a year. He would soon be assigned a range of committee work, little of which called on his particular talents as had his linguistic and diplomatic occupations. In November 1660, for instance, he was named to committees for bills related to settling the militia; endowing vicarages; examining petitions; preventing the voluntary separation and living apart of married persons; settling the debts of the Earl of Cleveland; and so on (see *Chronology*, 61). Such work was not without consequence, but it was hardly glamorous. Did Marvell feel peripheral to the new centres of power and influence?

Perhaps the most consequential bill on which Marvell worked under the Convention Parliament was the Worcester House Declaration, passage of which would have made effectual the king's promise of liberty to tender consciences. Marvell served as teller for the 'Yeas' in a vote of 24 November on bringing the bill to the floor. While not extending toleration as far as had the Protectoral Church, the king's proposals for a religious settlement were an attempt to reconcile moderate episcopal and Presbyterian opinion. They would have limited the influence of bishops within the restored episcopal Church; reintroduced a revised Book of Common Prayer while leaving its use to the discretion of ministers; and indulged the omission of those ceremonies deemed indifferent to salvation (the series of negotiations surrounding the Declaration are extensively discussed in Baxter 1696, 1.2.229-79). Such an agreement would have brought many Puritan godly into conformity, leaving Roman Catholics to one side and hotter Puritans to the other. The bill's reading on 28 November provoked 'the greatest dispute of any [parliamentary legislation] yet, and with much vehemency'; ultimately it was defeated, 183-157 (see Till 1997, at 226). Decisive in its demise was the counterintuitive alliance of the Independents ('the old Commonwealth Party') with the Cavaliers in a bid by Independents to prevent the Church's consolidation against unconformable dissenters. It was better for them that the Presbyterians remained on the outside looking in; there was safety in numbers (Winship 2018, 205). 'So there is an end of that bill', Marvell wrote to the Corporation, 'and for those excellent things therein' (*P&L*, 2:6). Marvell's evident disappointment in the bill's failure is consistent with his enduring support for a broad national church and his defence of 'sober liberty', from the Interregnum to as late as the mid-1670s, when the collapse of the tolerationist 'Cabal' government raised the spectre of a 'popish' church-state. Only in the last years of his life did Marvell abandon a position of moderate reform for one of outright opposition to and independence from the Church of England (see Connell 2019; Keeble and Harris 2019).

The failure to achieve a comprehensive church settlement at the outset of the Restoration is indicative of the splintering of consensus that would soon take hold in spite of the decade's auspicious beginnings and the new government's official policy of indemnity and oblivion. To the courtiers, politicians, and churchmen returning from exile, forgiving and forgetting was not the balm they desired, nor perhaps did they think erasing the past what their enemies deserved. A week after the Worcester House bill was voted down, on 4 December, the House exactingly engaged its power of memory in ordering 'That the several bodies of Oliver Cromwell, John Bradshaw, Henry Ireton, and Thomas Pride, be taken out of their graves, drawn on a hurdle to Tyburn, there to be hanged up from ten o'clock till sun-setting, and then buried under the gallows' (*HPHC*, 1:25). After their symbolic hanging, the corpses of Cromwell, Bradshaw, and Ireton were desecrated, their heads severed and placed on a twenty-foot spike above Westminster Hall where they would remain for more than two decades as grisly reminders of the reward for treason and rebellion.

These reprisals touched close to home for Marvell in the arrest of his Protectoral colleague John Milton, who was seized and imprisoned by the sergeant-at-arms of the Commons on 13 September. Milton had so far escaped being named among the exceptions to the king's general pardon, though a royal proclamation of 13 August had called for the suppression of two books written by Milton, *Eikonoklastes* and *Pro Populo Anglicano Defensio*, said to contain 'sundry treasonable passages against us and our government, and most impious endeavours to justify the horrid and unmatchable murther of our late dear father, of glorious memory' (*A Proclamation*, 1660). Some days later, several copies of these books were burned at the Sessions House in the Old Bailey by the common hangman. According to Milton's nephew, Edward Phillips, Marvell was foremost among those in Parliament and the Privy Council who came to the blind poet and provocateur's defence following his arrest; Phillips credits Marvell with making 'a considerable party' for his uncle (Darbishire 1932, 74). Milton was released on 15 December, and two days later Marvell continued to exert himself on Milton's behalf, complaining in Parliament of his excessive jailer's fees. Phillips's recollection may catch something of Milton's gratitude, Marvell's loyalty remaining vivid in Phillips's mind more than thirty years after the fact (his account of Milton's life was published in 1694). It would be nice if Milton had perhaps found occasion to memorialise such gratitude in verse: what would we give for a sonnet to Marvell? Moreover, what would Marvell have given? Such a gesture no doubt would have cost Milton less than the good offices done by Marvell cost him. As we will see, one of the chief tactics of Marvell's enemies in the debate over toleration was to associate him with Milton and rebellion, indeed to insinuate that Milton actually wrote his pamphlets, that Marvell was his minion. Marvell's defence of himself against these charges in the second part of *RT*, and his commendatory poem on *Paradise Lost*, are edgier performances than has been thought.

Edgy is also an apt way of describing the political atmosphere which came in with the election of the Cavalier Parliament, so-called for its hard Anglican and royalist majority, which first assembled in May 1661, and would not be dissolved until January 1679. Picking up where the Convention Parliament had left off in rejecting the Worcester House proposals, from 1661 to 1665 the House drafted and passed a series of penal statutes against nonconformists which came to be known (not altogether justly) as the Clarendon Code, after the king's first minister, Edward Hyde, Earl of Clarendon. The Corporation Act (1661) required all municipal officials to take Anglican communion, effectively disbarring Roman Catholics, Presbyterians, Independents, and those who belonged to smaller nonconformist groups from public office. The Act of Uniformity (1662) tightened the accepted forms of ministering within the Established Church, resulting in the expulsion of over 2,000 clergymen. The Conventicle Act (1664) forbade religious assemblies (conventicles) of more than five people other than immediate family outside the Church of England. The Five Mile Act (1665) prohibited ejected ministers from living within five miles of a parish from which they had been expelled. The vehemence with which high churchmen like Samuel Parker defended and enforced these statutes Marvell contemptuously ascribed to what he called 'push-pin divinity'. For such men 'would persuade princes that *there cannot be a pin pulled out of the Church but the State immediately totters*', though this pin '*signifies nothing in itself, but what the Commander pleases*, that even by the Church which commands it, is *declared to have nothing of religion in it* …' (*PW*, 1:109-10). Marvell's counter to such conformist zeal would be to paint arrogant, self-serving, intolerant divines of Parker's stripe as the true fanatics and moreover the true threat to the commonweal.

The fashioning of an official policy of religious intolerance by a revanchist Parliament would have depressed but not surprised Marvell, though as it turned out he would be absent from Parliament during much of the time this policy was being implemented. From May 1662 to April 1663, Marvell was posted in the Netherlands under the instructions of the Earl of Carlisle, Charles Howard, and Sir George Downing, Charles II's resident in the Hague. Only a few months after resuming his duties as MP, Marvell was appointed Carlisle's secretary in a Baltic embassy which lasted from August 1663 to January 1665. The first of these missions was of a decidedly clandestine nature, and Marvell came close to losing his seat through the Corporation's displeasure at his neglect of parliamentary business and his failure to explain himself. Marvell was acquainted with Downing from his time as a foreign secretary. Downing had been the Protectorate's man in the Hague and a zealous spy for Marvell's boss John Thurloe. As shrewd as he was self-serving, Downing had made overtures of his willingness to serve the king as early as March 1660. That May he was elevated to a knighthood and quickly set about demonstrating his worth to the new regime, telling Chancellor Clarendon, in a letter of 21 October 1661, 'if my father were in the way I would not avoid him for my loyalty' (see Catterall 1912, 269). Having hunted Cavaliers for Cromwell, he now set his nets for regicides sheltering in the Dutch Republic. (For Downing's life, see Scott 2008).

In this line of work, as Nigel Smith was the first to surmise, the MP was evidently Downing's servant: Marvell spoke Dutch, had travelled in the Netherlands, and was experienced in the art of discretion (recall the description of Marvell in Saumur as a 'notable English-Italo Machiavellian'). Smith suggests that he was acting as a double agent, tipping off old Cromwellian friends while he was employed to sniff out republican plots among English exiles (see *Chameleon*, 170-2). But it seems likely he had made a deal with the government or with certain of its ministers. In a letter to Hull Trinity House dated 8 May 1662, Marvell hastily explains that, on account of 'some persons too potent for me to refuse and who have great direction and influence upon my counsels and fortune, I am obliged to go beyond sea', and that the guild's interests will be looked after by his counterpart Colonel Gilby and by the Earl of Carlisle (*P&L*, 2:250). Carlisle was a member of the Privy Council, and Downing happened to be his brother-in-law. We know Downing was looking for effective assistance from Whitehall in 1661-1662—indeed, he wanted Clarendon to send over some assassins to take care of the fugitive regicides John Okey, Miles Corbet, and John Barkstead, sparing Downing the trouble of getting warrants from the reluctant Estates General (see Catterall 1912,

275-6). Presumably, this was not Marvell's function, or we have greatly misjudged his skillset. But for an intelligence operation, he might be useful, and Downing apparently thought he could trust him. Whether Downing was holding something over Marvell's head from Protectorate days is an open question, but from Marvell's letter, we do get a hint of coercion. In any case, he doesn't ask permission from the burghers of Hull, and he goes in a hurry.

Whatever deal Marvell had struck in going to the Hague, its upside was his appointment as secretary to Carlisle on the embassy to Russia, Sweden, and Denmark the following year. This was an important and well-publicised mission, and this time Marvell went 'with his Majesty's good liking, by leave from the House and with the assent of our Bench' (*P&L*, 2:254). We thus have a relatively full sense of what the Baltic voyage entailed, and indeed, an account of the embassy was later published by Guy Miège, who was under-secretary to Marvell on this occasion. Carlisle went to Moscow with the aim of re-establishing the trading privileges of the English Company at Archangel, the chief seaport of early modern Russia. The English had formerly traded there under a favourable tax immunity which had been vacated by the tsar in the time of the late civil war. For their part, the Russians were eager to secure English support in their war with Poland. In terms of its measurable outcomes, the embassy was a failure: neither side got what they wanted; afterward the tsar complained to the king about the insolence of his ambassadors and the English of their uncivil treatment by the tsar. But such diplomatic missions were as much political theatre as they were about specific quid pro quos, and the almost Swiftian absurdity of the wrangling over protocol Miège reports can be understood as a struggle to assert authority and prestige between the factotums of two insecure regimes (see Holberton 2019).

Linguistic and cultural differences were also a source of tension and diplomatic breakdown. As secretary, Marvell helped prepare letters and speeches for Carlisle to present to the tsar. Carlisle would read the speech in English, which the tsar's interpreter would translate sentence by sentence; a copy of the same speech in Latin was then presented to the tsar which served as the document of record for negotiations. It was the early modern equivalent of diplomacy by Google Translate, and little more reliable. For all Marvell's linguistic abilities, his Russian was hardly better than the next person's was, and none could say how faithfully the tsar's interpreter translated Carlisle's speeches. Carlisle himself had little Latin and may not have grasped the finer points of the language in which Marvell officially cast the embassy's business. No better were the Russian commissioners, who, Marvell thought, either wilfully or ignorantly misconstrued his meaning. Indeed, this provides one of the more memorable episodes in Miège's account, drawing together, and in a most surprising context—the glittering court of Tsar Alexey Michailovitz—Marvell's humanism, his irony, his ability to put on voices, and his astonishing grasp of the politics of language (see further von Maltzahn 2018 and Holberton 2019).

At issue was the English ambassador's styling of the tsar *Illustrissimus* ('most Illustrious') as opposed to *Serenissimus* ('most Serene'), as he had called Charles II, the former term of address, the tsar's commissioners complained, being 'much inferior to the dignity and grandeur' of his tsarskoy majesty (Miège 1669, 195). Marvell's reply on Carlisle's behalf (found on pages 215-19 of Miège) is a tour de force which wages international politics at the level of Lily's grammar and Erasmian copiousness, its tone couched, in a preview of Marvell's handling of Samuel Parker, 'betwixt jest and earnest'. 'Seeing we must here from affairs of state, fall into grammatical contests concerning the Latin tongue', Marvell's retort to the charge of mis-titling begins by making a show of how much higher a term is *Illustrissimus* compared to *Serenissimus*:

> For if the Sun be, as he is, the first fountain of light, and poets in their expressions (as is well known) are higher by much than those that write in prose, what else is it when Ovid in the [second book] of the *Metamorphoses* saith of Phoebus speaking with Phaeton, *Qui terque quaterque concutiens Illustre caput* [thrice and again he shook his illustrious head], and the Latin orators, as Pliny [*Epistles*] 139, when they would say the highest thing that can be expressed on any subject word it thus, *Nihil Illustrius dicere possum* [I can say nothing more illustrious]. So that hereby may appear to his tsarskoy majesty's near boyars and counsellors what diminution there is to his tsarskoy majesty (which far be it from my thoughts) if I appropriate *Serenissimus* to my master and *Illustrissimus* to him than which *nihil dici potest Illustrius* [nothing could be more illustrious].

Only in Latin's declining state, 'when there scarce could be found out words enough to supply the modern ambition of titles', did the appellation *Serenissimus* come to be used of princes, as the Russian commissioners might know if they understood 'the nicety of that most eloquent language'. But even were it allowed, which Marvell denies, that *Illustris* were 'by modern use … depressed from the undoubted superiority that it had of *Serenus* in the purest antiquity, yet being added in the transcendent degree to the word *Emperor*, the highest denomination that a prince is capable of, it becomes of the same value. So that to interpret *Illustrissimus* unto diminution is to find a positive in a superlative, and in the most orient light to seek for darkness'. Following a further set of points relating to the tsar's titles in High Dutch, Marvell brings this facetious discourse to a close by insisting (still of course affecting to speak for Carlisle), 'I would have used *Serenissimus* a hundred times concerning his tsarskoy majesty, had I thought it would have pleased him better', and that 'his majesty [Charles II] will upon the first information from me style him *Serenissimus*'. 'And so God grant all happiness to his most High, most Potent, most Illustrious, and most Serene tsarskoy majesty, and that the friendship may daily increase betwixt his said majesty and his most Serene majesty my master'.

Perhaps it is understandable that Carlisle did not come away with the prize of restored trading privileges with Russia. From Moscow, the embassy progressed to Riga, Stockholm, and Copenhagen, where the English found easier welcome and Marvell's fluency in French and Latin readier admiration. Bad weather prevented their sailing home from Copenhagen, forcing the worryingly under-supplied embassy to travel overland via Hamburg, Münster, Cologne, and Brussels to the French port of Calais, whence they arrived in London on 30 January 1665. The embassy's duration thus much exceeded Marvell's estimate of a year, and the stress of the mission, especially in its protracted Russian phase, clearly took its toll, as we may judge from Marvell's drawing a pistol on an unreasonable wagoner in Buxtehude (near Bremen), nearly precipitating a riot (see *Chronology*, 87-8). Marvell's diplomatic career was at an end; but his assault on the wagoner serves to introduce the final phase of this literary life, Marvell's resort to the paper bullets of satire and animadversion in combating what he called 'the quintessence of arbitrary malice'.

Plague, Fire, and War: Marvell's Instructions to a Painter

The Baltic embassy had hurried home under threat of renewed conflict with the Dutch, and some three weeks after its arrival in London, on 22 February, war was declared in defence of the honour, safety, and trade of the nation from England's rivals across the Channel. Tensions with the United Provinces had been rising year on year over trading rights on the west coast of Africa, with both sides engaging in blockades and seizures of contested settlements in Guinea. Following a raid by the Dutch admiral Michel de Ruyter in the course of which, Pepys heard, the Dutch fleet proceeded 'to take whatever we have – forts, goods, ships and men – and tied our men back to back and threw them all into the sea – even women and children also' (*Pepys*, 23 February 1665), those tensions burst into open war, and into waters much closer to home. The

Battle of Lowestoft, fought some forty miles off the Suffolk coast on 13 June, was nearly a decisive victory for the English fleet under the command of the Duke of York, resulting in the loss of 26 Dutch ships, set against that of a single English vessel. Neglected in panegyrics of the great victory was the failure of the English command to pursue the Dutch in retreat, a decision evidently taken on false authority by the Duke's groom of the bedchamber while the Duke was asleep. With the opportunity to review its tactics and refurbish its squadrons with heavier ships, the Dutch turned tables on the English, inflicting heavy losses against a divided English fleet in the Four Days' Battle of June 1666. With supply running short and the fleet laid up, Charles had little option but to open peace talks on conditions set by the Dutch. When the leaders of Holland discerned Charles's intent to cosy up to their sometime ally Louis XIV of France in hope of securing a more favourable peace, an aggressive counterstroke against the English was launched. On 13 June 1667, Admiral de Ruyter led a nervy raid on the English fleet moored at Chatham, sailing up the mouth of the Thames, destroying a dozen English ships, and towing away the *Royal Charles*, the ship on which the king had sailed for Dover. It was a total humiliation. (On the Second Anglo-Dutch War, see Hutton 1985; Rogers 1970; Jones 1996).

The maladministration of the Dutch War was set against the domestic calamities of plague and fire. Outbreaks of plague were of course a common if dreaded occurrence in early modern Europe, and we have already taken note of the arrival of plague in Cambridge and Hull during Marvell's time at university. But the scale and devastation of the epidemic which swept across England in 1665-1666, and which afflicted above all the densely populated capital, could only be described by contemporaries as Biblical. Pepys first mentions 'Great fears of the sickness here in the City' on 30 April 1665. By mid-July, the death toll was over 1000 a week, by mid-August over 3000, then 6000, then as high (Pepys estimated on 31 August) as 10,000 When at last the infection abated with the onset of winter, perhaps 70,000 Londoners had died from plague and another 30,000 from endemic diseases, or nearly a quarter of the city's inhabitants (see Shrewsbury 1970, 476, 487). The staggering loss of life would prove to be a harbinger of further destruction to come, this time to the fabric of the city itself. In a matter of four days, from the early morning hours of Sunday 2 September 1666 to the following Thursday, the Great Fire of London razed the city centre in a crescent extending from the Tower of London to as far north from the river as Cripplegate and as far west as Temple Bar. 'The burning still rages', a stunned John Evelyn recorded in his diary that Wednesday evening, 'and it is now gotten as far as the Inner Temple. All Fleet Street, the Old Bailey, Ludgate Hill, Warwick

Lane, Newgate, Paul's Chain, Watling Street, now flaming, and most of it reduced to ashes; the stones of [St] Paul's flew like grenados, the melting lead running down the streets in a stream, and the very pavements glowing with fiery redness, so as no horse, nor man, was able to tread on them, and the demolition had stopped all the passages, so that no help could be applied. The eastern wind still more impetuously driving the flames forward. Nothing but the Almighty power of God was able to stop them; for vain was the help of man' (2:21-2).

It was within this context of curdled hopes for the Restoration and its promise of liberty, abundance, and national regeneration that Marvell composed the linked series of poems known as the 'Advices to a Painter'. Marvell's authorship of 'The Last Instructions' (c. September 1667) is undisputed; current scholarship accepts that Marvell was involved in writing the 'Second' (c. April 1666) and the 'Third Advice to a Painter' (c. January 1667), though their unevenness as compared to 'The Last Instructions' leaves room for the involvement of other hands (see *Poems*, 323-8). Increasingly, however, the Second and Third Advice are treated as Marvell's work. These poems were clearly part of a well-organised propaganda campaign against the Earl of Clarendon and the conduct of the Dutch war; manuscript copies of the Second and Third Advice are relatively abundant, and they were also clandestinely printed (see Dzelzainis 2007). The longer, more daring, and more difficult 'Last Instructions' seems to have been confined to a much smaller coterie, with only a handful of manuscript copies surviving.

The Dutch war and the catastrophes which surrounded it obviously furnish much of Marvell's subject matter in these poems, but their satiric impetus and their conceit of 'advice to a painter' arise in response to other poetry, namely Edmund Waller's 'Instructions to a Painter for the Drawing of the Posture and Progress of His Majesty's Forces at Sea, under the Command of His Highness Royal; Together with the Battle and Victory Obtained over the Dutch, June 3, 1665', the fulsomeness of Waller's title giving some indication of its over-the-top praise for the Duke of York and the partiality of its description of the Battle of Lowestoft. Taking a longer view of the war's progress, Marvell transforms Wallerian panegyric into mock heroics and at the same insists on the veracity of so seeing the persons and events conjured by his speaking pictures. The brilliance of these performances was for a long time clouded by the perception that Marvell's poetic gifts were sacrificed on the altar of politics. 'Coming from the subtle and meditative detachment of the lyrics', wrote George deForest Lord in 1967, 'one finds the commitment to political action a real shock ... It is perhaps even harder to believe that a lyric poet of such unexcelled grace and sensitivity could have produced such a poem as *Last*

Instructions to a Painter, a poem that is often derisive, tendentious, cynical, and ugly' (209). Such shocks and disbeliefs are no longer as strongly felt, as more recent work has assiduously attended to the ideological contours and civil war contexts of Marvell's lyrics of the late 1640s and early 1650s. But it is not just responsiveness to politics which bridges the lyrics and the satires; for it is the Advices to a Painter, and above all 'The Last Instructions', that are heir to the perspectival poetics showcased to such superb effect in 'Upon Appleton House'.

Each of the Advices begins with ironic comment on the medium and technique appropriate to the painter's representing what the poet would show, in contrast to the artist instructed by Waller. 'Nay, Painter, if thou dar'st design that fight / Which Waller only courage had to write', Marvell drolls at the outset of the Second Advice,

> If thy bold hand can without shaking draw
> What ev'n the actors trembled when they saw;
> Enough to make thy colours change like theirs,
> And all thy pencils bristle like their hairs;
> First in fit distance of the prospect vain,
> Paint Allin tilting at the cost of Spain ...
> (ll. 1-8)

Waller's poem started by instructing the painter to limn the opposing British and Dutch fleets, a tableau surmounted by a heroic portrait of the Duke of York 'bestride the ocean' (l. 25), his 'armed hand' extended in a gesture of mastery reaching from the English Channel to the farthest Indies (ll. 27-8). Waller then calls on the painter's 'bold pencil' to illustrate the hope and courage spread 'Through the whole navy, by that hero led' (ll. 15-16). Notably, however, in describing the course of the battle, Waller abandons the trope of portraiture, begging the painter's excuse '... if I have awhile / Forgot thy art, and used another style; / For, though you draw armed heroes as they sit, / The task in battle does the Muses fit' (ll. 287-90). Marvell's exordium argues that the poet usurps the painter in Waller's poem because to draw the scene would give the lie to Waller's honeyed panegyric. A different kind of boldness is asked of Marvell's painter: 'to make thy colours change like theirs', that is, like the sailors who blanched at the fight. To denote the battle truly will make the hairs of the painter's brushes stand on end, Marvell says, the better to represent the frazzled English seamen.

In the sequel, which turns its attention from Lowestoft to the Four Days' Battle, Marvell signals the need for a change of painters to match the change of generals in the war, the English fleet having come under the joint command of the Duke of Albemarle (Monck) and Prince Rupert. 'Lely's a Dutchman, danger in his art: / His pencils may intelligence impart' (ll. 2-4), the speaker of the Third Advice reasons warily, alluding to the vividness of the court painter Peter Lely's style, and to the possibility of his being a Dutch agent. A better choice is Richard Gibson, a painter of miniatures and a dwarf:

> Thou Gibson, that among thy navy small
> Of marshalled shells commandest admiral;
> ....
> Come, mix thy water colours, and express,
> Drawing in little, how we do yet less.
> (ll. 5-10)

Gibson's soft and muted colours better suit the anaemic English navy than would Lely's, and his (Gibson's) littleness of stature and perspective likewise conform to the scale of English glory in the war. The 'marshalled shells' of Gibson's command refer to the use of sea shells for mixing paint and are at the same time emblems of maritime vessels, as depicted, for instance, in Botticelli's *Birth of Venus*, with its nude goddess riding a giant scallop shell to shore. Gibson's mock admiralty of the marshalled shells thus provides another fit image of the English command and invites us to imagine the English fleet reduced to the size of scallops, its dominion shrunk from the globe-spanning vision of Waller to the proportions of the bath, or narrow enough anyway to fit into one of Gibson's miniatures.

But Marvell's concern with perspective is not limited to ekphrasis; it is central to Marvell's explanation of the naval, political, and administrative blunders which followed the initial success at Lowestoft. The critical diagnosis comes in the section of 'The Last Instructions' which describes the parliamentary debates over the excise in October and November of 1666. Parliament had already voted the king grants of £2,500,000 and £1,250,000 in 1664 and 1665 to cover the costs of the war. By the third week of September 1666, however, amidst rumours of gross incompetence and malfeasance by the king's ministers, and with the city still in ruin from the Great Fire, the crown was forced to recall Parliament from a long recess to ask for further supply. In response to MPs' groaning on behalf of their constituents, the king made clear 'I do expect it from you, that you will use your utmost endeavours to remove all those false imaginations in the hearts of the people ... of I know not what jealousies and grievances. [...] If the taxes and impositions are heavy upon them, you will put them in mind, that a war with such powerful enemies cannot be maintained without taxes: and I am sure the monies raised thereby come not into my purse' (*HPHC*, 1:100). A grant of £1,800,000 was soon agreed; how to raise it was another question. The government's preferred instrument was a general excise tax, administration of which would have required a vast bureaucracy that consumed much of the revenue it produced, and 'will soon become as so many vermin and caterpillars to devour us', in the words of one contemporary (see Seaward 1989, 262). Marvell describes it as a monster with a 'thousand hands' and 'thousand eyes', the offspring of 'a female harpy' and the excise auditor John Birch, who, 'of his brat enamoured, as't increased, / Buggered in incest with the mongrel beast' (the portrait of Excise may be found at ll. 130-46).

Under the mists of morning, the court supporters of excise pack the House to try and force the bill through before its opponents are fully assembled. Here come the 'early wittols', led by Sir John Denham, next a squadron of 'old courtiers', then 'damning cowards', 'court officers' and 'procurers', 'the troop of Clarendon', 'the lawyers' mercenaries', 'debtors deep', politicos and 'sots', 'the rich', 'the projectors', 'the Eaters [of] Beef', and finally the 'Lords' sons', with Viscount Cornbury (Clarendon's heir) riding a hobby horse at their head. Rushing in to oppose them are 'forward Temple', the 'daring Seymour', 'Keen Whorwood', 'surly Williams', 'Lovelace young', 'Old Waller', and the Montezuma-like Edward Howard, the epithets of course recalling the gods and heroes of classical epic, 'white-armed Hera', 'swift-footed Achilles', 'great-hearted Aeneas'. Of the ensuing clash between these adverse parties, Marvell writes, and this is the key passage:

> Each thinks his person represents the whole
> And with that thought does multiply his soul,
> Believes himself an army, theirs one man
> As eas'ly conquer'd; and, believing, can;
> With heart of bees so full, and head of mites,
> That each, though duelling, a battle fights.
> Such once Orlando, famous in romance,
> Broached whole brigades like larks upon his lance.
> ('The Last Instructions', ll. 269-76)

The disinterestedness of the satire is rather remarkable in the context of the poem's abuse of Clarendon and his party at court ('His minion imps that, in his secret part, / Lie nuzzling at the sacramental war, / Horse-leeches circling at the haemm'rrhoid vein: / He sucks the King, they him, he them again', ll. 495-8). The MPs contesting over the excise on the floor of the Commons are shown to suffer from a quixotic (or rather 'Ariostan') delusion whereby they misapprehend their significance as historical actors—Homeric epithets attach to the immortal characters of the *Iliad* and *Odyssey*, Marvell's to a bunch of MPs destined to oblivion (see Gallagher 2011, at 96)—as well their own greatness relative to their opponents, each thinking himself an army, the other side but 'one man / As eas'ly conquer'd'. Marvell would use a similar device in describing Samuel Parker as 'stretched to such an height in his own fancy, that he could not look down from top to toe but his eyes dazzled at the precipice of his stature', or as suffering a crack in his skull that, 'as in broken looking-glasses, multiplied him in self-conceit and imagination' (*PW*, 1:75-6). Within the Advices, the ramifying of ego also serves to explain British naval failure: from Albemarle's decision to engage the Dutch with a reduced fleet, to the 'culpable unpreparedness' born of English overconfidence which led to the Medway disaster, to the confusions of Chatham dockyard, an utter failure of command despite the presence of multiple commanders. The passage also further upbraids Waller's heroic style, which would make 'a mite / Think he's the image of the infinite', to recall Rochester's 'A Satire against Reason and Mankind' (ll. 76-7), another poem and another poet demystifying of courtly pretension and indeed of all delusions of grandeur. We know Rochester read Marvell's Advices: was he thinking of Marvell's self-aggrandising statesman 'With heart of bees so full, and head of mites' when he wrote that line? Marvell unsparingly deflates Wallerian romance (hence the allusion to *Orlando Furioso*) to the scale of mock-epic, revealing the vertiginous distance between how his subjects see themselves and how we ought to see them.

The sexualised abuse of John Birch, buggered in incest with the mongrel Excise, and of Chancellor Clarendon and his minion imps, points to another of the poem's strategies, its twinning of sexual appetite and enormity with political corruption and dereliction of government (see Zwicker 1990; Riebling 1995). The poem opens with a scabrous sequence of portraits of court figures, the Earl of St Albans, 'full of soup and gold, / The new court's pattern, stallion of the old' (ll. 29-30), the Duchess of York, painted 'with oyster lip, and breath of fame, / Wide mouth, that 'sparagus may well pro-claim' (ll. 61-2), and most arrestingly, the Countess of Castlemaine and her sexually energetic footman. This last portrait displays most clearly a way of seeing alternative to Waller's, one linked to the microscope invoked at the poem's opening: 'to score out our compendious fame', counsels Marvell's speaker, 'With Hooke then, through the microscope, take aim: / Where, like the new Comptroller, all men laugh / To see a tall louse brandish the white staff' (ll. 15-18). One of the most famous illustrations in Robert Hooke's *Micrographia: or Some Physiological Descriptions of Minute Bodies Made by*

Magnifying Glasses, first published in January 1666, was Hooke's drawing of a louse, which folded out to four times the size of the book. Shown clinging to a human hair, it is said to resemble the Comptroller of the Household, who traditionally bore a white staff. It was none other than Peter Lely that Cromwell had (perhaps apocryphally) instructed, 'use all your skill to paint my picture truly like me and not flatter me at all. Remark all these roughnesses, pimples, warts, and everything as you see me'. Marvell's instructions to his painter go further still, urging him to reveal the lousy bodies of courtiers with the enhanced perspective of microscopy. Such looking provides a type for the poem's most scandalous acts of disclosure: peering into the private bedchambers of the good and great at Whitehall, and what's more, daring to probe into their inmost fantasies.

Barbara Villiers had married the royalist lawyer Roger Palmer on 14 April 1659, the bride being not yet nineteen years old (for Villiers's life, see Wynne 2008). By the following summer, the couple were living in King Street, next door to Whitehall palace. On the evening of 13 July 1660, having stayed late at Whitehall writing letters, Pepys heard music coming from the Palmer household, where the king and the Duke of York were being entertained by young Barbara, 'a pretty woman that they have a fancy to, to make her husband a cuckold'. On 7 December 1661, the diarist witnessed the sealing of the letters patent raising Roger Palmer to the Earl of Castlemaine and Baron of Limerick in Ireland; 'but the honour is tied up to the males got of the body of this wife, the Lady Barbary [Barbara], the reason whereof everybody knows'. Barbara had become the king's acknowledged mistress, and was pregnant with their first son, after whose birth Castlemaine would effectively separate from her husband, bearing Charles four more children. Following the king's marriage to Catherine of Braganza in May 1662, he would force his queen to accept his mistress as a lady of the bedchamber, advising Clarendon, amidst much infighting at court, 'whosoever I find to be my Lady Castlemaine's enemy in this matter, I do promise upon my word, to be his enemy as long as I live'. Next to the king, her most ardent appreciator was Peter Lely: she appears in at least ten portraits by Lely, most famously, or indeed infamously, in role portraits which cast her as the pensive Magdalene (c. 1662) and as the Madonna with Child, in a portrait with her infant son by the king, Charles Fitzroy (c. 1664). Popular rumour had it that the king and Lady Castlemaine diverted themselves by chasing a butterfly during the attack on the Medway.

These details help us understand the force and argument of Marvell's portrait of Castlemaine in 'The Last Instructions'. Paint her, Marvell's speaker commands, 'in colours that will hold / (Her, not her picture, for she now grows old):'

She through her lackey's drawers, as he ran,
Discerned love's cause and a new flame began.
Her wonted joys thenceforth, and court, she shuns,
And still within her mind the footman runs:
His brazen calves, his brawny thighs (the face
She slights) his feet shaped for a smoother race.
Poring within her glass she readjusts
Her looks, and oft-tried beauty now distrusts;
Fears lest he scorn a woman once assayed,
And now first wished she e'er had been a maid.
Great Love, how does thou triumph and how reign,
That to a groom couldst humble her disdain!
Stripped to her skin, see how she stooping stands,
Nor scorns to rub him down with those fair hands,
And washing (lest the scent her crime disclose)
His sweaty hooves, tickles him 'twixt the toes.
(ll. 79-96)

In his diary, Pepys frequently laments the king's enthrallment with Castlemaine and hopes for his reformation. Here Marvell partially fulfils such a wish in showing the king shut out and a new lover, the acrobat Jacob Hall, let in to the Countess's charmed circle. Yet her deportment with her lackey proves utterly disgraceful of the king's honour: her love is moved not by virtue or even beauty but by brazen calves, brawny thighs, and above all, by the bulge in Hall's drawers, a vision said to run constantly through the Countess's mind. In these lines, Charles is at once unmanned and indicted for embracing the tutelage of this most base 'counsellor of pleasure', as Pepys referred to Castlemaine and the king's debauched courtiers. The king's 'sceptre and his prick were of a length', to quote Rochester's famous lampoon, 'And she may sway the one who plays with t'other' ('In the Isle of Britain', ll. 11-12). Worse than swayed, he is Castlemaine's cully, his sexual dominion usurped by the acrobat, as indeed the king's sovereignty had been invaded and humiliated by the Dutch raid on the Thames. Thus is de Ruyter's passage upriver portrayed as an Ovidian conquest: 'Through the vain sedge, the bashful nymphs he eyed: / Bosoms, and all which from themselves they hide. / The sun much brighter, and the skies more clear, / He finds the air and all things sweeter here. / The sudden change, and such a tempting sight / Swells his old veins with fresh blood, fresh delight' (ll. 527-32).

But this relatively simple algebra of Jacob-for-Charles is compounded by far deeper and more scandalising laws of substitution. Pictured washing her lover's feet, Marvell's rendering of Castlemaine recalls Lely's modelling her after Mary Magdalene, a blasphemous doubling exceeded only by the doubling of the well-hung groom for the sinful woman's lord and saviour. But Castlemaine has also changed places with her lackey: she rubs down her stallion like a stable boy. Most grotesquely of all, her Magdalene-like laving of her lover's 'sweaty hooves' is undertaken as cover-up, '(lest the scent her crime disclose)'. The 'smoother race' for which Hall's feet are so ideally shaped is evidently sexual servicing of the Countess. The whole is an image of inverted values and disordered appetites in which the king is darkly implicated: his shadow consort figures the misrule of his court and the neglect of duty and country.

In a brilliant piece of design, the satirical portraits of Charles's courtiers with which the poem opens, and in particular the portrait of Castlemaine, are answered at its close by a portrait of the king with another doubled figure: the spectre of a young woman he divines was 'England or the Peace' (l. 906). 'The Peace' seems to refer to the Peace of Breda medal struck to commemorate the settlement of the war with the Dutch. On the front was the head of Charles II wearing a long wig and laureate wreath, on the reverse, Britannia with a spear in her right hand, her left hand resting on a shield. The sitter for the figure of Britannia was Frances Theresa Stuart, a great beauty of the restored court whom the king had fruitlessly pursued, and in this sense also a double for Castlemaine as a rival object of the king's attentions and as the inspiration for art. But unlike Castlemaine, Stuart provides an object lesson in what we might term the politics of the king's touch. Waking from an uneasy dream, Charles confronts a sudden shape with virgin's face raised up by Marvell's painter:

Naked as born, and her round arms behind
With her own tresses, interwove and twined;
Her mouth locked up, a blind before her eyes,
Yet from beneath the veil her blushes rise,
And silent tears her secret anguish speak;
Her heart throbs, and with very shame would break.
The object strange in him no terror moved:
He wondered first, then pitied, then he loved,
And with kind hand does the coy vision press
(Whose beauty greater seemed by her distress):

But soon shrunk back, chilled with her touch so cold,
And th' airy picture vanished from his hold.
In his deep thoughts the wonder did increase,
And he divined 'twas England or the Peace.
(ll. 890-906)

The virgin's abject distress first moves the king to pity and amazement, but through what the poem describes as a sort of affective processing error, these feelings turn into sexual arousal: the trembling body incites the touch of the king's 'kind hand', the adjective functioning as a heavily ironic hinge word. Rather than touching the girl kindly, as befits a gentle person and as befits the circumstance, the king touches her with a sense of entitlement, touches her as one captive to his pleasure (see *OED*, kind, *adj.* and *adv.*, AI3a-b, 'having a claim by birth or inheritance', AII7c, 'Designating a woman who is available to be a person's mistress, lover, or sexual partner'). Her coldness to the touch chills the king's ardour, prompting his recognition of her identity as a representation of England. In this remarkable scene, Marvell endeavours to perform what we recognise as a form of cognitive therapy on the king, to correct his prerogative, to recall him to his duty of kindness. What is required is nothing less than a second restoration, a restoration not so much political but moral, to answer fears 'that the whole kingdom is undone' by plague, fire, and war, trials befitting a new Sodom, as no few of Marvell's godly contemporaries remarked.

Not by accident, then, is the poem's redemptive centre an epyllion relating the valiant behaviour of Captain Archibald Douglas, who refused to abandon his command of the fire-bombed *Royal Oak* in the Battle of the Medway, eulogised by Marvell as a flaming beacon of androgynous purity:

Like a glad lover, the fierce flames he meets,
And tries his first embraces in their sheets.
His shape exact, which the bright flames enfold,
Like the sun's statue stands of burnished gold.
Round the transparent fire about him glows,
As the clear amber on the bee does close,
And, as on angels heads their glories shine,
His burning locks adorn his face divine.
But when in his immortal mind he felt
His altering form and soldered limbs to melt,
Down on the deck he laid himself and died,
With his dear sword reposing by his side,

And on the flaming plank, so rests his head
As one that's warmed himself and gone to bed.
(ll. 677-90)

By now the argument is clear: as Zwicker (1990) observes, 'Douglas is a denial of sexual desire', indeed a denial of sex altogether, and an embodiment of 'bravery and honour', 'fortitude and constancy, virtue in all its complex senses' (100). The married father we know Douglas to have been in life is said to try his first embraces amidst the blazing deck of the *Royal Oak*. But we should not gloss over the erotic heightening Marvell supplies to this reproof of Charles's sensuous court and its cognate failure to regulate and preserve the body politic. Indeed, Marvell's verse here approaches the sensuous exuberance of a Lely painting in its evocation of the handsome and fragile Douglas's demise. Too pure for this world, which seems to demand his sacrifice for its depravity, Douglas's beauty appears the greater to the poet for the distress of his circumstance, thus anticipating in a certain respect the king's response to the bound virgin. In 'Appleton House', the flooded River Wharfe licks its muddy back 'Till as a crystal mirror slick; / Where all things gaze themselves, and doubt / If they be in it or without' (ll. 636-9). The Douglas passage represents such a moment in 'The Last Instructions': regarding it, as we also regard the whole, it is difficult to say where we stand within the poem's argument about 'virtue in all its complex senses'.

This is also to confront an ambiguity about the poem's illocutionary force and indeed about the Advices as a group. The Second and Third Advice look like part of a 'country' campaign against Chancellor Clarendon, corrupt courtiers, and the Naval Administration (the 'country' opposition to the court in the 1660s and 1670s would coalesce into the Whig party in the wake of the Exclusion Crisis of 1679-1681). Clarendon would be the scapegoat of the Medway disaster, forced to resign the seals of his office and flee abroad to escape impeachment. But the Advices are notably exculpatory of Charles himself, and all three poems are framed by envois to the king which conventionally lay blame on wicked ministers and excuse the poet's rough satire as a form of parrhesia or free speaking. 'The Last Instructions' clearly goes far beyond the Second and Third Advice in its criticism of the court, the government, and the king—but the last, longest, most scabrous, and most brilliant of these poems was much restricted in its circulation, making it more of a coterie piece than a state satire meant to influence public opinion much less the monarch it purports to address.

Oft reprinted in the popular collections of 'poems on affairs state' compiled after the Glorious Revolution, the topicality of the Advices has rendered them largely illegible to non-specialist audiences. And though the prejudice against the Restoration satires, which critics under the influence of T. S. Eliot regarded as a betrayal of the lyric Marvell, has abated in its explicitness, the satires are rarely afforded the same kind of aesthetic attention as the lyrics, with a few notable exceptions. This has been to our cost, for we have not sufficiently appreciated how much the court lampoon and indeed the whole tradition of Augustan satire owe to Marvell's example. The state poems include several satires that were variously attributed to Marvell and to the Earl of Rochester, who were great admirers of each other and may have been personally acquainted through their association with Buckingham. From the perspective of literary history, Marvell's reported praise of Rochester is probably truer in reversion: that he was the only man in England that had the true vein of satire.

References

Baxter, Richard. 1696. *Reliquiae Baxterianae: or, Mr Richard Baxter's Narrative of the Most Memorable Passages of His Life and Times.* London.

Catterall, Ralph C. 1912. Sir George Downing and the Regicides. *American Historical Review* 17 (2): 268–289.

Connell, Philip. 2019. Marvell and the Church. In *The Oxford Handbook of Andrew Marvell*, ed. Martin Dzelzainis and Edward Holberton, 128–143. Oxford: Oxford University Press.

Darbishire, Helen, ed. 1932. *The Early Lives of Milton.* London: Constable.

Dzelzainis, Martin. 2007. Andrew Marvell and the Restoration Literary Underground: Printing the Painter Poems. *SC* 22 (2): 395–410.

Evelyn, John. 1901. *The Diary of John Evelyn.* Ed. William Bray. 2 vols. Washington and London: M. Walter Dunne.

Gallagher, Noelle. 2011. "Partial to Some One Side": The Advice-to-a-Painter Poem as Historical Writing. *ELH* 78 (1): 79–101.

History and Proceedings of the House of Commons from the Restoration to the Present Time. 1742. 14 vols. London: Richard Chandler.

Hobbes, Thomas. 1651. *Leviathan, or, The Matter, Form, and Power of a Common-Wealth, Ecclesiastical and Civil.* London.

Holberton, Edward. 2019. Marvell and Diplomacy. In *The Oxford Handbook of Andrew Marvell*, ed. Martin Dzelzainis and Edward Holberton, 96–113. Oxford: Oxford University Press.

Hutton, Ronald. 1985. *The Restoration: A Political and Religious History of England and Wales, 1658-1667.* Oxford: Clarendon Press.

Jones, J.R. 1996. *The Anglo-Dutch Wars of the Seventeenth Century*. London: Longman.

Keeble, N.H. 1990. "I would not tell you any tales": Marvell's Constituency Letters. In *The Political Identity of Andrew Marvell*, ed. Conal Condren and A.D. Cousins, 113–134. Aldershot: Scolar Press.

———. 1999. Why Transprose *The Rehearsal?* In *Marvell and Liberty*, ed. Warren Chernaik and Martin Dzelzainis, 249–268. Basingstoke: Macmillan.

Keeble, N.H., and Johanna Harris. 2019. Marvell and Nonconformity. In *The Oxford Handbook of Andrew Marvell*, ed. Martin Dzelzainis and Edward Holberton, 144–163. Oxford: Oxford University Press.

Lord, George de F. 1967. From Contemplation to Action: Marvell's Poetical Career. *Philological Quarterly* 46 (2): 207–224.

Ludlow, Edmund. 1894. *The Memoirs of Edmund Ludlow, Lieutenant-General of the Horse in the Army of the Commonwealth of England, 1625–1672*. Ed. C.H. Firth. 2 vols. Oxford: Clarendon Press.

Marvell, Andrew. 1971. *The Poems and Letters of Andrew Marvell*. Ed. H. M. Margoliouth, rev. Pierre Legouis with E. E. Duncan-Jones. 3rd ed. 2 vols. Oxford: Clarendon Press.

———. 2003. *Prose Works of Andrew Marvell*. Ed. Annabel Patterson, Martin Dzelzainis, Nicholas von Maltzahn, and N.H. Keeble. 2 vols. New Haven: Yale University Press.

———. 2007. *Poems of Andrew Marvell*. Ed. Nigel Smith. Rev. ed. London: Longman.

Miège, Guy. 1669. *A Relation of Three Embassies from His Sacred Majesty Charles II, to the Great Duke of Muscovy, the King of Sweden, and the King of Denmark*. London.

Monck, George. 1714. *A Collection of Letters Written by His Excellency General George Monk, afterwards Duke of Albermarle, Relating to the Restoration of the Royal Family*. London.

Pepys, Samuel. 1970–1983. *The Diary of Samuel Pepys*. Ed. Robert Latham and William Matthews. 11 vols. London: George Bell.

Proclamation for Calling in and Suppressing of Two Books Written by John Milton, A. 1660. London.

Riebling, Barbara. 1995. England Deflowered and Unmanned: The Sexual Image of Politics in Marvell's "Last Instructions". *SEL* 35 (1): 137–57.

Rogers, P.G. 1970. *The Dutch in the Medway*. Oxford: Oxford University Press.

Scott, Jonathan. 2008. Downing, Sir George, first baronet (1623-1684). *ODNB*.

Seaward, Paul. 1989. *The Cavalier Parliament and the Reconstruction of the Old Regime, 1661–1667*. Cambridge: Cambridge University Press.

———. 2019. Marvell and Parliament. In *The Oxford Handbook of Andrew Marvell*, ed. Martin Dzelzainis and Edward Holberton, 79–95. Oxford: Oxford University Press.

Shrewsbury, J.F.D. 1970. *A History of Bubonic Plague in the British Isles*. Cambridge: Cambridge University Press.

Till, Barry. 1997. The Worcester House Declaration and the Restoration of the Church of England. *Historical Research* 70 (172): 203–230.

von Maltzahn, Nicholas. 2005. *An Andrew Marvell Chronology*. London: Palgrave Macmillan.

———. 2018. Andrew Marvell's Paper Work: The Earl of Carlisle's Baltic Embassy (1664). *Marvell Studies* 3 (1): 1.

Waller, Edmund. 1893. *The Poems of Edmund Waller*. Ed. G. Thorn Drury. 2 vols. London: Routledge.

Wilmot, John, Earl of Rochester. 2013. *Rochester: Selected Poems*. Ed. Paul Davis. Oxford: Oxford University Press.

Winship, Michael P. 2018. *Hot Protestants: A History of Puritanism in England and America*. New Haven: Yale University Press.

Woolrych, Austin. 1958. The Collapse of the Great Rebellion. *History Today* 8 (9): 606–615.

Wynne, S. M. 2008. 'Palmer [née Villiers], Barbara, countess of Castlemaine and suo jure duchess of Cleveland (bap. 1640, d. 1709), royal mistress'. *ODNB*.

Zwicker, Steven N. 1990. Virgins and Whores: The Politics of Sexual Misconduct in the 1660s. In *The Political Identity of Andrew Marvell*, ed. Conal Condren and A. D. Cousins, 85–110. Aldershot: Scolar Press.

8

'The interest and happiness of the king and kingdom': London, 1667–1678

The last decade of Marvell's life was dominated by politics and prose. His letters attest the tumult of parliamentary business in these crisis-ridden years and the dedication with which he served his constituents. 'Really the business of the house hath been of late so earnest daily and so long, that I have not had the time and scarce the vigour left me by night to write to you', Marvell begins a typical dispatch of 14 November 1667, 'And today because I would not omit any longer I lose my dinner to make sure of this letter' (*P&L*, 2:59). When Parliament was out of session, Marvell occupied himself with the writing of pamphlets which resisted the forcing of conscience, cast light on court corruption, and sounded the alarm against tyranny and popery, thereby earning his posthumous reputation as a Whig hero and incorruptible patriot, 'a pattern for all free-born Englishmen', as Marvell's early biographer, the Whig author and translator Thomas Cooke, proclaimed in his 'Life' of 1726 (1:3). Marvell's antagonist Samuel Parker (1727), long after death had curbed the transproser's bitter pen, described him as someone who 'daily spewed infamous libels out of his filthy mouth against the King himself' and as a remorseless enemy in Parliament to the king's affairs (334–5). This tradition of remembering Marvell, witnessed by friend and foe alike in the eighteenth century, reaches down to the twentieth and twenty-first in different guises, from Legouis's 'poet, puritan, patriot', to Christopher Hill's Miltonic disciple, to David Norbrook's republican Marvell, to Annabel Patterson's (early) modern liberal. At first blush, Nigel Smith's 'chameleon'—various, variable, contradictory, elusive—would seem a revisionist departure from the solidly admirable image of the poet sustained by this Whiggish rear-guard of critics and commentators. But the heroic narrative of principled resistance to abso-lutism still sounds at times in Smith's account: when we come to the quick, 'Marvell stands for liberty—liberty of the subject, liberty in the state, liberty of the self, liberty from political and personal tyrannies' (*Chameleon*, 343). In this final chapter, I want to stand back from this tradition and allow into view the genuine perplexities of Marvell's negotiating of toleration and sovereignty, what we might think of as the lived dilemmas of conscience, of a moderate conscience like Marvell's.

Only occasionally in this last decade of his life, amidst the business of Parliament and pamphleteering, does Marvell the poet appear. It is disputed whether Marvell wrote 'The Garden' and perhaps other of his pastoral lyrics now, possibly while in retreat from the city at the country estate of his friend Philip, Lord Wharton; my own view is that the evidence is not sufficiently definitive to overturn the conventional and in many ways obvious dating of these poems to the early 1650s. What is sure is that he did write at least one great poem in these years, the verses 'On *Paradise Lost*', which were published with the second edition of Milton's epic in 1674. Not only does Marvell here telescope the reception history of *Paradise Lost*, poising Satanic ambition against pious achievement, he also turns his praise for Milton into a witty defence of his own poetic, self-effacement into self-vindication—an inimita-bly Marvellian farewell to verse, if such it was.

Finally, we shall come to the strange circumstances of Marvell's last months, which found him dividing his time between his lodgings in Covent Garden and a rented house in Great Russell Street which he shared with two disgraced bankers, Edward Nelthorpe and Richard Thompson, Thompson's wife Dorothy, and a widow called Mary Palmer. Subsequent to Marvell's abrupt death from malarial fever in August 1678, in the context of the Dickensian brangle which arose over the administration of Marvell's estate, Mary would claim to have been the poet's wife. The nature of the alleged marriage between Marvell and Mary Palmer remains something of a mystery—the registry book of the Church of the Holy Trinity in the Little Minories, where Mary said the two were married in secret in 1667, is missing for the years 1662 to 1683. Some have gone so far as to suspect that Mary disappeared it herself, thus ensuring her story could not be contradicted. But perhaps it is to Mary that we owe our possession of Marvell's true legacy, the *Miscellaneous Poems* of 1681, which appeared under a certificate of authenticity supposedly signed by Mary Marvell.

The Fall of Clarendon

In 'The Last Instructions', Marvell describes the immediate aftermath of the Medway disaster, another craven episode of finger-pointing and deflecting blame, the greatest share of which fell on the Commissioner of Chatham Dockyard, Peter Pett, imprisoned in the Tower and questioned by a committee of the Privy Council. The naval administrator Pepys, who was present at the interview, that night recorded his shame at having gone along with the farce of this kangaroo court: 'After having heard him for an hour or more, they bid him withdraw. I all this while showing him no respect, but rather against him, for which God forgive me! For I mean no hurt to him, but only find that these Lords are upon their own purgation, and it is necessary I should be so in behalf of the office' (19 June 1667). In a bravura passage most memorable for the eight couplets rhyming on Pett's name, Marvell sets this out with characteristic sharpness: 'All our miscarriages on Pett must fall: / His name alone seems fit to answer all' (ll. 767–8).

Having been pressured into recalling Parliament from its recess, Charles delayed the House's meeting; as soon as the treaty with the Dutch was ratified at the end of July, he prorogued Parliament until October. But it must have been clear to all that a greater sacrifice would be required for the appeasing of Parliament than the unfortunate Pett, who was quietly let off the hook with a fine. Parliament had voted the crown millions in supply the previous year for a war whose humiliating climax had played out in public view, and it would now be asked to make good on the monarchy's outstanding debts. The king well knew he could not afford a recalcitrant House, and he soon settled on the necessity of dismissing his chief minister, Chancellor Clarendon, a man with many enemies. To ambitious courtiers like Sir William Coventry, the Earl of Arlington, and the Duke of Buckingham, the three figures who most strongly urged Clarendon's downfall, the Lord Chancellor was an obstacle to their political advancement and that of their clients and placemen. Coventry and Arlington, as Secretary to the Admiralty and Secretary of State, respectively, were also concerned to save their own skins. In the House, Clarendon had made himself odious to a number of factions (see Roberts 1957)—old Cavaliers resentful of the Restoration settlement, Presbyterians chafing under the penal statutes, country gentlemen fed up with lethargy, peculation, and the miscarriage of the war. Clarendon was also hated by Lady Castlemaine, whose intimacy in the king's counsels he fiercely opposed.

Charles seems at first to have pursued Clarendon's removal reluctantly. He sent his brother York to break the news to his father-in-law (James had married Anne Hyde in September 1660). The king had received intelligence that the Parliament was resolved to impeach the Chancellor as soon as it met; such was their rage, and such was the king's need, he could neither protect Clarendon nor divert Parliament; he was thus bound to ask the Chancellor to deliver up the seals of his office (Hyde 1759, 3:825–6). The circumstance was presented as an opportunity to do the king one last good service and to retire in peace. Clarendon did not take the hint. First he demanded an audience with the king, and when it was granted, he gave the king a lecture: he was, he said, 'so far from fearing the justice of Parliament, that he renounced his majesty's protection or interpolation towards his preservation'; but he doubted not 'that the throwing off an old servant who had served the crown in some trust near thirty years ... would call his majesty's justice and good nature into question' (Hyde 1759, 3:831). Four days later, on 30 August 1667, the king sent the junior Secretary of State, Sir William Morrice, to collect the seals from Clarendon, but the Chancellor's stiff-necked posture had made escalations all but inevitable. Those courtiers who had lobbied for Clarendon's dismissal could hardly rest easy when the Duke of York, heir apparent, remained loyal to Clarendon who could perhaps regain office and favour. No less was Parliament adamant 'they will be revenged of my Lord Chancellor' (*Pepys*, 13 October 1667).

The next parliamentary session opened on 10 October, and on 26 October proceedings against the Earl were initiated by Sir Edward Seymour, a client of Buckingham's. On 6 November seventeen articles were brought against him; when none of these were deemed sufficient to try him on, a general charge of impeachment for high treason was put forward and carried up to the Lords on 12 November. But the Lords were not keen to arrest one of their own on a charge of capital treason without particular evidence, and a debate broke out between the two Houses on their respective powers and privileges. Thus far Clarendon had remained defiant, '(so much confidence he had in his own innocence, and so little esteem of the credit of his enemies), until he heard that the king himself expressed great displeasure towards him' (Hyde 1759, 3:838): it was rumoured that the king would dismiss Parliament and appoint a special tribunal of peers to try Clarendon for treason. On 29 November, the Chancellor was finally persuaded to flee for France on the promise that his honour and estates would not be assailed. Three weeks later, Parliament passed a bill banishing Clarendon from the kingdom for life, to which the king gave the royal assent (see Hutton 1989, 250–3; Roberts 1957).

The reasons for the king's taking so bitterly against his most devoted servant are not fully understood. It may be that Charles's tolerance for his paternalistic chief minister finally dissolved when he became a political liability. That the king wished to be more fully master of his prerogative is suggested by the fact that the post of Chancellor was kept vacant and other important offices broken into commissions, thus ensuring no one minister wielded undue power. The administration of this era, c. 1668–1673, accordingly came to be known as the Cabal, after the last initials of a junto of leading privy council-lors: Sir Thomas Clifford; Arlington; Buckingham; Lord Ashley (Anthony Ashley Cooper), later the first Earl of Shaftesbury; and John Maitland, first Duke of Lauderdale. As recent historians have stressed, however, this was by no means a unified group, politically or religiously; rather it was one whose personal interests—above all, an interest in toleration—happened to align over against their differences for a period of time. Clifford was a secret Catholic and a favourite of Arlington's, who was himself inclined to Rome; Buckingham, a self-aggrandising populist, had connections among Presbyterians and dis-senters, Levellers and republicans; Ashley was a former Cromwellian who would become the leader of the Whigs; Lauderdale a Scot and a Presbyterian, as well as a libertine and a willing instrument of absolutism. Nor was theirs a cabinet of equals: by September 1668, it seemed to Pepys that 'Buckingham and Arlington rule all' (9 September 1668), and indeed, Charles often pitted the two against each other, with Buckingham the leading figure at court, Arlington at the council table.

Comprehension and Indulgence

These manoeuvrings provide the context and coordinates for much of Marvell's political and literary programme from the Painter poems to the two parts of *Rehearsal Transpros'd* (1672/3). In February 1668, Arlington was the subject of an unusual outburst by Marvell in the House, during a debate on the report of the committee of inquiry into the conduct of the Dutch war. According to the parliamentary diarist Anchitell Grey, 'Mr Marvell, reflecting on Lord Arlington, somewhat transportedly said':

> We have had Bristol's and Cecil's secretaries, and by them knew the King of Spain's junto, and letters of the Pope's cabinet; and now such a strange account of things! The money allowed for intelligence so small, the intelligence was accordingly—A libidinous desire in men, for places, makes them think them-selves fit for them—The place of secretary ill-gotten, when bought with 10,000 l. and a barony—*He was called to explain himself; but said*, The thing was so plain, it needed not. (Grey 1769, 1:70–71)

Marvell's attack on Arlington, which juxtaposes the stinginess of his spending on intelligence as Secretary of State with the exorbitant cost of the emoluments he had received from the king, likely reflects Marvell's political alignment with Arlington's rival Buckingham. But if Marvell, 'as so often in these years, was speaking … to a brief' (Dzelzainis 2010, 166), his intervention nevertheless seems to betray the same explosive temper we glimpsed in the last chapter, which saw a frayed Marvell pulling a pistol on a wagon driver at the end of his mission to Muscovy and Sweden. Such vituperativeness makes sense in light of the Advices-to-a-Painter, which are exceptionally harsh in their treatment of Arlington and on the same score of providing bad intelligence—a judgement no doubt animated by Marvell's intimacy with that age-old art as a former diplomat and ex-spy.

If indeed Marvell was targeting Arlington on the Duke's behalf, what exactly was his relationship to Buckingham? It has become commonplace to speak of Buckingham as Marvell's 'patron'; Harold Love (1989) styles Marvell the Duke's 'long-term advisor' (225). *Rehearsal Transpros'd* was clearly written within that politician and wit's orbit, and the question 'whether, or to what extent, Buckingham actively sponsored' Marvell's anti-Clarendonian satires of the 1660s has been suggestively if circumstantially compassed (see Dzelzainis 2010, 162–6). But 'circumstantial' perhaps bears emphasising with regard to Marvell and Buckingham's association. In Chap. 4, we noted Marvell's encounter with the Villiers brothers at the English College at Rome in 1645–6; that they enjoyed a degree of familiarity there is suggested by Marvell's 'Elegy upon the Death of my Lord Francis Villiers' (1648). In September 1657, following his return from exile, the Duke had married Mary Fairfax, another point of connection to Marvell. But Buckingham's mis-devotion as a husband was notorious. In 1668, the Duke was at the centre of the duel of the century, in which he fatally wounded his mistress's husband, the Earl of Shrewsbury. Buckingham then proceeded to set up house with the Countess, and when Mary protested, he sent her to live with her father (*Pepys*, 15 May 1668). We find Marvell's and Buckingham's names occasionally drawn together in fugitive verse and in intelligence reports (see von Maltzahn 2005b, 59–60n95); the *Account of the Growth of Popery and Arbitrary Government* (1677) flatteringly casts Buckingham as a kind of Jeremiah figure, a voice crying out in the wilderness of parliamentary corruption and complaisance. But it is scarcely possible to imagine the private and diffident Marvell among the libertine wits in Buckingham's circle, and it is telling that no personal letter, no deposition, no proof positive testifies to this patronage relationship said to have endured more than a dozen years, in contrast to Marvell's clientage to such patrons as

Lord Wharton, Sir Edward Harley, and the Earl of Anglesey (cf. Hume and Marshall 2019; von Maltzahn 2019).

This is all to say that if Buckingham were Marvell's 'patron', it is less than clear exactly when and how he patronised him. That their projects aligned at several times is undeniable, that they worked to some extent in concert more than likely, but we might allow an element of provisionality and opportunism in both directions, an informal synergy as opposed to the quasi-sentimentalised exchange of benefits more characteristic of the early modern patronage economy (see Griffin 1996, Chap. 2). Marvell's Painter satires chime with Buckingham's anti-Clarendon, anti-Arlington interests, providing a public (though of course anonymous) accounting of the military and administrative failures soft-pedalled in propaganda like Waller's 'Instructions to a Painter' and deflected by self-serving ministers and their 'minion imps'. As Philip Connell justly observes, the Advices also contain ample evidence of Marvell's 'continued preoccupation with the Restoration church settlement of the 1660s' (Connell 2019, 135–6). The example Connell chooses comes from the Duchess of Albemarle's set-piece speech in the 'Third Advice', a broadside attack on disloyal ministers and persecuting bishops which neatly encapsulates the double-sidedness of Marvell's religious politics. For the distempered 'monkey Duchess' (l. 171), 'Half witch, half prophet', snarling like a 'Presbyterian sibyl' (ll. 198–9), is at once an object of satire but of a peculiar kind and a vehicle for views which will become key arguments in Marvell's prose writings. The main planks of Buckingham's oppositional stance in the Lords in the parliamentary sessions of 1666–7 were not obviously religious in nature—a bill against the importation of Irish cattle, inquiry into the bungled war effort, investigation of the Chancellor (see Yardley 1992, 321–2). But some historians have seen these issues as screens for Buckingham's tolerationist agenda, an agenda which would come to the fore in 1668 and again in 1672–3, pushes which coincide with Marvell's most exigent interventions in parliamentary debate (in the session of 1667–8) and with the writing of *Rehearsal Transpros'd*, his masterpiece of Buckinghamian satire.

With Clarendon in exile and his Anglican supporters on the back foot, during Parliament's Christmas recess of 1667–8, 'a project was prepared consisting chiefly of those things that the King had promised by his declaration of the year 1660', namely a liberty to tender consciences (Burnet 1753, 1:363). Quietly, a coalition was organised for the drafting of a new comprehension bill, whose sponsors at court included Charles, Buckingham, the Earl of Manchester, Sir Edward Montagu, and a number of other liberal and moderate peers. Among the clergy the chief negotiators were John Wilkins, Bishop of Chester, for the Anglicans, and for the Presbyterians and Independents,

William Bates, Richard Baxter, and Thomas Manton (see Simon 1962, 441–2). Notably, for our purposes, Herbert Croft, Bishop of Hereford, whom Marvell would defend in *Mr Smirke* (1676), was part of the wider Anglican congress involved in the discussions. The upshot of the bill was the comprehension of most Presbyterian clergy within the established church and the toleration of independent preaching and worship under a licensing scheme, though nonconformists would still be subject to civil penalties, including exclusion from office. The draft bill was written so as to exclude Catholics from its indulgence measures.

The bill's backers had counted on an element of surprise in attempting to secure its passage. But details of the proposed bill had leaked a few weeks before Parliament reconvened on 10 February and a hostile response had been prepared for it. In the morning, before the king had come to give his traditional speech to both Houses, the Commons passed a resolution 'That his Majesty be humbly desired to issue his proclamation, to enforce obedience to the laws in force, concerning religion and church government, as it is now established, according to the Act of Uniformity' (*CJ*, 9:44). Pepys records a member's pointed remark 'that, if any people had a mind to bring any new laws into the House, about religion, they might come, as a proposer of new laws did in Athens, with ropes about their neck' (10 February 1668). Speaking from the throne in the Lords, the king announced his making of a defensive alliance with Holland and Sweden against France and of a league for mediating peace between France and Spain. News of the alliance served as prelude to the inevitable request for supply, for the building of ships and fortifying of ports. To which the king somewhat gingerly added a final proviso for the settling of peace at home, 'That you would seriously think of some course to beget a better union and composure in the minds of my Protestant subjects in matters of religion; whereby they may be induced not only to submit quietly to the government, but also cheerfully give their assistance for the support of it' (*HPHC*, 1:114). Still, the majority declined to withdraw the morning's resolution, and in the coming weeks hopes for the bill would wither in the salted earth.

Marvell was nonetheless one of the most prominent voices for Protestant liberty in this session, working to redirect attention from the late war to the matter of toleration. Having hit at Arlington in his eruption of 14 February, on the 17th Marvell moved the taking into consideration of the king's speech, a step Arlington regarded as a tactical blunder on Marvell's part, letting him off the ropes when he was in danger of taking serious damage (see *Chronology*, 104). On 13 March, Marvell spoke against the renewal of the Conventicle Act, which had expired on 2 March. When the bill was brought in on the

30th, Marvell again opposed it. On 28 April it passed the lower House in a vote of 144 to 78, but its progress stalled in the Lords, which was focused on a jurisdictional dispute with the Commons, the case of *Thomas Skinner v. the East India Company*, in what, with a summer recess looming, amounted to a filibuster of the Conventicles Act by tolerationist peers, including Buckingham and Anglesey. As Marvell reported in a letter to Hull dated 9 May, 'The bill providing further for the City of London had not time to pass nor the bill for continuing the Act of Conventicles', and the king adjourned Parliament until 11 August (*P&L*, 75–6).

At this eleventh hour, we now know, thanks to the researches of Nicholas von Maltzahn, Marvell was working in secret with Lord Wharton to bring about liberty of tender conscience by other means, namely the exercise of the king's suspending powers. Our clue is the draft of an 'Address from the House of Peeres to the King to make use of his prerogative in Ecclesiastical affayres for the better composure and union of the minds of his protestant subjects in the intervall of the present adjournment', found among the Wharton papers in the Bodleian Library and written in Marvell's distinctive hand (in this instance I have forgone the convention of modernising spelling, so as to underscore the document's archival singularity). The extent to which Marvell was acting as secretary or ghost writer is unclear, but the two men were obviously working closely together. Citing the king's speech of 10 February and the prevention of its due consideration by Skinner's case, Marvell and Wharton come to the heart of the proposal:

> And therfore We do humbly beseech Your Mty that You will be graciously pleased in the intervall of this instant adjournment to take such course therein as to Your M^ty shall seem fit according to the Power inherent in You in Ecclesiasticall affairs by the Prerogatiue annext to Your Imperiall Crown. (Qtd. in von Maltazhn 2013, 256)

The speech was never read in the Lords, for reasons about which we can only speculate; but the crucial point is the readiness of these patrons of charity, comprehension, and liberty of conscience to see the king use his prerogative to effect a religious settlement that ran counter to the will of the elected assembly and the lords spiritual in Parliament. Indeed, Marvell and Wharton's rhetoric is downright Erastian, acknowledging the king's inherent power to suspend the law and the supremacy of the crown in matters ecclesiastical. This will be the ground on which Marvell's argument with Samuel Parker is most closely fought, and the *discordia concors* of arbitrary power as a tool of liberal government a recurring theme of Marvell's polemical prose.

The Rehearsal Transpros'd

'No man ought to be persecuted for matters of mere religion, honesty and sense. The interest of the nation, as well as the laws of Christianity require an absolute, universal, equal and inviolable liberty of conscience.' So wrote Marvell's nephew William Popple, the son of Marvell's second sister Mary and Edmund Popple, in 1688. The following year Popple's English translation of Locke's *Letter Concerning Toleration* (1689) was published in London and was subsequently printed in the first edition of Locke's works—no mean credentials for a seventeenth-century tolerationist (see Robbins 1967, 190–1). By the Restoration or shortly thereafter young Popple was just starting out in business in London and already one of his MP uncle's confidants: in March 1661, Marvell directed the Mayor of Hull to address letters to him 'only in these words *to be left with William Popple Merchant London* and not one word more of street sign or lodging' (*P&L*, 2:21). In 1670, to Marvell's grief, the Popples relocated from London to Bordeaux so that Will could take up a place in the family wine trade. Marvell's correspondence with his nephew across the Channel discloses a warmth of feeling and a sense of ease little seen elsewhere in Marvell's archive. The letters also speak to a breadth of shared interests in politics, news, poetry, philosophy, and not least, toleration. It is thus to Will that Marvell gives report, in March 1670, in typically canny fashion, of the king's latest horse trading with Parliament, his assent to legislation against the nonconformists in return for fresh supply: 'They are', he says, referring to the Lords, 'making mighty alterations in the Conventicle Bill, (which, as we sent up, is the quintessence of arbitrary malice) and sit whole days, and yet proceed but by inches, and will, at the end, probably affix a *Scotch* clause of the King's power in externals. So the fate of the bill is uncertain, but must probably pass, being the price of money' (*P&L*, 2:314–15).

Marvell's '*Scotch* clause' refers to the Scottish Act Asserting the King's Supremacy of November 1669. And indeed, the final statute of the Conventicles Bill after it emerged from the Lords made a point of stating that the new law in no way invalidated the king's 'powers and authorities in ecclesiastical affairs', which he may choose to exercise 'from time to time' and at any time hereafter (22 Car. II. c. 1), an escape hatch engineered in committee by peers opposed to the principle of the Act. The original text of the proviso drafted in the Lords had gone further still, and would, Marvell duly related to Popple, 'have restored [the king] to all civil or ecclesiastical prerogatives which his ancestors enjoyed at any time since the Conquest'. 'There was never so compendious a piece of absolute universal tyranny', he fumed. 'But the

Commons made them ashamed of it and retrenched it. The Parliament was never so embarrassed, beyond recovery. We are all venal cowards, except some few. What plots of state will go on this interval I know not' (*P&L*, 2:317). Scholars have tended to valorise Marvell's oppositional rhetoric while ignoring the queasy language of compromise ('We are all venal cowards'). But he seems to have read between the lines with considerable discernment, for plots of state were indeed afoot: an alliance with Catholic France, war with the Dutch, and a Royal Declaration of Indulgence suspending the penal laws against Catholics and nonconformists. Thus were combined arbitrary power, cousinage to France, and a tenuous state of toleration; in defending the last, as Marvell does so brilliantly in *Rehearsal Transpros'd*, he was accepting the rest into the bargain.

At the conclusion of the second Dutch war, England's international standing was at a low ebb. The Triple Alliance with Holland and Sweden was a shrewd move on the crown's part: it split the friendship between Louis XIV and the Dutch, who had become leery of the Sun King's ambitions in the Spanish Netherlands, and it made England a major player in peace talks between France and Spain. A Protestant defensive league was also pleasing to the Cavalier Parliament, which voted new taxes to refurbish the national defence. But no sooner had Charles strengthened his diplomatic hand, he opened secret negotiations with Louis via his (Charles's) sister Henrietta, who was married to Louis's brother, the Duke of Orléans. In return for steep French subsidies and revenge on the Dutch, Charles would renege on the Triple Alliance. But there was a kicker: in due time, Charles would declare himself a Catholic, a glory 'not only for the King of England, but for the whole of Catholic Christendom', for which Louis would pay a further two million French livres (see Ogg 1934, 345–6; also Hutton 1986). Under cover of a meeting between Charles and Henrietta at Dover, the secret treaty was concluded on 22 May 1670 and signed by the Catholic ministers Arlington and Clifford. Charles then engaged Buckingham to negotiate a cover treaty with Louis, which omitted the Catholic clause; the Duke's vanity was much gratified by the smoothness of the proceedings, and the sham treaty signed by all five members of the Cabal on 21 December. When Charles's conversion was not forthcoming, Louis moved ahead with preparations for war, dragging his English cousin with him. On 17 March 1672, England declared war against the United Provinces and on 6 April the French followed suit.

What I want to stress here is the coordinated nature of the Declaration of Indulgence and war against the Dutch, the religious act preceding the military by only two days. The Indulgence suspended all penal laws against recusants and nonconformists, providing for regulated public worship for nonconforming Protestants and, most alarmingly, allowing Catholics to worship privately in their own homes. These two events are perhaps most usefully seen as an attempt to play two sides against the middle, that is, to manage Anglican disaffection by mobilising support among nonconformists while also activating residual anti-Dutch sentiment. Accordingly, a series of prorogations would prevent Parliament from sitting for nearly two years, from 22 April 1671 to 4 February 1673. From a 'Country' MP who, in October 1670, lamented in a letter to a friend, 'We truckle to France in all things, to the prejudice of our alliance and honour' (P&L, 2:325), we might expect cries of popery and tyranny. But as Marvell's followers, contemporary and recent, have urged, 'a strong advocacy of religious toleration runs through and binds together his later career' (Hirst and Zwicker 2012, 157); and perhaps we should recall as well Marvell's authorship of 'The Character of Holland', expediently revised and republished at Marvell's direction in 1665 and republished again in 1672 (see Dzelzainis 2015). In any case, so welcome to the crown was Marvell's defence of the Indulgence and his satire on the prelacy of persecuting churchmen, when authorities sought to suppress publication of *Rehearsal Transpros'd* as an unlicensed religious pamphlet, a reprieve was issued by no less than the king himself, who insisted 'this man has done him right', whereas 'Parker has done him wrong' (*PW*, 1:23–4).

'Parker', of course, was Samuel Parker, domestic chaplain and polemical hatchet man to the Archbishop of Canterbury, Gilbert Sheldon, that zealous persecutor of nonconformity. Bishop Burnet, in his *History of His Own Times*, described Parker as 'the most virulent of all that writ against the sects ... afterwards made Bishop of Oxford by King James; who was full of satirical vivacity, and was considerably learned; but was a man of no judgment, and of as little virtue, and as to religion rather impious' (364–5). Both in terms of policy and personality, he was just the kind of man Marvell and Buckingham, though of different backgrounds and temperaments themselves, were bound to dislike: high-handed, high church, with literary and philosophical pretensions to boot. As would become clear in their exchange, Marvell also regarded Parker as a self-interested dissembler and turncoat: in the early 1660s, Parker had been a regular visitor to Milton's house in Jewin Street, where Marvell recalled meeting him (*PW*, 1:418), and had remained something of a Puritan himself until about 1663, when he began to seek preferment in the Church. The long title of Parker's most notorious work provides a good index to the style and content of the whole: *A Discourse of Ecclesiastical Polity Wherein the Authority of the Civil Magistrate over the Consciences of Subjects in Matters of External Religion Is Asserted: the Mischiefs and Inconveniences of Toleration are Represented, and All*

Pretences Pleaded in Behalf of Liberty of Conscience Are Fully Answered (1670). There followed a *Defence* of the *Ecclesiastical Polity* in 1671, and in 1672 a combative 'Preface' to an edition of Bishop John Bramhall's *Vindication of Himself and the Episcopal Clergy, from the Presbyterian Charge of Popery*, the work which would finally draw Marvell into the lists of prose controversy.

The Rehearsal Transpros'd was written between July and October 1672, with the aid of Anglesey's great library, of which more hereafter. Buckingham's play had debuted on 7 December the previous year and was published that summer (those interested in the play should consult Hume and Love's magnificent 2007 edition in the Oxford Buckingham). Parker's edition of Bramhall was entered in the Stationer's Register on 7 September. By early December 1672, the anonymous and unlicensed publication of *RT* had attracted the attention of the Stationer's Company and the Surveyor of the Imprimery, Sir Roger L'Estrange. Marvell's book was thus extremely current, a feature which distinguishes all his prose works. This strenuous contemporaneity helps explain the interest these works held for their original readers, but it has its costs for those who come to Marvell's prose without the benefit of native fluency in their dense topicality. If somewhat loosely, *RT* also belongs to the genre of animadversion, the point-by-point refutation of an interlocutor text or texts, here Parker's 'Preface' and, more briefly, the *Ecclesiastical Polity* and its *Defence*, a complexity compounded by *RT*'s imaginative debts to Buckingham's *Rehearsal*. In what follows, my concern will be to ask after the work's illocutionary force—that is, what Marvell was *doing in* writing what he wrote, in writing in this particular way—and to consider how *Rehearsal Transpros'd* and other of Marvell's prose works fit into our conception of this literary life.

It bears stating that Marvell's prose works, rhetorically impressive as they are, should not be confused for systematic ecclesiology or political philosophy. A consistency of arguments and ideas is not necessarily the aim of these works. This is not to say that they are unprincipled or merely cynical, but they were written above all to score points at a precisely calibrated moment in political culture, to provoke and to shape discourse and opinion. In the case of *Rehearsal Transpros'd*, Marvell's opening was the reverse suffered by an avowed defender of the king's ecclesiastical supremacy like Parker when that supremacy was exercised to ends antithetical to Parker and the high church bishops. That is, when crown and Church had been aligned against the nonconformists, Parker's writings (according to Marvell) had imagined the sovereign as enjoying little less ecclesiastical authority than St Peter. When the Declaration of Indulgence turned tables on the persecuting bishops, Parker was in the unenviable position of having to argue that the king could not or should not do as he had done in giving liberty to tender consciences. Marvell's strategy in

Rehearsal Transpros'd was thus to frame Parker and the bishops as disloyal hypocrites, and to tout his advocacy of indulgence as an expression of patriotic loyalism; he is, he says, 'much more a servant to the king's prerogative' than Parker, and more 'perfectly devoted to the foundations of our faith' (*PW*, 1:157). (Remember that Marvell is writing anonymously in the first part, and that his religious and political persona is part of *RT*'s apparatus of persuasion.) In *RT2*, the shoe will be on the other foot, as Marvell will find himself defending a policy which the king had by then withdrawn under pressure from Parliament.

Seen in these terms, the critical section of Marvell's argument in *RT* comes relatively late in the book, where Marvell ventures to connect the Restoration Church to the Laudian, and so to tell a story of rebellion and civil strife driven by ecclesiastical vainglory, a story being continued in the present tense by Archbishop Sheldon's *posse episcopatus*. In Marvell's telling of this story, Puritans and nonconformists are acquitted to be of 'republican principles, most pestilent, and *eo nomine* [as such], enemies to monarchy; traitors and rebels' (1:180), being found instead to embody a decidedly English Protestantism and a regard for the common weal at odds with clerical self-magnification (1:188–9). Here is another instance of Marvell writing against the grain of Whig history, disabling the explanatory force of a 'Puritan revolution' in favour of views that anticipate those of revisionist historians of recent memory: that Puritanism was not opposed to but rather a part of mainstream English Protestantism in the early seventeenth century (Patrick Collinson), and that Laudianism and Arminianism, not revolutionary Puritanism, had fuelled division in the English Church and ultimately in the body politic (Nicholas Tyacke).

Marvell rhetorically performs his own innocence of republican principles by hailing Charles I as 'the best prince that ever wielded the English sceptre' (191), a phrase unutterable by a regicide like Milton. Indeed, if we should happen to think of Milton's blast against the king's tenderness of conscience in *Eikonoklastes* (1649), it is rather wonderful to find Marvell arguing that the king's fault lay in his *excess* of piety, which led him to 'esteem and favour the clergy' so far as to make Archbishop Laud and his party ministers of state. '[But] they having gained this ascendant upon him, resolved whatever became on't to make their best of him; and having made the whole business of state their Arminian jangles, and the persecution of ceremonies, did for recompense assign him that imaginary absolute government, upon which rock we all ruined' (191). '[After] all the fatal consequences of that rebellion, which can only serve as sea-marks unto wise princes to avoid the causes', Marvell asks, coming to the sharp end of his point, 'shall this sort of men'—that is the neo-Laudian wing of the Church, the Sheldonian forcers of conscience—'still vindicate themselves as the most zealous assertors of the rights of princes?' (192).

'Arminian jangles, and the persecution of ceremonies': this is the brief of 'Bayes the Second', as Marvell christens Parker, after the buffoon playwright of Buckingham's *Rehearsal*. Arminianism was a liberal reaction to the Calvinist doctrines of total depravity and predestination which stressed instead the freedom of the individual to accept or reject God's grace. As embraced (disastrously) by Laud and supported by Charles I, however, Arminian theology was wed to the policy of 'Thorough', an insistence on sacerdotalism, uniformity of worship, and the beauty of holiness enforced by absolute royal and episcopal authority. Intent 'to *magnificate* the Church with triumphal pomp and ceremony', Marvell avers, 'The three ceremonies that have the countenance of law, would not suffice, but they [the Arminian clergy] were all upon new inventions, and happy was he that was endued with that capacity, for he was sure before all others to be preferred. There was a *second* service, the *table* set *altar-wise*, and to be called the *altar; candles, crucifixes, paintings, images, copes, bowing to the East, bowing to the altar*, and so many several cringes and genuflections, that a man unpractised stood in need to entertain both a dancing-master and a remembrancer' (188–9). Marvell harps on the issue of ceremonies more determinedly than has perhaps been acknowledged; he jeers ceremony as the *ousia* of Parker's 'push-pin divinity', which would 'persuade princes that *there cannot be a pin pulled out of the Church but the State immediately totters*' (109, 164). Ceremonies are both the occasion and the instruments of harassing nonconformists, at once 'pins' and 'pillories, whipping-posts, gallies, rods, and axes' (147). The image Marvell conjures up is that of a theatre of persecution; hence the need to entertain 'both a dancing master and a remembrancer' to be assured of grace. A remembrancer is a prompter, someone employed by a theatre company to cue the players' lines in rehearsal. In Buckingham's play, Bayes leads his actors in a dance, in the course of which he takes a tumble and breaks his nose; the original production was headlined by John Lacy, dancing master for the King's Company.

This brings us face to face with the literariness of *Rehearsal Transpros'd*, Marvell's styling of his polemical pamphlet after a hit stage play. It is hard to overstate the sheer unlikeliness and surprise of this conjunction in its original context, to say nothing of its success: try to imagine a work of political controversy in our own time which topped bestseller lists while also being read and debated by high-ranking officials, a work targeting a prominent right-wing politician and author under the name of a spoof character from a Hollywood film to which the text, while engaging in detailed policy argument, winkingly refers throughout. Such a work is perhaps not so hard to imagine in the twenty-first century; but achieving a like impact in the political and media landscape, perhaps impossible.

So why transpose *The Rehearsal*, as Neil Keeble (1999) asks in a classic essay. Buckingham's play, a collaborative work with wits of his circle, was a parody of popular drama, in particular the heroic plays of John Dryden, though its targets, literary as well as personal, were notably layered and multiple. The work's conceit is the rehearsal of a play-within-the-play led by the booby playwright Bayes for the benefit of two men of sense, Smith and Johnson, ironic foils to Bayes's foppish boasting. According to Bayes himself (1.1.105–24), the play is a mish-mash of coffee-house tittle-tattle and sententiae out of his commonplace book (the satirists' method is thus to plagiarise the plagiarist, the mock-play a garble of extracts from Dryden's and others' recent efforts upon the stage). But it's also Bayes's opinion that his play exemplifies an altogether 'new way of writing ... forty times better than the old plain way' (1.2.7–9). The main part of the farce targets the pretensions of heroic drama and its puffed-up protagonists; the hero of the play-within-the-play is called Drawcansir, after Dryden's Almanzor, the lead role in Dryden's two-part, ten-act *Conquest of Granada* (1670/71), a play famous for its rant and bombast. Buckingham and co. also make hay out of Dryden's argufying and opinion-making in essays, dedications, and prologues, his (Arminian-like) campaign to give (his own) new-fangled dramatic practice the appearance of ancient authority.

We are now in a position to apprehend the force of Marvell's casting choice, 'that instead of Author, I may henceforth indifferently call [Parker] Mr. Bayes as oft as I shall see occasion':

> And that, first, because he hath no name or at least will not own it, though he himself writes under the greatest security, and gives us the first letters of other men's names before he be asked them. Secondly, because he is I perceive a lover of elegancy of style, and can endure no man's tautologies but his own, and therefore I would not distaste him with too frequent repetition of one word. But chiefly, because Mr. Bayes and he do very much symbolise: in their understanding, in their expressions, in their humour, in their contempt and quarrelling of all others, though of their own profession. Because our divine the author, manages his contest with the same prudence and civility, which the players and poets have practiced of late in their several divisions. And lastly, because both their talents do peculiarly lie in exposing and personating the nonconformists. (*PW*, 1:51)

Parker had not signed the 'Preface' to Bramhall, though his authorship was immediately known, a circumstance Marvell exploits in assigning the anonymous 'Author' a name and identity of his own choosing. Parker's garrulous, overheated style is marked by that of Dryden/Bayes and their fizzing stage heroes (Dryden had described Almanzor as 'not absolutely perfect, but of an excessive and over-boiling courage'). The sole mystery is Marvell's claim that 'both their talents', that is Parker/Bayes, 'do peculiarly lie in exposing and personating the nonconformists'. This does not readily describe Dryden in 1672, a curious discrepancy, since it is the only hinge in Marvell's explanation to the pamphlet's central concern with ecclesiology. Fortunately, Derek Hirst (1999) has supplied the likely answer: Marvell appears to be thinking of Dryden's predecessor as poet laureate (under Charles I), Sir William Davenant (158–60). Marvell hits at Davenant twice in this first instalment of *RT*; in 'Appleton House', as may be recalled from Chap. 5, Marvell jests and jousts with Davenant's epic *Gondibert* (1651), whose plot allegorically shadows the English civil war. In the separately published *Preface* to *Gondibert*, Davenant had rather loftily pronounced on matters of epic style. There he also writes with revulsion against the Puritan godly, comparing them to headstrong Jews whose religion 'doth … consist in a sullen separation of themselves from the rest of human flesh, which is a fantastical pride in their own cleanness, and an uncivil disdain of the imagined contagiousness of others' (9). At the Restoration, Davenant was appointed one of Charles II's two theatre impresarios, leading the Duke's Men until his death in 1668; he was likely the original of Bayes in the earliest drafts of the group project that became *The Rehearsal*.

Rehearsal Transpros'd, then, consists of a puzzle and a game built on top of another puzzle and game, a 'labyrinth' of intertextual reference, court gossip, and political innuendo which invites and demands active unravelling and decoding. Exactly why this should have presented itself as an effectual discursive strategy deserves consideration. Written in concentrated bursts in 1672 and 1673, Marvell's two *Rehearsals* run to nearly 700 pages, and their dazzling literary architectonics surely exceed their utility. So, let us perhaps allow that there is something self-gratifying about these works, especially the first part; in the sequel, Marvell is more on the defensive, disadvantaged by shifting political circumstance, wounded by the libels of his opponents. But there *is* a utility, a strategy to Marvell's yoking of literary and theatrical hijinks to controversial divinity. The Declaration of Indulgence was widely interpreted as the policy of the Cabal, a policy unwelcome, as we have seen, to both the Cavalier Parliament and the episcopal establishment. In defending it, Marvell was making a bid to rally support among the 'grand jury ... of town wits', that section of London society most coextensive with the demesne of the Restoration theatre, a demographic distinct from that of the court and the city guilds (see Love 2004, esp. 66–79). His play is for 'those *gentlemen* who come so poorly out of the writing of Bunyan, for Mr Brisk and Mr Worldly-Wiseman', seeking to 'entice those who would never dream of opening a page of Stillingfleet or Parker, let alone Owen or Baxter' (Keeble 1999, 250–1). Marvell was inviting those who had laughed with Buckingham at Bayes and his ludicrous dramaturgy in turn to laugh with him at 'Bayes the Second' and his ecclesiastical bluster. There is an underappreciated subtlety to these manoeuvres. Enjoyment of Buckingham's arch wit required of its audience no little self-irony, for they were the same audiences which had made heroic drama popular in the first place. Marvell's aim is to reach those who did not directly benefit from the Indulgence, to convert the opinion of the better part of the Town; he is thus asking his readers to ironise the prejudice of their own Church leaders, indeed to hold at ironic distance their own intolerance.

It remains to ask *how* Marvell composed *Rehearsal Transpros'd*. For we are struck not only by the lushness of reference in these works but also by their exoticism. Obviously, Marvell would have had to hand Parker's writings and Buckingham's *Rehearsal*; the marshalling of additional ecclesiastical authorities is also to be expected, and extensive use is made in part one of John Hale's *Treatise of Schism* (1642), Archbishop Matthew Parker's *De Antiquitate Britannicae Ecclesiae* (1572), John Rushworth's *Historical Collections* (1629), and the works of John Owen, whose *Truth and Innocence Vindicated* (1669) had attracted Parker's ire. Church fathers, yes, the classics, of course, Shakespeare and Donne, Cervantes and Rabelais, *Il Pastor Fido* and *Dodona's Grove*, okay; but the range of sources mined for Marvell's many pungent anecdotes is decidedly eclectic and obscure. *Voyages* in the Mughal empire of Aurangzeb by Francois Bernier? John Selden's Latin works on Jewish antiquities? John Evelyn's *History of the Late Three Famous Impostors*? Martin Del Rio's *Disquisitionum Magicarum*? It is almost as if Marvell is flipping through curious works in a scholarly library—as indeed he was. Nearly all the works quoted in or alluded to in *RT* were owned by Anglesey, a prodigious bibliophile and book collector, as Annabel Patterson and Martin Dzelzainis (2001) discovered by cross-checking Marvell's references with the sale catalogue of Anglesey's library, down to the specific edition owned. Anglesey's patronage of Marvell had long been suspected from his intervention on behalf of Marvell and his publisher Nathaniel Ponder when the authorities threatened Ponder for printing the first part of *RT* without a license. It was but a short walk from Marvell's lodgings in Maiden Lane to Anglesey's mansion on the opposite side of Covent Garden, which happened to be in the same street as the Theatre Royal, where *The Rehearsal* was first performed.

The picture that emerges of the writer at work is thus one that combines rigour and system with more than a dash of expedience. Marvell worked at speed and he worked creatively with the materials to hand. If we step back from *Rehearsal Transpros'd*, we can see the resemblance to Marvell's mini-epics in verse, 'Appleton House' and the Painter poems, in their generic layerings, their multifarious intertextuality, their assembled quality, an insight which applies equally to the twinning of *Smirke* and the *Short Historical Essay* and to *An Account of the Growth of Popery*, described by its most recent editor as 'being in some part an assembly of preexisting documents, which it organizes into its fuller narrative' (*PW*, 2:207). Marvell was a sponge and a magpie, and so have we learned, and continue to learn, to read him by reconstructing his discursive diet, and moreover to do so without prejudice for 'literariness'. In the *Rehearsal Transpros'd*, Marvell is clearly intent on 'outdoing his opponent in education' (Patterson and Dzelzainis 2001, 713–14), writing circles around his less cosmopolitan foe. But the randomness, the pronounced strangeness of Marvell's anecdotes and examples, culled from texts in various languages, describing various times and places, also has its method. It amounts to a kind of secular typology, affirming at every turn Parker's role as universal knave: not only is he 'Bayes the Second', he is the second coming of every emperor, khan, and mogul, every churchman, magician, and conjuror 'stretched to such an height in his own fancy, that he could not look down from top to toe but his eyes dazzled at the precipice of his structure' (1:75). Under the power of Marvell's rhetorical art, such illusions are inexorably pierced, Parker shrunk down to size, swallowed, and disgorged for the general derision of the Town, to recall the anecdote on which Marvell ends the second part (1:437–8). Indeed, so successful was Marvell's book, it more or less swallowed his opponent for all time; 'so we still read Marvell's answer to Parker', says Swift in the 'Apology' to *A Tale of a Tub*, 'though the book it answers be sunk long ago'.

'Your Dear Friend Mr Milton'

In animadverting Parker, Marvell was, as we've seen, careful to position the anonymous transposer as a loyalist and a conformist, a better servant to the king's prerogative and more devoted to the Church of England than his opponent, whose party he derided as a 'canker and gangrene' on the Church's 'perfect beauty' (1:179). That party would be very active in the months following the publication of Marvell's book: by May 1673 some half-dozen responses had issued from the press, including Parker's authorised *Reproof* (1673) and another anonymous pamphlet called *The Transproser Rehears'd, or, The Fifth Act of Mr Bayes's Play* (1673) which Marvell also thought to have been written by Parker but which was probably the work of Samuel Butler (see von Maltzahn 1995). In their concerted attack upon the author of *Rehearsal Transpros'd*, whose identity was soon an open secret, the polemicists sought to undercut Marvell's finely calibrated self-presentation, to uncloak him as a Machiavel, an unregenerate republican and fanatic in loyalist's clothing. They also subjected him to cruel and sustained sexual satire and innuendo, casting him as 'Rosemary' to Parker's manly 'Bayes', a sexual eunuch, a Ganymede, evidence we considered in Chap. 5 in connection with Marvell's sexuality. These attacks converged around the figure and writings of John Milton (see Augustine 2014). Indeed, it can fairly be said that Marvell's high church enemies were the first to read him within what would come to be called the Whig tradition, as a scourge of kings and bishops, frequently adducing Milton's radical prose as gloss on Marvell's book. Of Marvell's notably equivocal account of the late war, 'p. 303. *Whether it were a war of religion or of liberty, is not worth the labour to enquire. Whichsoever was at the top, the other was at the bottom; but upon considering all, I think the cause was too good to have been fought for*', Butler scoffs, '[this] is nothing but *Iconoclastes* [Milton's *Eikonoklastes*] drawn in little, and *Defensio Populi Anglicania* in miniature' (251). This sense of Marvell as Milton's political minion is readily joined to sexual libel: Butler imagines Marvell as a 'gelding' to Milton's 'stallion' in a scabrous image of unnatural coupling which also doubles as an image of unnatural reproduction in Marvell's supposed plagiarism from Milton's writings.

Such provocations gave rise to a sequel, *The Rehearsal Transpros'd: The Second Part*, published under Marvell's name in late 1673, though both contemporary editions are dated 1674. The circumstances of this defence and continuation of Marvell's tolerationist arguments were very much changed from the previous summer. When Parliament was recalled on 4 February 1673, the king appeared resolute in his religious policy: while giving reassurance that he 'did not intend that it shall any way prejudice the Church', 'I shall take it very ill', he warned, 'to receive contradiction in what I have done. And I will deal plainly with you, I am resolved to stick to my Declaration' (*HPHC*, 1:163). The Commons were not impressed. On 14 February, a petition and address on the Declaration of Indulgence was read by the Speaker, wherein the House professed themselves 'bound in duty in inform your majesty, that penal statutes, in matters ecclesiastical, cannot be suspended but by Act of Parliament' (*CJ*, 9:252). By March it became clear that supply for the war would be withheld until the Declaration was withdrawn, its extension of liberty to Catholic conscience having fanned the flames of anti-popery, pushing moderate nonconformists back into alliance with the Anglican bloc. Fearing 'inevitable ruin' should supply 'be not speedily dispatched', Charles caved spectacularly. Not only did he vacate the Declaration of Indulgence, eliciting a unanimous vote of thanks from both Houses (*HPHC*, 1:174–5). He also submitted to a new *Act for preventing Dangers which may happen from Popish Recusants*, rendering persons refusing to take the Oaths of Supremacy and Allegiance and to take the sacrament according to the usage of the Church of England incapable of office (*HPHC*, 1:178). Without knowing it, Charles thereby sowed the seeds of a legitimacy crisis which would ultimately end in the Glorious Revolution: the Test Act forced James's resignation as Lord High Admiral and outed the heir apparent as a follower of Rome.

So as not to concede the impotence of the civil magistrate in view of future episcopal tyranny, Marvell essentially has to argue out of both sides of his mouth in *RT2*. We find him quoting Parker quoting the Declaration's insistence on the king's 'supreme power in matters ecclesiastical' while avowing that only one of them (Marvell) honours that quotation and indeed that he has 'come not long since from swearing religiously to own that supremacy' (*PW*, 1:276). Not confining himself to the question of right, he also urges the prudence and wisdom of exercising 'a relenting tenderness' over the people in point of religious obedience, reasoning that the 'wealth of the shepherd depends upon the multitude of his flock, the goodness of their pasture, and the quietness of their feeding: and princes, whose dominion over mankind resembles in some measure that of man over other creatures, cannot expect any considerable increase to themselves, if by continual terror they amaze, shatter, and hare their people, driving them into woods, and running them upon precipices' (325). At the same time, we need but turn the leaf to find Marvell working the opposite side of the equation, affirming the responsibility of 'society itself', as he puts it, to amend their own manners, preserve the public welfare, and redress corruptions in government. 'So that, whatever the power of the magistrate be in the institution', he here maintains, 'it is much safer for them not to do that with the left hand which they may do with the right, nor by an extraordinary what they may effect by an ordinary way of government' (326). This is to mince words with Parliament's resolution 'that penal statutes, in matters ecclesiastical, cannot be suspended but by Act of Parliament'. The king *can* enforce toleration by fiat, Marvell says, but it is advisable that he work his will through conventional means. The onus of good government is thus Whiggishly thrust back on king-in-Parliament. Such examples of constitutional see-sawing are mirrored in *RT2* by a newfound interest in the persecutions of tyrants as well as bishops, hinting at a fear that Charles would turn Nero to appease the parliamentary purse while his war was on. The withdrawal of the Declaration of Indulgence, in other words, obliged Marvell to hedge his bets as to whether king or Parliament gave the better odds for securing new toleration measures.

Notwithstanding its manifest tensions, Marvell's more scholarly and serious-minded sequel to his exuberantly literary and comic original effectively drew a line under his argument with the archidiaconal police force ('*Posse Archdiaconatus*'). According to Burnet (1753), Marvell's 'burlesque strain' not only 'humbled Parker, but the whole party: for the author of the *Rehearsal Transprosed* had all the men of wit (or, as the French phrase it, all the laughers) on his side' (365). The antiquary and gossip Anthony Wood (1691) saw things similarly, though he credits Parker with giving Marvell a better run for his money. Wood thought the debate 'a perfect trial of each other's skill and parts in a jerking, flirting way of writing, entertaining the reader with a great variety of sport and mirth ... And it was generally thought, nay even by many of those who were otherwise favourers of Parker's cause, that he (Parker) through a too loose and unwary handling of the debate (though in a brave, flourishing, and lofty style) laid himself too open to the severe strokes of his sneering adversary, and that the odds and victory lay on Marvell's side' (2:619). While two anonymous pamphlets did appear in rejoinder to *RT2*, Parker would not take up the cudgels against that 'lewd' and 'impudent' man until Marvell was safely dead, in Parker's posthumously published *History of His Own Time* (332).

But the aspersions cast by Marvell's enemies were not without their sting, as we may surmise from Marvell's reflection, near the beginning of *RT2*, on the ethics of undertaking to write satire and animadversion. He that 'does publish an invective, does it at his utmost peril', Marvell observes, 'and 'tis but just that it should be so':

> For a man's credit is of so natural and high concernment to him, that the pre-serving it better, was perhaps none of the least inducements at first to enter into the bonds of society, and civil government; as that government too must at one time or other be dissolved where men's reputation can be under security. 'Tis dearer than life itself, and (to use a thought something perhaps too delicate, yet not altogether unreasonable) if beside the law of murder, men have thought fit, out of respect to human nature, that whatsoever else moves to the death of man should be forfeit to pious uses, why should there not as well be deodands for reputation? (*PW*, 1: 236–7)

For the second time in this literary life, we encounter Marvell using that archaic word 'deodands'; the first was in the judgment of the nymph, 'Ev'n beasts must be with justice slain; / Else men are made their deodands' (ll. 16–17). Echoing his own unpublished and (evidently) uncirculated verse, Marvell here imagines himself into the psychology of the nymph, while his 'reputation' takes the place of her murdered fawn; Parker assumes the role of the 'wanton troopers', the wilfully destructive author not of real but of paper bullets, shot into Marvell's 'credit' ('a man's credit', no less); and our author muses uneasily on the justice that would make Parker his own deodand. As we have had frequent occasion to observe, the twinning of sexual libel and political insult was a common, indeed almost a defining feature of animadversive writing in this world. Marvell was hardly above such tactics, as the Painter poems and the first part of *Rehearsal Transpros'd*, with its satire on Parker as a '*Cock-Divine*', strutting in front of godly gentlewomen, well attest. Yet the psychic geometry of Marvell's complaint in *RT2* can't help but suggest, to readers of his poetry, something of the damaging force of the high church-men's jibes at Marvell's bodily integrity and sexual capacity. Wood faults Parker's 'too loose and unwary handling of the debate', but Marvell's warier and more sober approach in the second *Rehearsal* surely reflects an effort to limit his exposure, drawing his scholarly robes around him even as he savours whatever private prospects of wounding and loss underlay the public smart done to his reputation, his credit as a man.

Towards the close of his tract, Marvell turns aside from his main argument once more to answer the abuse directed at his association with Milton, in a passage famously characterised by Christopher Hill (1978) as 'the culmination of over twenty years of discipleship and friendship' born of 'a deference for Milton which was almost servile' (17). Hill is following and amplifying the view of Milton's great biographer David Masson; what they see, however, is surely clouded by their own convictions. For here we have not only prudent distancing but also traces of old resentments and a biography of Milton that one who had erewhile limned himself as a second Moses could scarcely have appreciated. 'You do three times at least in your *Reproof*, and in your *Transproser Rehears'd* well-nigh half the book through, run upon an author J. M. which does not a little offend me', Marvell bristles. 'For why should any other man's reputation suffer in a contest betwixt you and me? But it is because you resolved to suspect that he had an hand in my former book, wherein, whether you deceive yourself or no, you deceive others extremely. For by chance I had not seen him of two years before; but after I undertook writing, I did more carefully avoid either visiting or sending to him, lest I should any way involve him in my consequences' (*PW*, 1:417). Marvell is quick to indemnify Milton from liability or reproof for his attack on the bishops, but he also rather sharply asserts his own authorship and authority in his book, owning his friendship with 'J. M.' but precisely refusing 'discipleship' or junior status. Obviously the chafing is a reaction to Parker's condescension, but does Marvell also, perhaps, recall such treatment by Milton himself, was Milton always ready to credit the work of his under-secretary in view of what he, in his letter to President Bradshaw recommending Marvell for the job, called 'those jealousies and that emulation which mine own condition might suggest' (*CPW*, 4:860), meaning of course his blindness (see McWilliams 2006, 157–8; Zwicker 2022).

Such hints are only deepened by Marvell's ensuing précis of Milton's career. 'J. M. was, and is', he asserts, 'a man of great learning and sharpness of wit as any man. It was his misfortune, living in a tumultuous time, to be tossed on the wrong side, and he writ *Flagrante bello* [in the heat of war] certain dangerous treatises … At His Majesty's happy return, J. M. did partake, even as you yourself did for all your huffing, of his regal clemency, and has ever since expiated himself in a retired silence' (417–18). What might Milton have made of this, one wonders. Here Marvell puts him on the 'wrong' side of the civil war, and moreover, says that he was 'tossed' there by 'misfortune', which is a rather astonishing way to describe Milton's commitment to the Good Old Cause. In *The Ready and Easy Way* (1660), issued and then reissued in the final weeks of the Commonwealth, Milton had compared the 'happy' restoration of Charles Stuart to 'choosing a captain back for Egypt'. He did partake of the royal clemency, but only after Marvell had pleaded on his behalf; and his so-called retired silence muffles the publication, in 1667, of *Paradise Lost*, which was pulled up by the episcopal licenser for 'imaginary treason'. It may be that Marvell is in some way confessing and regretting how far *he* had been drawn, in those tumultuous times, towards Milton's cause, but Milton would not have thanked him for being so remembered. Even allowing for the performativity of these gestures in their argumentative context, the detuning of attacks on *RT* associating its author with republican values, Marvell's motives and intentions in this passage seem distinctly mixed.

Hill saw the 'defence' of Milton in *RT2* and the lines 'On *Paradise Lost*' as companion pieces, and he was right to do so, if for the wrong reasons; for they are threaded not on servility and deference but on irony and passive aggression. Critics more often refer to the commendatory poem as 'On Mr Milton's *Paradise Lost*', the title under which it appeared in the 1681 Folio. But the honorific 'Mr Milton' is an artefact of the Folio's Whiggish origins (on which see von Maltzahn 1999); as published in the second edition of *Paradise Lost* in 1674, the poem bore the prominent title 'ON *Paradise Lost*', which suggests

Marvell titled it this way in his copy text or that he omitted a title altogether, leaving the matter to Milton's publisher Samuel Simmons. This may seem overly punctilious, but it makes a difference in judging the poem's angle of origin—'Mr Milton' is how Marvell would have referred to his senior colleague in the Office of Foreign Tongues, 'J. M.', as he chooses to refer to him in 1673/4, are the personal initials of a social equal. It is also important to the poem's sense of drama. 'On Mr Milton's *Paradise Lost*' will undoubtedly praise a successful performance; 'On *Paradise Lost*' does not announce its tenor or its character.

And indeed, the poem begins in a place of anxious expectation, with Marvell worrying that Milton 'would ruin (for I saw him strong) / The sacred truths to fable and old song' (ll. 7–8). As the succeeding couplet makes clear, that worry amounts to the possibility that Milton might be diverted from his pious task to settle scores with worldly foes: '(So Sampson groped the Temple's posts in spite / The world o'erwhelming to revenge his sight)' (ll. 9–10). This figure and its attendant anxiety find their resolution in the eventual exchange of blind Samson for the blind prophet Tiresias: 'Where couldst thou words of such a compass find?', the poet wonders, having surveyed the majesties of Milton's poem, 'Whence furnish such a vast expanse of mind? / Just heaven thee like Tiresias to requite / Rewards with prophecy thy loss of sight' (ll. 41–4). Royalists had of course jeered Milton's blindness as divine punishment for his efforts on behalf of regicide and the republic, service which Marvell here redeems; though in so doing, he is also redeeming Milton from the biography he supplied for him the previous year. But the poem's ironies around vastness and sublimity and not least around the epic's bold neglect of rhyme do not permit of such neat solutions and so unsettle the poem's tacit endorsement of Milton's political virtue, a virtue conspicuously tethered by Milton to the poetry Marvell would praise.

The encomiast's initial misgivings concern the blind poet's 'vast design', 'Messiah crowned, God's reconciled decree, / Rebelling angels, the forbidden tree, / Heaven, hell, earth, chaos, all' (ll. 2–5). He trembles, in Masson's words (1880), 'for [Milton's] failure, great as he knew his powers to be': 'how could the blind man compass such a union of grandeurs?' (6:713). Of course, what Marvell has done is to compress this union of grandeurs into a conspectus of three lines, and with an economy virtuosic in its own right, tapering the polysyllables of lines three and four into the staccato diction of line five. That Marvell is being playful here is signalled by the fact that 'Heaven, hell, earth, chaos, all' is afforded only three feet, less than a full line. The modern edition of Marvell's poetry from which I've been quoting obscures a further instance of metrical wit: both Simmons and *Miscellaneous Poems* print not 'Heaven' but 'Heav'n', the contraction contracting God's kingdom to a single syllable. To observe this winking quality, so foreign to Masson's account of the poet's trembling before Milton's monumental work, allows us to appreciate Marvell's lines as an ironic recasting of the breathless proem to Book I, in which Milton states his ambition to outwing Homer and outgo Moses in pursuit of 'Things unattempted yet in prose or rhyme' (1.16). That ambition is at once feared, admired, and held up to lightly comic scrutiny in verse that demonstrates the puny lyricist's powers to invest a scant few lines with whole worlds.

The clipping of 'Heav'n' also reduces Marvell's pentameter line to its proper quantity of syllables, ensuring it stays within its metrical bounds. Marvell's tiny graphic joke thus opens the compendious subject of versification in *Paradise Lost*, a subject his commendatory poem prefaces in the most literal sense: the second page of 'On *Paradise Lost*' (A3ᵛ) opposes the first page of Milton's 'Note on the Verse' (A4ʳ) in the second and third editions. (The 'Note on the Verse' was first added by Simmons to unsold copies of the first edition in 1668, so it was certainly known to Marvell when he composed his poem.) Simmons had solicited the note from Milton to inform would-be buyers 'why the poem rhymes not', an expectation reinforced by the hegemony of heroic rhyme in Restoration literary culture. In the Preface to *Annus Mirabilis* (1667) and in his *Essay of Dramatic Poesy* (1668), Dryden had touted heroic rhyme as 'the noblest kind of modern verse'. Responding to his bookseller's prompt, Milton places his unrhymed poem in the company of Homer's and Virgil's Greek and Latin epics as well as that of 'our best English tragedies', a reference to Shakespeare's masterpieces in blank verse. 'This neglect then of rhyme', he says by way of conclusion, 'so little is to be taken for a defect, though it may seem so perhaps to vulgar readers, that it rather is to be taken for an example set, the first in English, of ancient liberty recovered to heroic poem from the trouble and modern bondage of rhyming' (Milton 1674, sig. A4ᵛ). Talk of bondage returns us to the idea of choosing a captain back for Egypt: Milton thus charges his poem and specifically his prosody with a polemical energy that opposes Stuart monarchy and Stuart play-poetry in equal measure.

These issues, personalities, and politics are all gathered together in the close of Marvell's poem, which is also, for our purposes, the functional close of this literary life:

> Well mightst thou scorn thy readers to allure
> With tinkling rhyme, of thine own sense secure;
> While the town-Bayes writes all the while and spells,
> And like a pack-horse tires without his bells:
> Their fancies like our bushy points appear,

The poets tag them, we for fashion wear.
I too transported by the mode offend,
And while I meant to praise thee must commend.
Thy verse created like thy theme sublime,
In number, weight, and measure, needs not rhyme.
(ll. 45–54)

The 'town-Bayes' is of course Marvell and Milton's old acquaintance and fellow secretary, John Dryden, whose heroic opera *The State of Innocence* was circulating in manuscript in early 1674. *The State of Innocence*, based on *Paradise Lost*, 'constituted a kind of competing version of Milton's matter', and Dryden had received permission from Milton himself to 'tag his verses' (Freedman 1955, 101). Marvell counterpoints Dryden's 'tinkling rhyme' and literary drudging—his service as poet laureate and historiographer royal, his slavery to fashion, his padding in Milton's footsteps—with Milton's poetic liberty and sublime substance. This is rather mean to Dryden, but its praise—well, not quite praise—for Milton is variously complicated by Marvellian irony. 'Well mightst thy scorn thy readers to allure': sure of his own sense, Milton need not rely on chiming line endings to reinforce his meanings. Yet Marvell's phrase also highlights the indignant rudeness of Milton's note, with its scorn for 'vulgar readers', and it serves to glance at the fact that the first edition of *Paradise Lost* had not exactly flown off booksellers' shelves. Simmons issued the poem with a succession of different title pages, always of fresh date, and the interpolated front matter in later issues was clearly meant to make the text more vendible. Moreover, even as he vindicates Milton's use of blank verse, Marvell's own rhymed couplets compel him to 'commend' where he would 'praise'. To commend, as some have argued, is perhaps more disinterested than to praise, and so the higher compliment. Then again, isn't praise what we would like from tributary verse? And this is hardly a poet whose hand is clumsily forced by the constraints of rhyme, the couplet's ingenuity a sign not of 'bondage' or ineptitude but of prosodic mastery. The final distich outdoes all: 'Thy verse created like thy theme sublime, / In number, weight, and measure, needs not rhyme'. Milton's poem needs it not, but Marvell gives it anyway, a gift which is also a theft, appropriating 'sublime' for his own rhyme. Defining his own poetic against Dryden's drudging couplets and Milton's surging blank verse, Marvell also threads a politics independent at once of royalist aesthetics and the republican sublime.

At the outset of this book, I said that Marvell's whole poetic may be summed up in the Latin prefix *trans*—crossing from one place, person, thing, or state to another. 'Even at his most openly committed, as a Restoration pamphleteer defending freedom of conscience in the Restoration', Joanna Picciotto (2020) observes, 'Marvell released a transpersonal phantasmagoria so protean that it actually earned him the nickname "Trans"' (388). Over the last eight chapters, we have charted the creative character of Marvellian *imitatio*, the play of his echoing song. This tendency towards transversion only becomes more pronounced in his writing after the Restoration, witness his fashioning of the Painter poems in mockery of Waller, his transprosing of the *Rehearsal*, his rhyming tribute to Milton's blank verse epic. 'On *Paradise Lost*' is the last time we meet with the lyric poet, though not quite Marvell's last poem; there are some scattered verses in English and Latin, mostly satirical, of later date. But surveying the table of contents of Marvell's *Poems*, we are struck by the disappearance of the lyric Marvell after leaving Nun Appleton in the late summer or autumn of 1652. Not absolutely, not totally: there are the 'Two Songs' Marvell composed for the marriage of Lord Fauconberg and Mary Cromwell, the Latin epitaphs for Jane Oxenbridge and the sons of John Trott, the pastoral sequence from 'Last Instructions'. Still, though few now subscribe to the once-standard notion that politics and political commitment irrecoverably dissipated Marvell's poetic genius, it is hard not to wish for a few more of those perfect lyrics, which he seems once to have written with almost unrivalled ease, and indeed to wonder what happened to stop his lyric muse. To that question, this book has no answer; but perhaps we can thus read something more into that striking collocation of Cromwell's Latin secretaries in the last lines of 'On *Paradise Lost*'. Yes, we can see the opportunity here for one more hit at 'Bays', but this seems a rather indecorous mingling of generic purposes at this moment in the poem, unless it were moreover an occasion for Marvell to place himself once more in the company of his great contemporaries, to wing past them on his humble ode.

An Account of the Growth of Popery and the Birth of Whig Legend

The failure of the indulgence and the imposition of the Test spelled the beginning of the end for the Cabal government. James's failure to take Anglican communion at Easter 1673 sparked rumours of his conversion, and on 12 June he duly resigned all his offices. A widower since 1671, on 20 September he married by proxy the Italian princess Mary of Modena, raising the spectre of a perpetual Catholic monarchy should the duchess bear him an heir. England was gripped with a wave of anti-popery, in no small part fomented by Dutch propaganda which sought to turn English public opinion against the war and to demonise the Catholic menace (France). In January 1674, the House began proceedings for the removal of Buckingham, Arlington, and Lauderdale from their employments and from the king's councils. Arlington and Lauderdale survived but at the loss of considerable face and influence; Buckingham was dismissed and became a leading figure of opposition to the government, along with Shaftesbury, who had been ousted as Lord Chancellor the previous November for opposing the Catholic match. In the last years of his life, Marvell seems to have detached somewhat from the erratic Duke, moving closer to the highly active Shaftesbury's sphere of influence. With the drift of his patrons, especially Shaftesbury, into full-blown resistance to a monarchy evidently bent on enhancing its powers in collusion with a tyrannical Church, Marvell abandoned the strategic loyalism and unqualified irenicism of his *Rehearsals* for full-throated oppositional polemic in *An Account of the Growth of Popery and Arbitrary Government* (published 'about Christmas' 1677), the most explosive of his prose writings and the basis for his posthumous legend as Whig patriot.

Three other prose interventions date to this late stage of Marvell's career: *Mr Smirke* and the *Short Historical Essay*, published together in 1676, and *Remarks upon a Late Disingenuous Discourse*, the last work from Marvell's hand, which was licensed in April 1678. In *Smirke*, Marvell defended the Latitudinarian bishop Herbert Croft against the hardliner Bishop of Ely, Francis Turner. Its pendant piece was a tendentious account of early Christian history deflating of councils, creeds, and the churchmen who sought to impose them. The *Remarks* mediated yet another religious quarrel, this one between two dissenting ministers, John Howe and Thomas Danson, on the issue of Calvinist soteriology. These works are not now much read, though *Smirke* stands to become better known with the printing of this text in full in the forthcoming 21st-Century Oxford Authors edition of Marvell, the first classroom edition to include meaningful selections of Marvell's prose in thirty years. *Smirke* undeniably had a notoriety in its own time, and it extends Marvell's marriage of controversial divinity with the theatre: Mr Smirk is chaplain to 'my Lady Bigot' in Etherege's *Man of Mode*, the smash hit of the spring theatrical season of 1676. But it was the *Account* which roiled the opening of Parliament in January 1678 and provided the basic language and framework of the Exclusion Crisis which was to follow. It is here that we owe our remaining attention.

The Third Anglo-Dutch War had lasted from April 1672 to February 1674, when the renewed anti-popery of the Cavalier Parliament threatened supply, forcing the king to conclude a peace with the Dutch with little to show for his trouble. The shuffle of ministers brought a new personality to the fore, Thomas Osborne, from June 1674 known as the Earl of Danby, who succeeded Clifford as Lord Treasurer and was by September of that year, following Arlington's resignation as Secretary of State, the unchallenged chief minister. A staunch royalist and uncompromisingly Anglican, Danby urged a rapprochement between king and Parliament on the basis of a Protestant foreign policy and unwavering support for the Church of England against nonconformists and Catholic recusants. But Danby could not alter the fact of the Duke of York's religion, nor was he able to detach Charles unambiguously from his alliance with France. Moreover, in assiduously cultivating a bloc of loyal supporters of the Court in the Cavalier Commons—Danby is often credited with inventing the modern art of parliamentary management—and in somewhat too eagerly allying with the bishops in the Lords, Danby also succeeded in consolidating an embryonic opposition committed to defending parliamentary independence and resisting the coalescence of an authoritarian church-state.

Cries of 'popery and arbitrary government' in the 1670s were thus less about the fear of Catholicism being reintroduced into England than about England sliding into popish absolutism of the kind associated with Louis XIV's France. In the set-piece 'character' of popery which opens the *Account* (pages 227 to 241 in the Yale edition), Marvell thus largely ignores matters of confession, hammering instead on questions of political theology. 'It is almost inconceivable', he writes, 'how princes can yet suffer a power so pernicious, and doctrine so destructive to all government', referring to the authority claimed and exercised by the pope over Catholic subjects. 'But, as far as I can apprehend, there is more of sloth than policy on the princes' side in this whole matter: and all that pretence of enslaving men by the assistance of religion more easily, is neither more nor less than when the *Brahmin*, by having the first night of the bride assures himself of her devotion for the future, and makes her more fit for the husband' (233–4). In this unpleasant, orientalising analogy, Marvell makes the prince a willing cuckold of the priest, in a bargain that works to ensure the passive obedience of the bride.

Fears of such an unholy bargain between Church and crown are apparent in the furore over two bills which figure prominently in Marvell's *Account*. The first of these was a *Bill to prevent Dangers from disaffected Persons*, which was contrived by Danby and the bishops and introduced into the House of Lords in April 1675. The bill would have required all members of Parliament and other officeholders to declare '*That it is not lawful upon any pretence whatsoever to take up arms against the King*', and what's more, '*that I will not at any time endeavour the alteration of the government either in Church or State*', as

Marvell transcribes the oath in his tract (*PW*, 2:281). After the 'greatest and longest debate' Burnet could remember, the bill passed the Lords on 31 May and 'very probably it would have passed in the House of Commons', were it not for the jurisdictional dispute of *Shirley v. Fagg* which broke out between the two Houses, a dispute which may have been enflamed by Country MPs determined to derail the progress of the Test (539, 541–2). With all business grinding to a halt, on 9 June the king disgustedly prorogued Parliament for fifteen months, laying blame for these unhappy differences on 'the ill designs of our enemies' (*Lord's Journal*, 12:729). While clearly a rebuke for the fruitless session, the long discontinuance itself became another piece of evidence in a purported plot to undermine Parliament.

The existence of such a plot was first mooted in the notorious *Letter from a Person of Quality* (1675), now known to be the work of Shaftesbury, which promised in its ringing opening sentences to give 'a perfect account of this STATE MASTERPIECE', meaning the origins and progress of the test bill. 'It was first hatched (as almost all the mischiefs of the world have hitherto been) amongst the *Great Church Men*', the pamphlet declared, 'and is a project of several years' standing, but found not ministers bold enough to go through with it, until these *new ones*'. Thus met, they have designed '*to have the government of the Church sworn to as unalterable*', 'to declare the government *absolute* and *arbitrary*', 'And to secure all this they resolve to take away the power, and opportunity of *Parliaments* to alter anything in Church or State' (1–2, emphasis in original). The same conspiratorial tone and even some of the same language show through in the magnificent period with which Marvell begins the *Account*: 'There has now for diverse years, a design been carried on, to change the lawful government of England into absolute tyranny, and to convert the established Protestant religion into downright popery: than both which, nothing can be more destructive or contrary to the interest and happiness, to the constitution and being of the King and kingdom' (*PW*, 2:225). Not without justice can Marvell's pamphlet be regarded as a kind of pseudo-sequel to Shaftesbury's *Letter* with the perspective changed to that of a Country MP. In both cases, the contents of the bills extensively reported therein and of the debates surrounding them were protected by parliamentary privilege, and the frisson of forbidden disclosure achieved by means of these illicit publications was obviously a great driver of their interest and influence. Shaftesbury's *Letter* was burnt by the public hangman and a committee established to inquire into its author, publisher, and printer. In a June 1678 letter to William Popple, Marvell related, with evident satisfaction, 'There have been great rewards offered in private, and considerable in the *Gazette*, to any who could inform of the author or printer [of the *Account*], but not yet discovered' (*P&L*, 2:357).

Yet more exercising to Marvell than the Test was the so-called Bishop's Bill, *An Act for further securing the Protestant Religion, by Education of the Children of the Royal Family therein, and providing for the Continuance of a Protestant Clergy*, first read in the Lords on 1 March 1677 and sent to the Commons two weeks later. In debate there, Marvell was provoked to much his longest parliamentary speech in more than twenty years as an MP, and the text of the bill is exhibited at almost obscene length in the pages of the *Account* as the smoking gun of an episcopal plot (2:313–23). ''Tis an ill thing, and let us be rid of it as soon as we can', Marvell is said to have protested of the bill. 'He could have wished it had perished at the first reading rather than have been revived by a second. He is sorry the matter has occasioned so much mirth. He thinks there was never so solemn and sad an occasion, as this bill before you' (Grey 1769, 4:322). At the end of his lengthy and somewhat disconnected remarks, Marvell apologised for speaking with unbecoming abruptness—he was, it seems, practically beside himself. That Marvell should return to this scene in his narrative of a plot 'to change the lawful government of England into absolute tyranny, and to convert the established Protestant religion into downright popery' does not surprise, and von Maltzahn comments shrewdly on the bill's intermittence in full amidst Marvell's recounting of the late proceedings in Parliament: 'the longer the bill goes on, page after page, the more demented seems the bishops' fantasy in making every kind of provision for their own role or rule' (*PW*, 2:192). But the narrative deforming thus observed points us deeper into Marvell's writing and psyche. As the full title of the Bishop's Bill indicates, key among its provisions was that entrusting the education and care of any royal children born to a Catholic successor, from the age of seven to the age of fourteen, to the bishops and archbishops of the Church of England (2:319). Contemplating Marvell's visceral response to the bill's reading in Parliament, we find something like a match in the gothic intensities of Marvellian lyric at its most importunate, but above all, in that baffled, baffling scene of deputed care in the biography of the Unfortunate Lover:

> IV
> While Nature to his birth presents
> This masque of quarr'lling elements;
> A num'rous fleet of corm'rants black,
> That sailed insulting o'er the wrack,
> Received into their cruel care
> Th'unfortunate and abject heir:
> Guardians fit to entertain
> The orphan of the hurricane.

V

They fed him up with hopes and air,
Which soon digested to despair;
And as one corm'rant fed him, still
Another on his heart did bill.
Thus while they famish him, and feast,
He both consumed, and increased:
And languished, with doubtful breath,
Th'amphibium of Life and Death.
       (ll. 25–40)

Earlier, we countenanced this episode as a layering of different lineaments of story, that of Charles I's betrayal by the Laudian clergy, who fed and famished him on dreams of absolutism; and that of Andrew Marvell, orphan of the hurricane, the beneficiary, or so it would seem on the evidence of the poem, of the black-coated cormorants' indecipherable but surely devastating care. Marvell's prose testifies at length to his concern with episcopal presumption, with religious persecution he frequently and insistently equated with violence, and with the Church's predatory self-interest in enhancing royal authority. This is a story Marvell tells with brio and conviction in *An Account of the Growth of Popery and Arbitrary Government*, but it is a work animated as well by forces and sympathies that go beyond matters of conscience or politics, brandishing wounds even as it plays at sharp with cruel guardians and would-be tyrants.

The extent of that animus and its potential effects upon the public sphere may be gauged by the government's response to the publication of Marvell's pamphlet. The bounty of £100 for information leading to the discovery of the author of this '*seditious, and scandalous libel against the proceedings of both Houses of Parliament, and other His Majesty's Courts of Justice, to the dishonour of His Majesty's government, and the hazard of the public peace*', represented something like four times Marvell's annual salary as an MP (*London Gazette*, no. 1288, 21–25 March 1678). One of Danby's hired pens, Marvell's old acquaintance Marchamont Nedham, rushed to incorporate attacks on the *Account* in pamphlets published in February and March. Roger L'Estrange, who as Surveyor of the Press had been dogging Marvell's footsteps for years, took it upon himself to animadvert its falsehoods in a style altogether Marvell's own, in *An Account of the Growth of Knavery, under the Pretended Fears of Arbitrary Government, and Popery* (1678), published in April.

This response perhaps invites in turn some brief reflection on Marvell's political trajectory after the Restoration. We have no reason to doubt the sincerity of his grief at Cromwell's death, a grief at once personal and political; yet nor is there any sign of principled resistance in the way he greets the return of the king. This is not the profile of a junior Milton, the blind secretary having clearly become disillusioned with Cromwell and risked his already precarious future safety in defying the Restoration as the Commonwealth crumbled. The Painter poems record Marvell's movement towards a position we can identify as 'Country' or 'proto-Whig', but the Second and Third Advice are more accurately described as anti-Clarendon than anti-government, and they seem to solicit the readership of the king. 'The Last Instructions' does not, but its closely limited copying suggests it was a coterie piece written for Buckingham's circle, and its high-wire risks evidently not ventured with a view to wide circulation or public influence. As a prose writer, Marvell tirelessly opposes Church aggression, but he begins, as we have seen, as the champion of Court interest in *The Rehearsal Transpros'd*, and the influence exerted on its behalf in the dust-up surrounding the pamphlet's unlicensed publication gave him the confidence to issue the sequel under his own name. With *Smirke*, Marvell was clearly treading dangerously, and his printer John Darby and bookseller Nathaniel Ponder were continually harassed and threatened by the Stationer's Company and government licensers. But even here and indeed as late as the *Remarks* there is at least the appearance of moderate views: *Smirke* defends one Anglican divine against another, while the *Remarks* side with the temperate Presbyterian Howe against the bitterly nonconformist Danson.

It thus behoves us to ask, without the *Account of the Growth of Popery*, would Marvell be remembered in the annals of Whig heroes? Indeed, would his political career be remembered at all? Marvell scholars have of late done much to persuade us of the great moment of that career and its associated writings, but it is perhaps instructive to note that the best political history of the Restoration, Ronald Hutton's study *Charles II*, neglects to mention Marvell at all. Historians whose concerns more actively embrace cultural politics in addition to high politics and political narrative—Neil Keeble (2002) and John Spurr (2000), for instance, in their respective histories of the 1660s and 1670s—make of him a rather larger figure. But this should give us due pause not to read Marvell's career backward from the *Account*, to outfit him with Whig armour before he ever thinks of putting it on. Recognition of Marvell as a prose writer of great style and substance was, to be sure, essential and overdue, but this should in no way inhibit our continued investment in the lyric inheritance, as this book has argued. Indeed, in Marvell's case, lyric attention is a form of politics by other means, supplying the coin for the maintenance of a political Marvell.

Life in Death

The lasting impact of *The Account of the Growth of Popery*, along with Marvell's reputation as an indomitable patriot and truth-teller, were secured by two events which now fell out: one was his death, on 16 August 1678, following a sudden fever; the other was the revelation by Titus Oates, from 28 September, of a supposed Popish Plot to assassinate Charles II in order to bring the Catholic Duke of York to the throne, to reduce all his Majesty's dominions to the Roman religion, and to extirpate all good Protestants root and branch. Shaftesbury and his followers would rally around the fictitious Plot in attempting to force James's exclusion from the succession, under pressure of which the parties of Whig and Tory first sprang into existence. Marvell's death allowed the reprinting of a weighty folio edition of the *Account* under his name in late 1679, with a colophon that read, 'Printed at *Amsterdam*, And Recommended to the Reading of all English Protestants' (original punctuation). Accordingly, the 'thrice-worthy' Marvell's name became a kind of badge of virtue in early Whig polemic as well as a convenient bluff: a discerning enemy, L'Estrange (1679) noted the design of Shaftesbury's faction 'to canonise Mr Marvell (now in his grave) if not for a saint, yet for a prophet, in showing how pat the Popish Plot falls out to his conjecture' (sig. A2^v) , and elsewhere complained of the ease with which malefactors now cast seditious pamphlets 'upon Mr Marvell, who is lately dead, and there the inquiry ends' (*Chronology*, 215).

However, it was not only the *Account* which gained life from the Popish Plot and Exclusion Crisis. According to Anthony Wood (1691), 'This *Andr. Marvell*, who is supposed to have written other things ... died on the 18 [sic] of Aug. 1678, and was buried under the pews in the south side of the Church of St Giles-in-the-Fields, near London. Afterwards, his widow published his composition *Miscellaneous Poems*. Lond. 1681. fol., which were then taken into the hands of many persons of his persuasion, and by them cried up as excellent' (2:620). That Whig associates of Marvell's should have sought to publish his poems after his death is intelligible enough, and there was obviously a marketplace for Marvelliana (L'Estrange again: 'there is money to be got by it, and that's five and fifty reasons in one'). But the mechanism of that happy event provides one last puzzle: Marvell's wife.

Marvell died in the house on Great Russell Street where, as mentioned at the beginning of this chapter, he was living with two Hull-born merchants, his long-time friends Edward Nelthorpe and Richard Thompson, Thompson's wife, and two servants, the senior of whom went by the name of Mary Palmer. Nelthorpe and Thompson's banking venture, the firm of Nelthorpe,

Thompson, Farrington, and Page, had gone bust in early 1676. Thereafter they became the target of numerous lawsuits and commissions of bankruptcy 'and were become by this means in the compass of one year the sad objects of common obloquy, or pity', as Thompson later deposed (in Tupper 1938, 369). Hounded and harried by their creditors, in June 1677 Nelthorpe and Thompson resorted to the rather desperate measure of seeking to disappear, in which project they were abetted by their honoured friend Mr Marvell, a sometime spy, intelligencer, and author of seditious pamphlets. Marvell enlisted Mary Palmer, the landlady of his lodgings in Westminster and apparently an associate of some trust, to take the lease of the house in Great Russell Street in her name. At this time, Marvell also took out a bond for £500 from a London goldsmith, in trust for Nelthorpe. Government authorities offered rewards for knowledge of the bankrouts' whereabouts; so great was the storm, parliamentary legislation aiming at their punishment was referred to committee, a committee to which Marvell was named, as he drily reported in a report to the Hull Corporation.

These are curious circumstances enough, but the plot really begins to thicken upon Marvell's death. A few days after his decease, one of the other partners in the bank, Michael Farrington, allegedly prevailed upon Mary Palmer for the keys to Marvell's lodgings in Covent Garden, removing, according to Mary's later testimony, 'all hampers, trunks, bonds, bills, and other goods', leaving behind only 'a few books and papers of small value', among which, almost certainly, were the manuscripts of Marvell's poems (Tupper 374). The next shock came when Nelthorpe himself died on 18 September. Perhaps glad to be free of further entanglements in her husband's ruinous affairs, Nelthorpe's wife, who had taken their children to live with relatives, relinquished administration of the estate to Farrington, in actions dated 30 April and 31 October 1679. Farrington then tried to collect the £500 bond from the goldsmith, only to be rebuffed when the goldsmith claimed it had already been repaid. It was at this point that he became concerned in Marvell's estate, about which nothing had so far been done; it was he who paid the fee to take out the administration naming Mary *Marvell* and John Greene, an attorney well known to the firm, as Marvell's executors, in actions dated 30 September 1679 and 31 March 1680. The late member for Hull in this way acquired a wife.

So Fred Tupper reconstructed these events nearly eighty years ago, and though his account is imperfect in various respects and deeply coloured by historical prejudice, it still seems to me the most plausible way of reading the available evidence. On Tupper's theory, Mary Palmer's marriage to Marvell was a legal fiction which was concocted as an expedient to securing Marvell's assets, specifically the disputed goldsmith's bond. The advantage to Farrington as administrator of Nelthorpe's estate was that he might redeem the bond while shielding it from creditors, and to Mary, who was retained at a salary of £10 a year, presumably some portion of the proceeds. But by the middle of 1681, Mary seems to have had other ideas, and sought to collect the bond in her own right as Marvell's 'widow and relict'. So begins the train of suits and countersuits involving Farrington, Mary Palmer, Greene, the goldsmith Charles Wallis, and John Morris, the owner of the house in Great Russell Street, with whom Mary was said to have conspired. It was in the course of these filings and depositions that the authenticity of Mary Palmer's marriage to Marvell was litigated. According to Farrington, it was in no way likely that Marvell, 'who was a member of the House of Commons for many years together and a very learned man would undervalue himself to intermarry with so mean a person as the said Mary then was, being the widow of a Tennis Court Keeper in or near the City of Westminster who died in mean condition. And in truth the said Andrew Marvell did not at any time in his lifetime own or confess that he was married to the said Mary or any other person nor did he cohabit with the said Mary at any time as man and wife use to do'. In retort, Mary claimed that it was their difference in station which disposed her husband 'to have the marriage kept private', and therefore 'she did sometimes attend upon him more like a servant than a wife' while they lived with Nelthorpe and the Thompsons, though she did 'very often and so often as she pleased sit down with them at meals and eat her meat with them' (Tupper 380).

Phil Withington (2005) is right when he says that the rejection of the marriage by modern commentators is consonant with 'the orthodoxy of an older tradition of Whig hagiography that, in eulogising the "dignity, honour, sense, genius, fortitude, virtue and religion" of Marvell, dismissed Mary as a mercenary' (225). Farrington's arguments work on the sexist assumptions of the twentieth and twenty-first centuries nearly as well they did on those of the seventeenth. Still, the evidence seems against the secret marriage: when the row over Marvell's estate was ended, Mary reverted to using the name Palmer, and it is under that name that she was buried in 1687. But we might consider whether she and Marvell were perhaps something like civil partners, that they enjoyed an unconventional intimacy and familiarity which did not, possibly does not consort with cohabiting 'as man and wife use to do'. Theirs was a relationship of long standing, if the date of 1667 which Mary gave for their alleged marriage is any indication, and Marvell evidently trusted her not only with his life but with the lives of those friends he was sheltering in what must have been the very strange months in which he also completing work on the *Account of the Growth of Popery*.

Nelthorpe and Thompson were decidedly Whiggish in outlook, said to be great frequenters of coffee houses and addicted to the hearing and telling of news, and it may be through this connection that Mary Palmer brought Marvell's poems to be printed by the Whig bookseller Robert Boulter in the autumn of 1680. As published by Boulter the following year, *Miscellaneous Poems | By Andrew Marvell, Esq; Late Member of the Honourable House of Commons*, was prefaced by Mary's testimonial note: 'These are to certify every ingenious reader, that all these poems, as also the other things in this book contained, are printed according to the exact copies of my late dear husband, under his own handwriting, being found since his death among his other papers, witness my hand this 15th day of October, 1680', signed, '*Mary Marvell*'. In a manner suiting the brilliantly enigmatic poems to which the note gives imprimatur, Mary's words are full of ambiguous meaning. Manifestly, they signify that the honest and honourable reader will find Andrew Marvell's words herein exactly as he wrote them. But there is also an air of defensiveness about 'ingenious', anticipating readers perhaps inclined to construe the book sceptically or tendentiously. The note thus answers the surprise many readers may have felt on encountering the lyrics which comprise the bulk of the volume. Marvell had no reputation as a lyrist, and the deliberate witnessing of their origins insists the poetry is no counterfeit introduced to pad—and profit from—Marvell's fame as a political writer. 'My late dear husband' does other work, warding off the sexual libel and innuendo which had swirled around Marvell in the controversy with Parker. Of course, the note also serves to advance Mary's legal claim to be the poet's 'widow and relict'. In the last accounting, however, 'to every ingenious reader' may be thought of as a shibboleth of inheritance: as Marvell's heirs and administrators of his poetic estate, we are called upon to give voice to these poems with the same integrity of spirit, the same ingenuity which first informed them and which, indeed, informed the whole of this literary life.

References

Augustine, Matthew C. 2014. The Chameleon or the Sponge: Marvell, Milton, and the Politics of Literary History. *SP* 111 (1): 132–162.

Burnet, Gilbert. 1753. *Bishop Burnet's History of His Own Times*. 4 vols. London.

Connell, Philip. 2019. Marvell and the Church. In *The Oxford Handbook of Andrew Marvell*, ed. Martin Dzelzainis and Edward Holberton, 128–143. Oxford: Oxford University Press.

Cooke, Thomas. 1726. The Life of Andrew Marvell, Esq. In *The Works of Andrew Marvell, Esq.* 2 vols. London.

Davenant, William. 1651. *Gondibert: An Heroick Poem.* London.

Dzelzainis, Martin. 2010. Andrew Marvell and George Villiers, Second Duke of Buckingham. *Explorations in Renaissance Culture* 36 (2): 151–169.

———. 2015. Marvell and the Dutch in 1665. In *A Concise Companion to the Study of Manuscripts, Printed Books, and the Production of Early Modern Texts*, ed. Edward Jones, 249–265. Chichester: Wiley Blackwell.

Freedman, Morris. 1955. Dryden's "Memorable Visit" to Milton. *HLQ* 18 (2): 99–108.

Grey, Anchitell. 1769. *Debates of the House of Commons, from the Year 1667 to the Year 1694.* 10 vols. London.

Griffin, Dustin. 1996. *Literary Patronage in England: 1650–1800.* Cambridge: Cambridge University Press.

Hill, Christopher. 1978. Milton and Marvell. In *Approaches to Andrew Marvell*, ed. C.A. Patrides, 1–30. London: Routledge.

Hirst, Derek. 1999. Samuel Parker, Andrew Marvell, and Political Culture, 1667–73. In *Writing and Political Engagement in Seventeenth-Century England*, ed. Derek Hirst and Richard Strier, 145–164. Cambridge: Cambridge University Press.

Hirst, Derek, and Steven N. Zwicker. 2012. *Andrew Marvell, Orphan of the Hurricane.* Oxford: Oxford University Press.

History and Proceedings of the House of Commons from the Restoration to the Present Time. 1742. 14 vols. London: Richard Chandler.

Hume, Robert D., and Ashley Marshall. 2019. Marvell and the Restoration Wits. In *The Oxford Handbook of Andrew Marvell*, ed. Martin Dzelzainis and Edward Holberton, 687–702. Oxford: Oxford University Press.

Hume, Robert D., and Harold Love, eds. 2007. *Plays, Poems, and Miscellaneous Writings associated with George Villiers, Second Duke of Buckingham.* Oxford: Oxford University Press.

Hutton, Ronald. 1986. The Making of the Secret Treaty of Dover. *HJ* 29 (2): 297–318.

———. 1989. *Charles II: King of England, Scotland, and Ireland.* Oxford: Clarendon Press.

Hyde, Edward, Earl of Clarendon. 1759. *The Life of Edward Earl of Clarendon, Lord High Chancellor of England.* 3 vols. Oxford.

Journal of the House of Lords (1509-1773). 1767–1830. 39 vols. London: His Majesty's Stationary Office.

Journal of the House of Lords. 1767–1830. London: His Majesty's Stationary Office.

Keeble, N.H. 1999. Why Transprose *The Rehearsal*. In *Marvell and Liberty*, ed. Warren Chernaik and Martin Dzelzainis, 249–268. Basingstoke: Macmillan.

———. 2002. *The Restoration: England in the 1660s.* Oxford: Blackwell.

L'Estrange, Roger. 1678. *An Account of the Growth of Knavery.* London.

———. 1679. *The Parallel, Or, An Account of the Growth of Knavery.* London.

Love, Harold. 1989. Scribal Texts and Literary Communities: The Rochester Circle and Osborn b. 105. *Studies in Bibliography* 17: 219–235.

———. 2004. *English Clandestine Satire, 1660–1702*. Oxford: Oxford University Press.

Marvell, Andrew. 1971. *The Poems and Letters of Andrew Marvell*. Ed. H. M. Margoliouth, rev. Pierre Legouis with E. E. Duncan-Jones. 3rd ed. 2 vols. Oxford: Clarendon Press.

———. 2003. *Prose Works of Andrew Marvell*. Ed. Annabel Patterson, Martin Dzelzainis, Nicholas von Maltzahn, and N. H. Keeble. 2 vols. New Haven: Yale University Press.

———. 2007. *Poems of Andrew Marvell*. Ed. Nigel Smith. Rev. ed. London: Longman.

Masson, David. 1859–80. *The Life of John Milton: Narrated in Connexion with the Political, Ecclesiastical, and Literary History of His Time*. 6 vols. Cambridge and London: Macmillan.

McWilliams, John. 2006. Marvell and Milton's Literary Friendship Reconsidered. *SEL* 46 (1): 155–177.

Milton, John. 1674. *Paradise Lost: A Poem in Twelve Books*. London.

———. 1953–82. *Complete Prose Works of John Milton*. Ed. Don M. Wolfe et al. New Haven: Yale University Press.

Ogg, David. 1934. *England in the Reign of Charles II*. Oxford: Clarendon Press.

Parker, Samuel. 1727. *Bishop Parker's History of His Own Time in Four Books*. London.

Patterson, Annabel, and Martin Dzelzainis. 2001. Marvell and the Earl of Anglesey: A Chapter in the History of Reading. *HJ* 44 (3): 703–726.

Picciotto, Joanna. 2020. Truth-Telling, Mass Media, and the Poet's Office. *ELH* 87 (2): 375–404.

Robbins, Caroline. 1967. Absolute Liberty: The Life and Thought of William Popple, 1638–1708. *William and Mary Quarterly* 24 (2): 190–223.

Roberts, Clayton. 1957. The Impeachment of the Earl of Clarendon. *Cambridge Historical Journal* 13 (1): 1–18.

Simon, Walter G. 1962. Comprehension in the Age of Charles II. *Church History* 31 (4): 440–448.

Smith, Nigel. 2010. *Andrew Marvell: The Chameleon*. New Haven: Yale University Press.

Spurr, John. 2000. *England in the 1670s: 'This Masquerading Age*. Oxford: Blackwell.

Tupper, Fred S. 1938. Mary Palmer, Alias Mrs. Andrew Marvell. *PMLA* 53 (2): 367–392.

von Maltzahn, Nicholas. 1995. Samuel Butler's Milton. *SP* 92 (4): 482–495.

———. 1999. Marvell's Ghost. In *Marvell and Liberty*, ed. Warren Chernaik and Martin Dzelzainis, 50–74. Basingstoke: Macmillan.

———. 2005a. *An Andrew Marvell Chronology*. New York: Palgrave Macmillan.

———. 2005b. Andrew Marvell and the Prehistory of Whiggism. In *"Cultures of Whiggism": New Essays on English Literature and Culture in the Long Eighteenth Century*, ed. David Womersley, assisted by Paddy Bullard and Abigail Williams, 31–61. Newark: University of Delaware Press.

———. 2013. Andrew Marvell and the Lord Wharton. *SC* 18 (2): 252–265.

———. 2019. Marvell and Patronage. In *The Oxford Handbook of Andrew Marvell*, ed. Martin Dzelzainis and Edward Holberton, 43–60. Oxford: Oxford University Press.

Withington, Phil. 2005. *The Politics of Commonwealth: Citizens and Freemen in Early Modern England*. Cambridge: Cambridge University Press.

Wood, Anthony. 1691. *Athenae Oxonienses*. 2 vols. London.

Zwicker, Steven N. 2022 (forthcoming). "Let Us Now Praise Famous Men": Andrew Marvell and the Problem of Panegyric. In *Imagining Andrew Marvell at 400*, ed. Matthew C. Augustine, Giulio J. Pertile, and Steven N. Zwicker. Oxford: Oxford University Press for the British Academy.

Index

Horace, 20, 21, 37, 62, 93–95, 102,
132, 148
Howard, Charles, 1st Earl of
Carlisle, 169
Hull Charterhouse, 10
Hull Grammar School, 10, 12,
19–26, 29
Hutton, Ronald, 173, 190, 220
Hyde, Edward, 1st Earl of Clarendon,
118, 168, 190

J

James I and VI of England, 12
James II and VII of England, *see* James,
Duke of York
James, Duke of York, 79, 173–175,
178–179, 189–190, 207,
214, 221
Jardine, Lisa, 33, 34
Jonson, Ben, 73, 84, 85, 100–105, 108

K

Keeble, N. H., 165–167, 202,
204, 220
Kenner, Hugh, 149

L

Lambert, John, 67, 144, 145
Langton, Prioress Anna, 111, 118
Laud, William, Archbishop of
Canterbury, 13
See also Laudianism
Lauderdale, 1st Earl of, *see*
Maitland, John
Laudianism, 200
See also Laud, William
Lawes, Henry, 141
Legouis, Pierre, 1, 2, 155, 187
Leishman, J. B., 39
Lely, Peter, 59, 117, 176, 179, 181, 183

L'Estrange, Sir Roger, 199, 219, 221
Levellers, 92, 117, 191
Lilburne, John, 92
Lord, George deForest, 174
Louis XIV of France, 173, 197, 216
Love, Harold, 61, 69, 192, 204
Lovelace, Richard, 51, 72–77, 80, 84,
85, 99, 105
Loxley, James, 40
Lucan, 95, 96, 102–105

M

Mack, Peter, 20, 34
Maitland, John, 1st Earl of Lauderdale,
191, 215
Marvell, Andrew
dating of his poetry, 39,
40, 60, 188
diplomatic service, 140, 145, 166,
170, 172
and the Dutch, 58, 59, 139, 145,
154, 169, 171–174, 178,
181, 197
Latin secretary, 139, 152–153
MP, 2, 9, 46, 97, 99, 162, 164–172,
177, 178, 198, 217–219
parliamentary speeches, 218
Petrarchism, 36, 77, 78, 135, 136
Platonism, 41–44
political allegiances, 3
sexuality, 70, 107, 108, 132,
137, 206
traveling tutor, 52
works by
*Account of the Growth of Popery
and Arbitrary Government, An*,
69, 192, 205, 214–221, 223
'Ad Regem Carolum Parodia,' 20,
21, 47, 93
'Ametas and Thestylis Making
Hay-Ropes,' 35
'Bermudas,' 141, 142

Made in the USA
Middletown, DE
07 May 2021